—— Prehistoric Crete ——

Regional and Diachronic
Studies on Mortuary Systems

— Prehistoric Crete —
Regional and Diachronic Studies on Mortuary Systems

edited by

Joanne M.A. Murphy

contributions by

Philip P. Betancourt, Gerald Cadogan, Melissa Eaby,
Borja Legarra Herrero, and Katia Perna

Published by
INSTAP Academic Press
Philadelphia, Pennsylvania
2011

Design and Production
INSTAP Academic Press

Library of Congress Cataloging-in-Publication Data

Prehistoric Crete : regional and diachronic studies on mortuary systems / edited by Joanne
M.A. Murphy.
  p. cm.
Includes index.
ISBN 978-1-931534-61-1 (pbk. : alk. paper)
1. Tombs—Greece—Crete. 2. Funeral rites and ceremonies—Greece—Crete. 3. Antiquities,
Prehistoric—Greece—Crete. 4. Excavations (Archaeology)—Greece—Crete. 5. Crete
(Greece)—Antiquities. I. Murphy, Joanne M. A., 1971-
DF221.C8P69 2011
939'.18—dc23

                                                                              2011017839

Chapter icon: tholos tomb from Erganos, after F. Halbherr, "Cretan Expedition XI. Three
Cretan Necropoleis: Report on the Researches at Erganos, Panaghia, and Courtes," *AJA* 5
(1901), pp. 259–293, fig. 6.

Table of Contents

List of Figures. vii

Acknowledgments. ix

Abbreviations. xi

1. Introduction, *Joanne M.A. Murphy*. 1

2. Landscape and Social Narratives: A Study of Regional Social
   Structures in Prepalatial Crete, *Joanne M.A. Murphy*. 23

3. The Secret Lives of the Early and Middle Minoan Tholos
   Cemeteries: Koumasa and Platanos, *Borja Legarra Herrero*. 49

4. Tomb 4 at Pseira: Evidence for Minoan Social Practices,
   Philip B. Betancourt. 85

5. A Power House of the Dead: The Functions and Long Life
   of the Tomb at Myrtos-Pyrgos, *Gerald Cadogan*. 103

6. The LM IIIC Burial Culture in Crete: A Socio-Economic
   Perspective, *Katia Perna*. 119

7. Regionalism in Early Iron Age Cretan Burials, *Melissa Eaby*. 165

Index. 203

List of Figures

Figure 2.1. Map of South-Central Crete showing location of tombs. . . . 24

Figure 2.2. Plan of Mochlos Prepalatial cemetery. 29

Figure 3.1. Tholos tombs in Crete and Pre- and Protopalatial
cemeteries in South-Central Crete. 50

Figure 3.2. Koumasa cemetery. 57

Figure 3.3. Platanos cemetery. 64

Figure 3.4. Non-ceramic assemblages in selected burial contexts
in Central Crete. 68

Figure 4.1. Map of East Crete. 86

Figure 4.2. Plan of the Pseira cemetery. 87

Figure 4.3. Plan of Tomb 4 and its courtyard. 88

Figure 4.4. Vasiliki Ware pottery found inside and near Tomb 4. 90

Figure 4.5. Fragmentary fenestrated stand found at Tomb 4. 91

Figure 4.6. Incomplete pottery vessels found inside the terrace in
front of Tomb 4. 92

Figure 4.7. Complete vessels of clay and stone found buried
upright in the terrace in front of Tomb 4. 95

Figure 4.8. Fragments of a burial jar from the Pseiran cemetery. 100

Figure 5.1.   The region of East-Central Crete. 104

Figure 5.2.   Myrtos-Pyrgos: general plan. 105

Figure 5.3.   Myrtos-Pyrgos: Tomb complex. 106

Figure 5.4.   Ossuary 1 (Space 106). 107

Figure 5.5.   Forecourt (Space 100) and dove rhyton group. 108

Figure 5.6.   Dove rhyton group. 109

Figure 5.7.   Street VI, leading to the Forecourt and Tomb. 110

Figure 5.8.   Steps 8 and 9. 111

Figure 5.9.   Fallen objects in the tomb chamber over the
                upper burial layer. 112

Figure 5.10.   Stone drill guides. 113

Figure 6.1.   LM IIIC/SM mortuary areas on Crete. 122

Figure 6.2.   LM IIIC/SM sites on Crete. 123

Figure 6.3.   Cemetery distribution and types of tombs. 127

Figure 6.4.   Distribution of LM IIIC cremations and inhumations. 129

Figure 6.5.   Distribution of SM cremations and inhumations. 129

Figure 6.6.   LM IIIC/SM tombs with valuable goods. 130

Figure 7.1.   Map of EIA burial sites on Crete. 167

Figure 7.2.   Relative frequency of EIA tomb types by percentage
                of sites at which they appear. 168

Figure 7.3.   Relative frequency of EIA tomb types by total
                number of tombs. 168

Figure 7.4.   Distribution of large and small tholos tombs. 169

Figure 7.5.   Distribution of large tholos tombs. 170

Figure 7.6.   Date of construction of new tholos tombs. 171

Figure 7.7.   Potential EIA burial regions. 173

Figure 7.8.   Relative frequency of EIA tomb types by region. 174

Acknowledgments

I would like to thank the INSTAP Academic Press for its support in publishing this volume. I am grateful to the external reviewers who made insightful comments on the papers, which helped the authors make it a more thoughtful work. I especially thank the contributors for their patience and perseverance during the process of bringing the volume to completion.

Abbreviations

Bibliographic abbreviations follow the conventions suggested in the *American Journal of Archaeology* 111.1 (2007), pp. 14–34.

ca.	approximately	inv. no.	inventory number
cm	centimeter	km	kilometer
EBA	Early Bronze Age	LG	Late Geometric
EIA	Early Iron Age	LH	Late Helladic
EM	Early Minoan	LM	Late Minoan
EO	Early Orientalizing	pers. comm.	personal communication
FN	Final Neolithic		
ha	hectare	pers. obs.	personal observation
MBA	Middle Bronze Age	PG	Protogeometric
m	meter	PGB	Protogeometric B
MM	Middle Minoan	SM	Subminoan
IA	Iron Age		

1 | Introduction

JOANNE M.A. MURPHY

Since the inception of Minoan archaeology, studies pertaining to tombs and tomb deposits have played seminal roles in our understanding of Minoan culture and the reconstruction of Bronze Age society (e.g., Hall 1912; Seager 1912, 1916; Xanthoudides 1918, 1924; Marinatos 1930–1931; Levi 1961–1962). For several geographical areas and chronological periods of Cretan history, tombs are the most abundant source of data: for example, South-Central Crete in the Prepalatial period and eastern Crete at the end of the Bronze Age into the Early Iron Age. In addition to studies that explored one tomb type and traced it chronologically and to other works that examined tombs in one region in detail during a given period (Branigan 1970a; Soles 1973, 1992; Coldstream and Catling, eds., 1996; Relaki 2003), several scholars have produced synthetic works that examine Bronze Age Cretan tombs either from all of Crete or from one period or area (Pini 1968; Branigan 1993; Löwe 1996; Vavouranakis 2002). While many articles that focused on the different types of graves in different periods and areas have been published in various journals and edited volumes (Andreadaki-Vlasaki 1985; Alberti 1999, 2001, 2004; Agelarakis, Kanta, and Moody 2001; Perna 2001; Goodison 2004; Hatzaki 2005), there have been very few multi-authored volumes dedicated to the regional and diachronic diversity of mortuary practices (for a rare example, see Branigan 1998). This lacuna in scholarship concerning mortuary practices, combined with fragmentation of the field induced by specialization, has resulted in a lack of communication between scholars working on death in different time periods and regions. Such divided scholarship further prevents beneficial discourse among colleagues confronting similar problems in different data sets and in historiographical issues in the field. The papers in this volume expand the current discussion by presenting scholarship that examines Cretan mortuary systems from diverse spatial, temporal, and theoretical perspectives.

The issues addressed in the papers in this book are broad and varied. The theme for this edited volume is expansive in order to present a diverse sample of contemporary archaeological scholarship on Crete. The aim is not to present all tombs in all periods on Crete comprehensively, although much of the bibliography can be gleaned from the references. Neither the periods nor the regions of prehistoric Crete are represented evenly in this publication; there are three articles on the Early–Middle Bronze Ages (EBA–MBA), two that focus on Late Minoan (LM) Crete, and one that discusses mortuary practices from the Iron Age (IA). Three of the papers take a regional comparative approach; two others focus on tombs in East Crete, and one examines two cemeteries in South-Central Crete. This range of articles in the volume produces an overview and introduction to the various methodological and theoretical approaches currently used to interpret and re-create Minoan burials, and it contextualizes Minoan studies within broader archaeological research.

The History and Theoretical Development of Mortuary Studies

In the early years of Minoan archaeology, the publication of material relating to mortuary activity was most commonly structured into comprehensive catalogs of artifacts and tomb architecture (Paribeni 1904; Savignoni 1904; Evans 1906, 1914; Seager 1912, 1916; Forsdyke 1927). The goal of these publications, implied or stated, was to make the results of their explorations widely available to an international audience (Evans 1924, v). This tradition of publishing monographs or large articles containing the results of an excavation continues in recent years

(Demargne 1945; van Effenterre 1948; Hood, Huxley, and Sandars 1958–1959; Vasilakis 1989–1990; Sakellaraki and Sakellarakis 1991; Sakellarakis and Sapouna-Sakellaraki 1991, 1997; Hallager and McGeorge 1992; Betancourt, Davaras, and Hope-Simpson, eds., 2002, 2003; Alexiou and Warren 2004; Davaras and Betancourt 2004). These publications provide detailed knowledge of the artifacts, or, especially in the earlier volumes, of the selection of artifacts that the excavator chose to keep and publish; their greatest asset to the field is in their description of the finds and the dissemination of excavation results. Interpretations of these data sets in the early publications were limited, and they often consisted of uncritical correlations between the type of grave or of artifacts in the grave with the social personae of the deceased. A tomb with rich artifacts was interpreted as the remains of a high echelon in the society burying elites or leaders, and a tomb with poorer artifacts was thought to be from the lower echelons.

From the 1960s, artifacts from the tombs were often included in separate publications focused on those types of objects rather than on a holistic view of the social context of the objects or of their place of interment (Branigan 1965, 1968a, 1968b, 1970b, 1971; Warren 1965, 1969; Pelon 1976; Wiencke 1981; Yule 1981; Betancourt 1985). These early publications established a foundation of detailed information about the artifacts in the tombs and about the architecture or construction of the tombs upon which the greater theoretical sophistication of later works could be built. Recent research on mortuary practices stresses the simplicity of earlier correlations between rich burials and the upper echelons of society; instead, the social processes behind the burials are examined and explicated, and the mechanisms that led to the creation and maintenance of an elite are questioned. This scholarship also draws attention to the diversity within elite structures and the sophistication in trade, religion, ideology, and landscape (Branigan 1984, 1987, 1991; Maggidis 1994; Wilson and Day 1994; Karytinos 1998; Murphy 1998; Sbonias 1999; Panagiotopoulos 2002; Bardsley 2004; Papadatos 2005).

In the past few decades the archaeology of death on Crete, like most other areas of archaeological inquiry, has been changing under the influence of the paradigmatic and philosophical shifts in the academy. Up until the 1960s, archeological reconstructions of the past assumed that societies were populated by elites and plebs in a strictly evolution-ary model with little variation in modes of hierarchy. This world view had largely been derived from Victorian ideals and the remnants of the work of Spencer (1860, 1876–1896), Tylor (1903), and Morgan (1877). Since the 1960s, archaeologists have become acutely aware of the dis-parity between their knowledge of the past as it was lived and the verac-ity of the past as they had been re-creating it. Clarke's (1973) *Loss of Innocence* summarized the increased variety of new technologies and theories available to archaeologists since World War II, which had altered the way archaeologists classified, questioned, and interpreted past patterns and behaviors; contemporary with Clarke's revolutionary work in Europe, scholars in the United States were also emphasizing the complexity and inadequacy of the archaeological reasoning behind reconstructions of the past (Willey and Philips 1958; Binford 1962, 1971, 1972; Watson, LeBlanc, and Redmond 1971).

In the past half-century, the results of this close scrutiny of archaeolo-gy during the 1960s and early 1970s have combined with a growing inter-est in the archaeology, sociology, and anthropology of death to produce a large body of scholarship on different approaches to death and diverse theories on methodologies for the analysis and interpretation of mortuary activities. Many of the developments in mortuary theory derive from— and coincide with—major shifts in the academic paradigm from mod-ernism to post-modernism. According to the seminal work of Huntington and Metcalf (1979), the scholarship of the 1960s pushed death into the forefront of academic focus. Included in scholarly literature from the 1960s was the English translation of Hertz's 1907 paper on collective rep-resentations of death. Hertz, a follower of Durkheim, had stressed the complexity of death, giving examples of societies that do not see death as instantaneous, but as part of a process of dying. Turner (1967, 1969; see also Goody 1962; Miles 1965; Bloch 1971) expanded Hertz's acknowl-edgement of the social depth and complexity of death and incorporated the ideas of van Gennep (1909), who had emphasized death as a rite of passage and the rituals surrounding death as a means to control the biological inevitability of death. Durkheimian sociology, through its re-introduction to the study of death in the 1960s via the works of Hertz (1907, 1960), inspired studies of death that emphasized the solidarity and sustenance of society in the face of death. Archaeologists argued that social structure and hierarchy were reflected in rituals relating to death that functioned to recreate society.

Drawing on sociological theories and anthropological functionalism, cultural anthropologists discussed death and the use of the rituals around death by communities to control social bonding and expressions of emotions (Raddclife-Brown 1964, 32; Durkheim 1965, 385–392). Huntington and Metcalf (1979, 27) criticized such static and universal interpretations of death and rituals because they removed them from the actual cultural context, thereby suggesting that context was not important. Huntington and Metcalf disagreed with Durkheim and Radcliff-Brown, who claimed that one could either explain all ritual solely as a means of social bonding or as sentimental response. Huntington and Metcalf argued that while both interpretations may be partially valid, they are not entirely sufficient nor universal; the symbolic and sociological contexts and cultural particulars of the corpse must be studied to achieve a fuller appreciation of it.

In tandem with the increased use of ethnography both to generate generalizing social principles and to provide parallels for ancient societies, critical admonitions against simplistic applications of ethnographic analogy were also published during the 1960s and 1970s. Ucko (1969) presented scenarios in the fields of both interpretation and analogy that would constitute an archaeologist's nightmare. For example, he cited the varying practices of the Ashanti tribe in western Africa (Ucko 1969, 273), who lay out some bodies facing the village in the belief that they will turn to face the forest after the burial, but orient others facing the forest, and he criticized the common assumptions that burial practices are synonymous with religious beliefs and that the wealth or poverty of the grave goods reflect different statuses and wealth within the society. Binford (1972) illustrated the weaknesses in the supposition that similarities in burial practices in different geographical areas reflect their cultural inter-relationship. Similarly, Hodder (1989) warned against liberal and simplistic use of analogies between cultures since similar objects may be used in similar ways, but each group may attach a different meaning to those objects. Huntington and Metcalf (1979, 122) critiqued the assumed correlation between energy expenditure at the funeral and in post-funerary rituals and the social position of the deceased, noting the kings of Saudi Arabia who are buried simply with a pile of stones over them. Huntington and Metcalf (1979, 34, 44) also argued against the Durkheimian (1965, 385–392) view that funerals universally act as a means of social cohesion, citing the Nyakyusa of Tanzania, where funerals frequently disrupt the community and break bonds rather than reinforcing them.

By the beginning of the 1970s, there was a major shift in the appreciation of the complex information about ancient societies that archaeologists could glean from studying tombs and mortuary rituals. Tombs were increasingly viewed as accessible reflections of many aspects of the related society. Several major works addressed such issues as ancestors, ranking, and social cohesion through burials during this period. The now-renowned work of Saxe (1970), which was developed by Goldstein (1976, 1980) and somewhat refined by Morris (1991), played a major role in changing the appreciation of the wealth of social/cultural information that could be gained by anthropologists and archaeologists from studying mortuary activities. Saxe's dissertation, which focused on the relationship between the dead and the living and on the value of the former to the latter, introduced into the archaeology of death hypotheses about the use of formal disposal areas for the dead by agricultural groups to legitimize rights to critical resources. His dissertation promoted consideration of the ancestors and their importance to the living in the application of theoretical models to archaeological data. Since Saxe's work, ancestors have been seminal to the reconstruction of many societies by archaeologists. Discussions of the expression of the social ranking of individuals through their burials also became prominent in the 1970s (e.g., Binford 1971; Brown 1981; O'Shea 1981). Binford (1971) examined the variables in the funerary remains of a society in order to reveal divisions within the society. These variables may be equated to the social persona of the deceased. By virtue of their membership in the structural components of a social system, individuals acquire social identities and statuses— father, brother, chief, teacher (Tainter 1978, 106–110)—and these multiple personae are expressed through the rituals surrounding their death (Tainter 1975, 1978). Social ranking of the deceased in tombs was also discussed during the 1970s in a critical and theoretical manner and the processes involved in the causes for hierarchies were elucidated (Brown 1971; Peebles and Kus 1977; O'Shea 1984).

Beginning with Chapman, Kinnes, and Randsborg's (1981) publication on the archaeology of death, there has been a plethora of publications and conferences on this topic. Several of these volumes fruitfully questioned the assumptions and arguments that had been prevalent since the 1960s. In this renewed interest in the archaeology of death since the 1980s, archaeologists have emphasized the multifaceted nature of death and the rituals involved with it. The realization that death rituals are carried out by the living for the living and that the disruption to the existing hierarchy by a death provides an opportunity for the living to re-position themselves in society have been particularly influential. A current and well-received body of archaeological scholarship posits that death rituals do not simply reflect and reproduce society, but they instead are employed in the active creation of ideologies and of socially, politically, and economically desired positions (see Bartel 1982; Hodder 1982a, 1982b; Pader 1982; Parker Pearson 1982, 1999; Carr 1995). As Hodder demonstrates, the deceased, through the elaboration of the funerary and post-funerary rituals, may gain a status and position in death that they never held in life (Hodder 1982c, 142). Barrett (1990, 179) proposed that ". . . material culture does not so much reflect social conditions as it participates in the structuring and transformation of those conditions." Incorporating post-modern explorations of rituals as modes of communication, Arnold (2001) underlined the attention they bring to the living, who are the participants and agents of action in the ritual, in contrast the more traditional academic focus on the dead; it is the living that wish to recreate society through the displays and activities at the cemetery. Since the 1980s the relations between archaeological theory and cultural anthropological theory have also shifted. In the 1960s and 1970s archaeologists derived much of their theory from cultural anthropology and sociology, and, since the 1980s, most of the theories used by archaeologists have been generated by archaeologists.

In the past 30 years the application of the developments in archaeology have revolutionized the methods for interpreting the role and function of mortuary data in the related society. Recent archaeological scholarship has acknowledged and explored the cultural dependability and variability of each community's reaction to the inevitability of death (Reid, Schiffer, and Rathje 1975; Peebles and Kus 1977; Chapman, Kinnes, and Randsborg, eds., 1981; O'Shea 1984). This contextual approach to archaeology advocates not just removing artifacts from seriations of similar data, but placement of the whole scene within the social context and examination of it as an area for the display of the drama of social behavior (Shanks and Tilley 1987a, 1987b). Since the 1990s, archaeologists have begun to interpret cemeteries as arenas for the performance and the display of social strategies and as mechanisms for the negotiation of social roles and power (Miller and Tilley 1984; Parker Pearson 1993; Beck, ed., 1995; Chesson, ed., 2001). They argue that at cemeteries and tombs related communities make multi-dimensional and multi-scalar cultural statements about the dead and the living through the objects buried with the dead or used in the rituals, the building and topographical locations of the burial place, and the funerary and post-funerary activities (Barrett 1994; Rainville 1999). In the past 20 years, various prominent themes have also penetrated mortuary studies, including gender (Arnold and Wicker 2001), agency (Flannery 1999; Dobres and Robb, eds., 2000), landscape, and memory (Barrett 1990; Knapp and Ashmore 1999; Silverman and Small, eds., 2002; Van Dyke and Alcock 2003; Williams, ed., 2003). Incorporating post-modern understandings of the material world, these studies demonstrate the communication of cultural ideas through material culture and the landscape and their involvement in the processes of social reproduction (Hodder, ed., 1982; Tilley 1999).

During this period of growth and awareness in archaeological theory, a perceived division emerged between archaeologists trained in classics departments and those from anthropology departments. Clarke's work (1973) along with contemporary works by Binford and others fuelled the perception of a distinction between anthropologically trained archaeologists and classically trained archaeologists, which was named the "great divide" by Renfrew (1980). In his article "Archeology as Anthropology," Binford (1962) argued that archaeology is anthropological and is scientific in the sense that it generates hypotheses to be tested against collected archaeological data, it explicitly formulates theories, and it clearly states its assumptions; these procedures became the norm in the anthropological archaeology. While Binford argued that anthropological archaeologists approached their data with explicit, theoretically-shaped questions and methods, it was suggested that classically trained archaeologists approached the data in order to organize them into clear categories so that patterns would emerge from the data almost as if bidden. Renfrew (1980) suggested that Greek archaeology differed from other archaeologies because, in the Greek world, most of the archaeological reasoning was inductive and the data was allowed to "speak for itself." In this distinction between anthropological archaeology on the one hand and Greek/classical archaeology on the other, archaeologists working in Greece were criticized as too focused on data and too limited culturally on the grounds that they had not attempted to place the Greek world into larger frameworks of similar or different societies (most recently, see Galaty and Parkinson, eds., 2007, 1–3, 21–23; see also Morris 1994). Whatever validity this polarization of archaeologies had in the third quarter of the twentieth century, many recent compendia in Aegean archaeology, partly as a defense against such attacks, have focused on distinctly theoretical issues (see, e.g., Spencer 1995; Hamilakis 2002; Galaty and Parkinson, eds., 2007). The papers in the present volume indicate that many Aegean scholars are incorporating newer theories in their work; other scholarship provides close readings of the data and presents valuable detailed information on the types of material found at their sites/regions on which further analysis may rely.

With the introduction of New Archaeology, post-modernism, and post-processualism into the archaeology of death in Greece, archaeologists have explored the complexity of cultural functions and ideological statements expressed through burials. Initially the literature on mortuary systems addressed the use of tombs in legitimizing and maintaining the rights of the living (e.g., Morris 1987; Antonaccio 1995; Murphy 1998); but recently, the creation of power and rights for the living through the burial of the dead has been discussed (e.g., Voutsaki 1993, 1995a, 1995b, 1998; Preston 1999, 2004a, 2004c). The impact on Cretan studies of this theoretically explicit and developed style of scholarship is visible in the themes discussed in the archeology of death: rituals and social cohesion (Branigan 1991), feasting (Hamilakis 1998), ranking and elites (Blasingham 1983; Soles 1988; Maggidis 1994, 1998; Karytinos 1998; Dimopoulou 1999; Preston 2004a; Papadatos 2005), and mortuary systems and their various roles in social negotiations and performances (Preston 1999, 2004a, 2004b; Borgna 2003; Relaki 2003).

Toward a Current Understanding of Cretan Mortuary Practices

Minoan studies are frequently divided either by region or time period—as is common in most geographical areas of the archaeological world—and there has often been a lack of communication between the scholars pursuing diverse aspects of the field. This volume is intended to promote dialogue between scholars specializing in different time periods and regions. Most of authors in this volume presented their papers at the Archaeological Institute of America (AIA) meetings in January 2007 at San Diego, after which the participants had a lively discussion about different aspects of the death on Crete. This volume, like the AIA session, includes papers from all areas on Crete, ranging in scale from a single tomb to large regions such as the Mesara area or East Crete, or indeed the entire island, and from the Early Minoan (EM) period to the Early Iron Age (EIA). The papers by volume contributors who did not participate in the session (Betancourt, Ch. 4; Eaby, Ch. 7), expand the scope of the volume both geographically and chronologically.

The variety of papers in this volume represents current thinking on the archaeology of death on Minoan Crete. The breadth and diversity of these papers was achieved by separate open invitations sent to group lists and to individual scholars known to be working on Cretan mortuary issues, first for participants in the AIA colloquium and subsequently for papers for the edited volume. Some scholars who participated in the colloquium were unable to submit papers for the volume, and some scholars included in the volume did not participate in the colloquium. The resulting publication demonstrates clearly that scholarship on Crete is not unified in its approach to archaeology. This multiplicity applies not only to approaches to the data, but also to the questions asked of that data and to the interpretational limits imposed on the data and the scholarship. In Minoan archaeology, cultural historical approaches, post-modern interpretations, regional studies, and detailed single-site examinations coexist and have academic value. These papers illustrate the rich understanding of past activity obtainable by embracing a variety of approaches.

In addition to presenting a diversity of voices, the studies published here transcend the early scholarship that focused on superficial differences between various types of cemeteries, tombs, and burials, and the quantities and categories of grave goods. Many of the earlier works shared an often-explicit understanding that tombs acted as a direct reflection of the hierarchy and religious activity in the related society, and they postulated that superficial differences or changes in the mortuary activity mirrored significant differences or changes in the related community or culture. This compendium also builds on more recent studies of Minoan mortuary systems that have combined earlier observations with anthropological paradigms and theories, emphasizing the insights into the complexities of social structure and stratification, ideologies, and economics of the related communities afforded by mortuary analysis. Issues such as regionalism, intra-island and/or diachronic studies, construction of identity, territoriality, the cemetery as religious space, manifestation of power struggles, mechanisms for the control of resources and people, and legitimization and normalizations of hierarchies are addressed in these papers.

Through a post-modern interpretation of landscape, Joanne Murphy (Ch. 2) elucidates the uses of landscape in conjunction with mortuary systems to create and encode social structures in Lebena in South-Central Crete and at Mochlos in eastern Crete during the Prepalatial and Protopalatial periods. She argues that although the communities in both areas manipulated landscape and cemeteries in similar ways—as tools of communication and visual metaphors for the ideal social structure and organization—those social structures were distinctly different, as were the sizes of the family groups using the tombs. She discusses burials as a social mechanism to disguise the fluidity and fragility of small-scale societies.

Borja Legarra Herrero (Ch. 3) reassesses Platanos and Koumasa in South-Central Crete, reviewing the history of scholarship on the EM and Middle Minoan (MM) cemeteries with an emphasis on the uncritical assumptions subsumed by the literature. With a post-processual understanding of the creative social functions of cemeteries, he reconstructs their roles as complex social arenas for interaction and for the negotiation of social relationships. He stresses variability in the cemeteries, accentuates the implications of poor chronology for the tholos cemeteries, emphasizes the need for an analysis of these cemeteries that underlines their heterogeneity and their constantly changing social roles, and argues that these two cemeteries are examples of mortuary activities at different times with diverse social uses.

The unpublished Tomb 4 on the island of Pseira in the bay of Mirabello in northeastern Crete is the focus of Philip Betancourt's paper (Ch. 4). He presents the evidence for the long duration of this communal rock shelter tomb, which was first used in the Final Neolithic (FN) or EM I period. In MM II, a court, which was unique in this cemetery, was built in front of its entrance. He argues that this court, along with the vessels found buried in it, was used in rituals that venerated the dead, and that this evidence for a ritual of veneration at this relatively poor site demonstrates that such rituals were not limited to monumental burial places.

In a diachronic study of the long-used Tomb at Pyrgos in eastern Crete, Gerald Cadogan (Ch. 5) presents models for the functions of the tomb in the social arena. He contends that the changing mortuary behavior at this Tomb, in which burials were made from the EM period until the LM period, justifies it being called a power house and reflects its varying roles in manipulating memory and tradition and in creating identity at local, regional, and inter-regional levels. He presents his interpretation of the multiple roles of the Tomb in relation to the nearby settlement, including the location and construction of the Tomb in a newly nucleated settlement, its role in legitimizing control of the settlement and surrounding territories, and the changing uses of the Tomb over time. In an analysis of the skeletal remains from the last phase of the Tomb's use (LM I), Cadogan argues for the prominence of a male elite.

Katia Perna's discussion (Ch. 6) of material from LM IIIC provides a link between the previous papers in this volume on earlier mortuary evidence and Eaby's paper about Iron Age practices. Perna highlights the radical social transformation of the island during the LM IIIC period, which is characterized in the mortuary realm by a lack of uniformity. In order to place the tombs in a broader context and to analyze their relationship to the political and economic development of the Cretan centers, she discusses the difficulties of linking the cemeteries with settlements and gives a detailed analysis of the tomb and burial types.

And finally, Melissa Eaby (Ch. 7) adds breadth to the chronological scope of this volume by examining the mortuary practices on Crete dating to the Iron Age, which she defines as LM IIIC to the Early Orientalizing period. In addressing the diversity in burial behavior, she identifies six distinct mortuary regions and three border zones, stresses the regionalism of practices, and emphasizes the cultural differences on the island. She argues that the formative factors propelling this diversity include socio-political organization, cultural identity, previous traditions in the region, and the development of city-states. In her assessment of these patterns she contends that the greatest diversity in burial activity is related to areas with early evidence of city-state formation, while homogeneity is linked to a lack of social diversity and a simple socio-political organization.

Conclusion

Death is an inevitable fact of life and a popular scholarly subject. The preceding introduction to this volume provides a synthetic overview of scholarship on mortuary studies in archaeology and in Cretan studies, and on mortuary activity as reported and interpreted in these papers. One of the most salient themes to surface from post-modern studies is the multi-valency of all aspects and objects in life; a tomb or mortuary ritual can therefore both reflect one social structure and create others at the same time. The patterning and variability in these papers of mortuary activity and the theoretical frameworks used to question and interpret this activity are as diverse as the uses of the tombs they discuss. Each author in this volume takes a clear and distinct approach to the data, including some that emphasize political geography on multi-regional and multi-scalar levels, some that examine the commemoration of the dead and of the community for legitimizing purposes but also for maintaining and/or creating elite positions in social systems, and others that underline the overlap between mortuary rituals and religion. The breadth of these papers is intended generate a discourse not just among archaeologists working in different areas and time periods on Crete but also among archaeologists in Greece and a broader anthropological audience.

References

Agelarakis, A., A. Kanta, and J. Moody. 2001. "Cremation Burial in LM IIIC–Sub Minoan Crete and the Cemetery at Pezoulos Atsipadhes, Crete," in *Καύσεις στην Εποχή του Χαλκού και την Πρώιμη Εποχή του Σιδήρου, Ρόδος, 29 Απριλίου–2 Μαΐου 1999*, N. Ch. Stampolidis, ed., Athens, pp. 69–82.

Alberti, L. 1999. "L'alabastron nelle necropoli di Cnosso del TM II–IIIA1," in *Epi ponton plazomenoi. Simposio italiano di studi egei, dedicato a Luigi Bernabò Brea e Giovanni Pugliese Carratelli (Roma, 18–20 febbraio 1998)*, V. La Rosa, D. Palermo, and L. Vagnetti, eds., Rome, pp. 167–175.

———. 2001. "Costumi funerari medio minoici a Cnosso: La necropoli di Mavro Spileo," *SMEA* 43, pp. 163–187.

———. 2004. "The Late Minoan II–IIIA1 Warrior Graves at Knossos: The Burial Assemblages," in Cadogan, Hatzaki, and Vasilakis, eds., 2004, pp. 127–136.

Alexiou, S. and P. Warren. 2004. *The Early Minoan Tombs of Lebena, Southern Crete* (*SIMA* 30), Sävedalen.

Andreadaki-Vlasaki, M. 1985. "Γεωμετρικὰ νεκροταφεῖα στὸ Νομό Χανίων," in *Πεπραγμένα του Ε' Διεθνούς Κρητολογικού Συνεδρίου* Α', Herakleion, pp. 10–35.

Antonaccio, C. 1995. *An Archaeology of Ancestors: Greek Tomb and Hero Cult*, Lanham, Md.

Arnold, B. 2001. "The Limits of Agency in the Analysis of Elite Iron Age Celtic Burials," *Journal of Social Archaeology* 1 (2), pp. 210–224.

Arnold, B., and N.L. Wicker, eds. 2001. *Gender and the Archaeology of Death*, Walnut Creek, Calif.

Bardsley, C.S. 2004. "Cognitive and Cultural Evolutionary Perspectives on Religion: A Socio-Communicative Approach to the Archaeology of the Mesaran Tholos Tombs," in *Belief in the Past. The Proceedings of the 2002 Manchester Conference on Archaeology and Religion* (*BAR-IS* 1212), T. Insoll, ed., Oxford, pp. 17–26.

Barrett, J.C. 1990. "The Monumentality of Death: The Character of Early Bronze Age Mortuary Mounds in Southern Britain," *WorldArch* 22 (2), pp. 179–189.

———. 1994. *Fragments from Antiquity: An Archaeology of Social Life in Britain, 2900–1200 B.C.*, Oxford.

Bartel, B. 1982. "A Historical Review of Ethnological and Archaeological Analyses of Mortuary Practices," *JAnthArch* 1, pp. 32–58.

Beck, L.A., ed. 1995. *Regional Approaches to Mortuary Analysis*, New York.

Betancourt, P.P. 1985. *The History of Minoan Pottery*, Princeton.

Betancourt, P.P., C. Davaras, and R. Hope Simpson, eds. 2002. *Pseira VI: The Pseira Cemetery 1. The Surface Survey* (*Prehistory Monographs* 5), Philadelphia.

———, eds. 2003. *Pseira VII: The Pseira Cemetery 2. Excavation of the Tombs* (*Prehistory Monographs* 6), Philadelphia.

Binford, L. 1962. "Anthropology as Archaeology," *AmerAnt* 28 (2), pp. 217–225.

————. 1971. "Mortuary Practices: Their Study and their Potential," in *Approaches to the Social Dimensions of Mortuary Practices*, J.A. Brown, ed., pp. 6–29.

————. 1972. *An Archaeological Perspective*, New York.

Blasingham, A. 1983. "The Seals from the Tombs of the Mesara: Inferences as to Kinship and Social Organization," in *Minoan Society*, O. Krzyszkowska and L. Nixon, eds., Bristol, pp. 11–21.

Bloch, M. 1971. *Placing the Dead: Tombs, Ancestral Villages, and Kinship Organization in Madagascar*, London.

Borgna, E. 2003. "Regional Settlement Patterns, Exchange Systems and Sources of Power in Crete at the End of the Late Bronze Age: Establishing a Connection," *SMEA* 45, pp. 153–183.

Branigan, K. 1965. "Four 'Miniature Sickles' of Middle Minoan Crete," *CretChron* 19, pp. 179–182.

————. 1968a. *Copper and Bronze Working in Early Bronze Age Crete*, Göteborg.

————. 1968b. "Silver and Lead in Prepalatial Crete," *AJA* 72, pp. 219–229.

————. 1970a. *The Tombs of Mesara*, London.

————. 1970b. "Minoan Foot Amulets and Their Eastern Counterparts," *SMEA* 11, pp. 7–23.

————. 1971. "Cycladic Figurines and Their Derivatives in Crete," *BSA* 66, pp. 57–78.

————. 1984. "Early Minoan Society: The Evidence of the Mesara Tholoi Revised," in *Aux origines de l'hellénisme: La Crète et la Grèce. Hommage à Henri van Effenterre*, Paris, pp. 29–37.

————. 1987. "Ritual Interference with Human Bones in the Mesara Tholoi," in *Thanatos: Les coutumes funéraires en Égée à l'Age du Bronze* (*Aegaeum* 1), R. Laffineur, ed., Liège, pp. 43–50.

————. 1991. "Funerary Ritual and Social Cohesion in Early Bronze Age Crete," *Journal of Mediterranean Studies* 1, pp. 183–192.

————. 1993. *Dancing with Death: Life and Death in Southern Crete, c. 3000–2000 B.C.*, Amsterdam.

————, ed. 1998. *Cemetery and Society in the Aegean Bronze Age* (*Sheffield Studies in Aegean Archaeology* 1), Sheffield.

Brown, J.A. 1971. "The Dimensions of Status in the Burials at Spiro," in *Approaches to the Social Dimensions of Mortuary Practices* (*Society for American Archaeology Memoir* 25), J.A. Brown, ed., Washington, D.C., pp. 92–112.

————. 1981. "The Search for Rank in Prehistoric Burials," in *The Archaeology of Death*, R. Chapman, I. Kinnes, and K. Randsborg, eds., 1981, Cambridge, pp. 25–37.

Cadogan, G., E. Hatzaki, and A. Vasilakis, eds. 2004. *Knossos: Palace, City, State. Proceedings of the Conference in Herakleion Organised by the British School at Athens and the 23rd Ephoreia of Prehistoric and Classical Antiquities of Herakleion, in November 2000, for the Centenary of Sir Arthur Evans's Excavations at Knossos* (*BSA Studies* 12), London.

Carr, C. 1995. "Mortuary Practices: Their Social, Philosophical-Religious, Circumstantial and Physical Determinants," *Journal of Archaeological Method and Theory* 2, pp. 105–200.

Chapman, R., I. Kinnes, and K. Randsborg, eds. 1981. *The Archaeology of Death*, Cambridge.

Chesson, M., ed. 2001. *Social Memory, Identity, and Death: Anthropological Perspectives on Mortuary Rituals* (*Archeological Papers of the American Anthropological Association* 10), Arlington.

Clarke, D. 1973. "Archaeology: The Loss of Innocence," *Antiquity* 47, pp. 6 –18.

Coldstream, J.N., and H.W. Catling, eds. 1996. *Knossos North Cemetery: Early Greek Tombs* I–IV (*BSA Suppl.* 28), London.

Davaras, C., and P.P. Betancourt. 2004. *The Hagia Photia Cemetery* I (*Prehistory Monographs* 14), Philadelphia.

Demargne, P. 1945. *Fouilles exécutées à Mallia: Exploration des nécropoles (1921–1933)* (*ÉtCrét* 7), Paris.

Dimopoulou, N. 1999. "The Neopalatial Cemetery of the Knossian Harbour-Town at Poros: Mortuary Behavior and Social Ranking," in *Eliten in der Bronzezeit: Ergebnisse zweier Kolloquien in Mainz und Athen*, I. Kilian-Dirlmeier and M. Egg, eds., Mainz, pp. 27–36.

Dobres, M.-A., and J.E. Robb, eds. 2000. *Agency in Archaeology*, London.

Durkheim, É. 1965. *The Elementary Forms of the Religious Life*, J.W. Swain, trans., 5th ed., London.

Evans, A.J. 1906. "The Prehistoric Tombs of Knossos," *Archaeologia* 59, pp. 391–562.

————. 1914. "The 'Tomb of the Double Axes' and Associated Group, and the Pillar Rooms and Ritual Vessels of the 'Little Palace' at Knossos," *Archaeologia* 65, pp. 1–94.

————. 1924. "Preface," in *The Vaulted Tombs of the Mesara*, S.A. Xanthoudides, London, pp. v–xiii.

Flannery, K.V. 1999. "Process and Agency in Early State Formation," *CAJ* 9 (1), pp. 3–21.

Forsdyke, E. J. 1927. "The Mavro Spelio Cemetery at Knossos," *BSA* 28, pp. 243–296.

Galaty, M. L. and W. A. Parkinson, eds. 2007. *Rethinking Mycenaean Palaces II: Revised and Expanded Second Edition*, Los Angeles.

Goldstein, L. 1976. *Spatial Structure and Social Organization: Regional Manifestations of the Mississippian Society*, Ph.D. diss., Northwestern University.

———. 1980. *Mississippian Mortuary Practices: A Case Study of Two Cemeteries in the Lower Illinois Valley*, Evanston, Ill.

Goodison, L. 2004. "From Tholos Tomb to Throne Room: Some Considerations of Dawn Light and Directionality in Minoan Buildings," in Cadogan, Hatzaki, and Vasilakis, eds., 2004, pp. 339–350.

Goody, J. 1962. *Death, Property and the Ancestors: A Study of the Mortuary Customs of the LoDagaa of West Africa*, Stanford.

Hall, E. 1912. *Excavations in Eastern Crete: Sphoungaras*, Philadelphia.

Hallager, B.P., and P.J.P. McGeorge. 1992. *Late Minoan III Burials at Khania. The Tombs, Finds and Deceased in Odos Palama* (*SIMA* 93), Göteborg.

Hamilakis, Y. 1998. "Eating the Dead: Mortuary Feasting and the Politics of Memory in the Aegean Bronze Age Societies," in Branigan, ed., 1998, pp. 115–132.

———, ed. 2002. *Labyrinth Revisited: Rethinking Minoan Archaeology*, Oxford.

Hatzaki, E. 2005. "Postpalatial Knossos: Town and Cemeteries from LM IIIA2 to LM IIIC" in *Ariadne's Threads: Connections between Crete and the Greek Mainland in Late Minoan IIIC (LM IIIA2 to LM IIIC). Proceedings of the International Workshop Held at Athens, Scuola archeologica italiana, 5–6 April 2003*, A.-L. D'Agata and J.A. Moody, eds., Athens, pp. 65–95.

Hertz, R. 1907. "Contribution à une étude sur la représentation collective de la mort," *L'Année Sociologique* 10, pp. 48–137.

———. 1960. "A Contribution to the Study of the Collective Representation of Death," in *Death and the Right Hand*, trans. by R. Needham and C. Needham, Aberdeen, pp. 29–76.

Hodder, I. 1982a. *Symbols in Action*, Cambridge.

———. 1982b. "The Identification and Interpretation of Ranking in Prehistory: A Contextual Perspective," in *Ranking, Resource and Exchange*, A.C. Renfrew and S. Shennan, eds., Cambridge, pp. 150–154.

———. 1982c. *The Present Past*, London.

————. 1989. *The Meaning of Things: Material Culture and Symbolic Expression*, London.

Hodder, I., ed. 1982. *Symbolic and Structural Archaeology*, Cambridge.

Hood, S., G. Huxley, and N. Sandars. 1958–1959. "A Minoan Cemetery on Upper Gypsadhes," *BSA* 53–54, pp. 194–269.

Huntington, R., and P. Metcalf. 1979. *Celebrations of Death: The Anthropology of Mortuary Ritual*, Cambridge.

Karytinos, A. 1998. "Sealstones in Cemeteries: A Display of Social Status?" in Branigan, ed., 1998, pp. 78–86.

Knapp, A.B., and W. Ashmore. 1999. *Archaeologies of Landscape: Contemporary Perspectives*, Oxford.

Levi, D. 1961–1962. "La tomba a tholos di Kamilari presso a Festos," *Annuario* 23–24, pp. 7–148.

Löwe, W. 1996. *Spätbronzezeitliche Bestattungen auf Kreta (BAR-IS* 642), Oxford.

Maggidis, C. 1994. *Burial Building 19 at Archanes: A Study of Prepalatial and Early Protopalatial Funerary Architecture and Ritual*, Ph.D. diss., University of Pennsylvania.

————. 1998. "From Polis to Necropolis: Social Ranking from Architectural and Mortuary Evidence in the Minoan Cemetery at Phourni, Archanes," in Branigan, ed., 1998, pp. 87–102.

Marinatos, S. 1930–1931. "Δυὸ πρώιμοι Μινωικοὶ τάφοι," *ArchDelt* 13 [1933], pp. 137–170.

Miles, D. 1965. "Socio-Economic Aspects of Secondary Burial," *Oceania* 35 (3), pp. 161–174.

Miller, D., and C. Tilley. 1984. *Ideology, Power and Prehistory*, Cambridge.

Morgan, L.H. 1877. *Ancient Society*, New York.

Morris, I. 1987. *Burial and Ancient Society*, Cambridge.

————. 1991. "The Archaeology of Ancestors: The Saxc/Goldstein Hypothesis Revisited," *CAJ* 1 (2), pp. 147–169.

————. 1994. "Archaeologies of Greece," in *Classical Greece: Ancient Histories and Modern Archaeologies*, I. Morris, ed., Cambridge, pp. 8–48.

Murphy, J.M. 1998. "Ideology, Rites and Rituals: A View of Prepalatial Minoan Tholoi," in Branigan, ed., 1998, pp. 27–40.

O'Shea, J.M. 1981. "Social Configurations and the Archaeological Study of Mortuary Practices: A Case Study," in *The Archaeology of Death*, R. Chapman, I. Kinnes, and K. Randsborg, eds., Cambridge, pp. 39–52.

————. 1984. *Mortuary Variability: An Archaeological Investigation*, New York.

Pader, E.J. 1982. *Symbolism, Social Relations and the Interpretation of Mortuary Remains*, Oxford.

Panagiotopoulos, D. 2002. *Das Tholosgrab E von Phourni bei Archanes: Studien zu einem frühkretischen Grabfund und seinem kulturellen Kontext* (*BAR-IS* 1014), Oxford.

Papadatos, Y. 2005. *Tholos Tomb Gamma: A Prepalatial Tholos Tomb at Phourni, Archanes* (*Prehistory Monographs* 17), Philadelphia.

Paribeni, R. 1904. "Ricerche nel sepolcreto di Haghia Triada presso Phaestos," *MonAnt* 14, pp. 677–756.

Parker-Pearson, M. 1982. "Mortuary Practices, Society and Ideology: An Ethnoarchaeological Study," in *Symbolic and Structural Archaeology*, I. Hodder, ed., Cambridge, pp. 99–113.

————. 1993. "The Powerful Dead: Archaeological Relationships between the Living and the Dead," *CAJ* 3 (2), pp. 203–229.

————. 1999. *The Archaeology of Death and Burial*, College Station.

Peebles, C.S., and S.M. Kus. 1977. "Some Archaeological Correlates of Ranked Societies," *AmerAnt* 42 (3), pp. 421- 448.

Pelon, O. 1976. *Tholoi, tumuli et cercles funéraires: Recherches sur les monuments funéraires de plan circulaire dans l'Égée de l'Âge du Bronze (IIIe et IIe millénaires av. J.-C.)*, Athens.

Perna, K. 2001. "Rituali funerari e rappresentazione del potere nella Creta del TM III A2/B," *Creta Antica* 2, pp. 113–125.

Pini, I. 1968. *Beiträge zur minoischen Gräberkunde*, Wiesbaden.

Preston, L. 1999. "Mortuary Practices and the Negotiation of Social Identities at LM II Knossos," *BSA* 94, pp. 131–143.

————. 2004a. "A Mortuary Perspective on Elites in Final and Post-Palatial Crete," *AJA* 108, pp. 321–348.

————. 2004b. "Final Palatial Knossos and Post-Palatial Crete: A Mortuary Perspective on Political Dynamics," in Cadogan, Hatzaki, and Vasilakis, eds., 2004, pp. 137–145.

————. 2004c. "Contextualising the Larnax: Tradition, Innovation and Regionalism in Coffin Use on Late Minoan II–IIIB Crete," *OJA* 23 (2), pp. 177–197.

Raddclife-Brown, A.R. 1964. *The Andaman Islanders*, New York.

Rainville, L. 1999. "Hanover Deathscapes: Mortuary Variability in New Hampshire, 1770–1920," *Ethnohistory* 46 (3), pp. 541–597.

Reid, J.J, M.B. Schiffer, and W.L. Rathje. 1975. "Behavioral Archaeology: Four Strategies," *American Anthropologist* 77, pp. 864–869.

Relaki, M. 2003. *Social Arenas in Minoan Crete: A Regional History of the Mesara from the Final Neolithic to the End of the Protopalatial Period*, Ph.D. diss., University of Sheffield.

Renfrew, C. 1980. "The Great Tradition Versus the Great Divide: Archaeology as Anthropology," *AJA* 84, pp. 287–298.

Sakellaraki, E., and Y. Sakellarakis. 1991. "Ἀνασκαφὴ Ἀρχανῶν 1986–1988," *ArchEph* 130 [1993], pp. 169–218.

Sakellarakis, J., and E. Sapouna-Sakellaraki. 1991. *Archanes*, Athens.

————. 1997. *Archanes: Minoan Crete in a New Light*, Athens.

Savignoni, L. 1904. "Scavi e scoperte nelle necropoli di Phaestos," *MonAnt* 14, pp. 501–675.

Saxe, A. 1970. *Social Dimensions of Mortuary Practices*, Ph.D. diss., University of Michigan.

Sbonias, K. 1999. "Social Development, Management of Production, and Symbolic Representation in Prepalatial Crete," in *From Minoan Farmers to Roman Traders: Sidelights on the Economy of Ancient Crete*, A. Chaniotis, ed., Stuttgart, pp. 25–52.

Seager, R. 1912. *Exploration on the Island of Mochlos*, Philadelphia.

————. 1916. *The Cemetery of Pachyammos, Crete*, Philadelphia.

Shanks, M., and C. Tilley. 1987a. *Social Theory and Archaeology*, Cambridge.

————. 1987b. *Reconstructing Archaeology: Theory and Practice*, Cambridge.

Silverman, H., and D.B. Small, eds. 2002. *The Space and Place of Death (Archaeological Papers of the American Anthropological Association* 11), Arlington, Va.

Soles, J. 1973. *The Gournia House Tombs*, Ph.D. diss., University of Pennsylvania.

————. 1988. "Social Ranking in Prepalatial Cemeteries," in *Problems in Greek Prehistory*, E.B. French and K.A. Wardle, eds., Bristol, pp. 49–61.

————. 1992. *The Prepalatial Cemeteries at Mochlos and Gournia and the House Tombs of Bronze Age Crete (Hesperia* Suppl. 24), Princeton.

Spencer, H. 1860. "The Social Organism," *Westminster Review* 17, pp. 51–68.

———. 1876–1896. *The Principles of Sociology* I–III, London.

Spencer, N. 1995. *Time, Tradition and Society in Greek Archaeology: Bridging the "Great Divide,"* London.

Tainter, J. 1975. "Social Inference and Mortuary Practices: An Experiment in Numerical Classification," *WorldArch* 7, pp. 1–15.

———. 1978. "Mortuary Practices and the Study of Prehistoric Social Systems," in *Advances in Archaeological Method and Theory* 1, M. Schiffer, ed., London, pp. 105–141.

Tilley, C. 1999. *Metaphor and Material Culture*, Oxford.

Turner, V. 1967. *The Forest of Symbols: Aspects of Ndembu Ritual*, Ithaca.

———. 1969. *The Ritual Process*, Chicago.

Tylor, E. 1903. *Primitive Culture*, London.

Ucko, P.J. 1969. "Ethnography and Archaeology Interpretation of Funerary Remains," *WorldArch* 1 (2), pp. 262–280.

Van Dyke, R., and S. Alcock. 2003. "Archaeologies of Memory: An Introduction," in *Archaeologies of Memory*, R. Van Dyke and S. Alcock, eds., Oxford, pp. 1–13.

van Effenterre, H. 1948. *Nécropoles de Mirabello* (*ÉtCrét* 8), Paris.

van Gennep, A. 1960. *The Rites of Passage*, trans. M.B. Vizedom and G.L. Caffee, Chicago.

Vasilakis, A. 1989–1990. "Προϊστορικές Θέσεις στη Μονή Οδηγήτριας, Καλοί Λιμένες," *Kretike Estia* 3 [1990], pp. 11–79.

Vavouranakis, G. 2002. "Towards an Elemental Approach to Early Minoan Funerary Architecture: The Enduring Bedrock," in *Symposium on Mediterranean Archaeology* (*BAR-IS* 1040), G. Muskett, A. Kolisida, and M. Georgiadis, eds., Oxford, pp. 39–46.

Voutsaki, S. 1993. *Society and Culture in the Mycenaean World: An Analysis of Mortuary Practices in the Argolid, Thessaly and Dodecanese*, Ph.D. diss., University of Cambridge.

———. 1995a. "Value and Exchange in Pre-monetary Societies: Anthropological Debates and Aegean Archaeology," in *Trade and Production in Pre-Monetary Societies* (*SIMA* 134), C. Gillis, C. Risberg, and B. Sjöberg, eds., Jonsered, pp. 7–17.

———. 1995b. Social and Political Processes in the Mycenaean Argolid: The Evidence from the Mortuary Practices," in *Politeia: Society and State in the Aegean Bronze Age. Proceedings of the 5th International Aegean Conference, University of*

Heidelberg, Archäologisches Institut, 10–13 April 1994 (*Aegaeum* 12), R. Laffineur, and W.-D. Niemeier, eds., Liège, pp. 55–66.

―――. 1998. "Mortuary Evidence, Symbolic Meanings and Social Change: A Comparison between Messenia and the Argolid in the Mycenaean Period," in Branigan, ed., 1998, pp. 41–58.

Warren, P. 1965. "The First Minoan Stone Vases and Early Minoan Chronology," *CretChron* 19, pp. 7–43.

―――. 1969. *Minoan Stone Vases*, Cambridge.

Watson, P.J, A.J. LeBlanc, and C.L. Redmond. 1971. *Explanation in Archaeology: An Explicitly Scientific Approach*, New York.

Wiencke, M.H. 1981. "Typology and Style of Prepalatial Seals," in *Studien zur minoischen und helladischen Glyptik* (*CMS Beiheft* 1), Marburg, pp. 251–261.

Willey, G., and P. Phillips. 1958. *Method and Theory in American Anthropology*, Chicago.

Williams, H., ed. 2003. *Archaeologies of Remembrance: Death and Memory in Past Societies*, New York.

Wilson, D.E., and P.M. Day. 1994. "Ceramic Regionalism in Prepalatial Central Crete: The Mesara Imports from EM IB to EM IIA Knossos," *BSA* 89, pp. 1–87.

Xanthoudides, S. 1918. "Παράρτημα Πρωτομινωικός Τάφος Μεσαράς," *ArchDelt* 4, pp. 15–23.

―――. 1924. *The Vaulted Tombs of the Mesara*, London.

Yule, P. 1981. *Early Cretan Seals: A Study of Chronology*, Mainz.

2 | Landscape and Social Narratives: A Study of Regional Social Structures in Prepalatial Crete

JOANNE M.A. MURPHY

This paper explores two Prepalatial tomb groups—Mochlos in East Crete and Lebena in South-Central Crete—in order to demonstrate the similarities between the manipulations by these communities of their mortuary systems and landscapes in an attempt to encode their social ideologies despite the regionally-based differences in their social structures (Fig. 2.1).* The former group emphasized eternal and stable community membership, while the latter stressed the constructed elite status of individual families. The arguments for these conclusions build on the regional and local studies that have been the focus of much recent scholarship on Cretan mortuary systems (Wilson and Day 1994; Murphy 1998; Relaki 2004; Legarra Herrero 2009) and on the accepted understandings of the different social divisions in these two areas of Crete (Soles 1988; Branigan 1991b), and they employ recent theories about the uses of landscape and mortuary systems. Theories of memory and landscape are discussed to

*I would like to thank Carol Hershenson, Evi Gorogianni, Julie Fairbanks, and the anonymous reviewers for their helpful comments and suggestions on earlier drafts of this paper. I would also like to thank Jeffrey Soles for reading the section on Mochlos and generously discussing it with me.

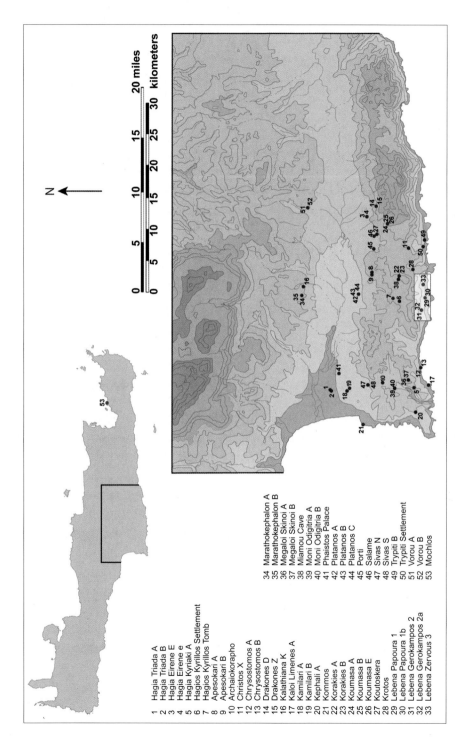

1   Hagia Triada A
2   Hagia Triada B
3   Hagia Eirene E
4   Hagia Eirene e
5   Hagia Kyriaki A
6   Hagios Kyrillos Settlement
7   Hagios Kyrillos Tomb
8   Apesokari A
9   Apesokari B
10 Archaiokorapho
11 Christos X
12 Chrysostomos A
13 Chrysostomos B
14 Drakones D
15 Drakones Z
16 Kalathiana K
17 Kaloi Limenes A
18 Kamilari A
19 Kamilari B
20 Kephali A
21 Kommos
22 Korakies A
23 Korakies B
24 Koumasa A
25 Koumasa B
26 Koumasa E
27 Koutoskera
28 Krotos
29 Lebena Papoura 1
30 Lebena Papoura 1b
31 Lebena Gerokampos 2
32 Lebena Gerokampos 2a
33 Lebena Zervous 3
34 Marathokephalon A
35 Marathokephalon B
36 Megaloi Skinoi A
37 Megaloi Skinoi B
38 Miamou Cave
39 Moni Odigitria A
40 Moni Odigitria B
41 Phaistos Palace
42 Platanos A
43 Platanos B
44 Platanos C
45 Porti
46 Salame
47 Sivas N
48 Sivas S
49 Trypiti B
50 Trypiti Settlement
51 Vorou A
52 Vorou B
53 Mochlos

Figure 2.1. Map of South-Central Crete showing location of tombs. Lebena tombs highlighted.

elucidate the manipulation of these elements by societies in order to make social statements that are intended to appear natural and unquestionable.

Theoretical Framework

Three areas of recent anthropological and archaeological research are relevant to the case studies that follow of mortuary systems at Mochlos and Lebena: (1) the ways in which different cultures encode their ideologies on the landscape; (2) the interplay between social memory and landscape; and (3) the stability and time-depth of social hierarchies and ideologies.

Recent studies on the uses of landscape to communicate social ideologies (Bradley 1998, 2000; Cooney 2000; Scarre, ed., 2002) stress the interactions of community members with the natural and cultural landscapes and underline how societies socialize the landscape and embed social paradigms within it (Barrett 1990). Earlier interpretations of the landscape as a passive stage whereon the culture under study acted out its life—used by the people for sustenance (such as farming and fishing), for the performance of their rituals, and for building settlements, religious sites, and tombs (which was not engaged in any reciprocal relationship with the people living in it)—have been supplanted by views of the landscape as an inherent element of the community that was used and manipulated to make statements about the identity and world-views of the community (Brady and Ashmore 1999; Kealhofer 1999) and for the creation and maintenance of cultural narratives.

It is apparent from landscape studies that landscapes are culturally constructed (Knapp and Ashmore 1999, 10) and are politically, ideologically, and culturally contingent (Rabinowitz 1997). Foucault (1984) contends that the control of space is the key to social power, while Mann (1986) argues that landscapes are arenas of social power. The cultural stories—along with both their statements of power and attacks on the power holders—are visible in the landscape because it is multi-vocal and embedded with the various narratives of the related community—on one hand emphasizing the community as a whole and on the other accentuating the different groups within the community (Kealhofer 1999; Snead and Preucel 1999).

An exploration of memory is necessary for understanding the significance of the relationship between cultural narratives and the landscape and of the support by the latter of cultural paradigms (Rowlands 1993; Edmonds 1999). In his seminal work on memory, Halbwachs (1992, 51) argues that an individual's memory is created and exists only within a collective context, and it must be evoked by events, places, and people. He stresses (1992, 51) that "the mind reconstructs its memories based on the pressure of society"; not only can society induce people to alter their memories by embellishing or shortening them and therefore adjusting their reality and importance, but groups within a society can also recall and restructure long-forgotten events so that they seem like eternal group memories. This further enables groups to re-invent themselves and to derive legitimacy by drawing on otherwise long-forgotten events, attitudes, or beliefs. Collective memory is, in fact, a reconstruction of the past.

Basso's work on the Apache (1996, 67) illustrates the influence of the land on their concept of themselves and vice versa; the memory-filled landscape re-creates their identity, working almost like a mnemonic device by reminding them of their history and how they connect and relate to the world and to one another. In an experiential approach, Archibald (1999) demonstrates how the sensual elements of a landscape and place can act as creators and stimulators of memories. He argues (Archibald 1999, 14) that "familiar places become repositories of memory both personal and communal," and he gives multiple examples of how elements of the socially constructed environment can act as symbolic memory devices.

The landscape and built environment are constant reminders of the grand narrative of culture and community, because they connect sensorily with the people in the community. The agency of the landscape and its significance had been related in many archaeological works to Bourdieu's (1977) concept of *habitus*, the commonplace basis for social reproduction. Through its everyday relationship with the members of a community, the landscape plays a powerful role in the creation of the identity of a group, which is reinforced on a daily basis (Parker Pearson 1982; Knapp and Ashmore 1999, 16). The impartial power or effect of the landscape on people performs a central role when arguing that all members of the community become socialized to the dominant narrative (Barrett 1990;

Taçon 1994). The normalization of this dominant narrative is especially significant in relation to mortuary systems or ritual activity, although some community members may disagree with the hegemonic narrative (Moore 1977). For example, ethnographic works on religion show that it is highly unlikely that all members of a community will subscribe to religious beliefs or participate in the associated rituals; religious systems are open to change and influence (Hayden 2003, 15), and ethnographies from areas as disparate as South America, New Guinea (Reay 1959, 131), and Southeast Asia (Izikowitz 1951, 321) demonstrate that large portions of the populations (10%–20%) are self-identified atheists and agnostics, despite belonging to communities that are overtly religious, while other community members also do not participate in or are uninformed about the communal rituals. Rappaport (1999), however, points out that the impact of a ritual equally affects those who participate and believe and those who do not. Likewise landscape, the built environment, and the sensual embeddedness of these constructs in the people who occupy the area are transcendent of an individual's beliefs in the dominant religious system or ideology.

Because of the fragility and precariousness of any society's social ideology and of the power and status of a group or individual in a society, groups and individuals must constantly defend and support their favored positions by projecting the illusion that these are simultaneously natural and permanent; the same mechanisms, however, can be used to support different social ideologies. In contrast to studies on small-scale societies during the 1970s and 1980s, which stressed the rigidity of ranking (Earle 1987; Levy 1999, 62), more recent investigations have underlined the fluidity and fragility of ranking in small-scale societies. The latter studies show that ranking is unstable and in a constant state of flux, and its creation and maintenance therefore requires many social mechanisms. One way to create and reinforce an impression of permanence is to express the social ideology through the landscape and the mortuary system, thereby using both of those social constructs as tools of communication and as visual metaphors for the ideal social structure and organization (Baker and Biger, eds., 1992; Tilley 1994, 1999; Brady and Ashmore 1999).

The landscape and mortuary systems were used in both East Crete at Mochlos and in South-Central Crete at Lebena during the Prepalatial period to create and enforce their respective social ideologies and social hierarchies, although the social structures of the associated communities differed fundamentally. Lebena projected a more egalitarian ideology where the community as a whole was the most important social unit, while Mochlos was divided into a clear hierarchy based on small family groups. Despite the distinct differences in their social structures, both populations used the landscape in conjunction with their mortuary systems to reinforce those social structures and their respective ideologies.

Mochlos

This study of the mortuary system at the Prepalatial site on the islet of Mochlos in eastern Crete and its use of the landscape to express the social ideology of the community examines the distribution of the tombs, the social unit of burial, and evidence for ranking in the artifacts from the tombs, the architecture of the tombs, and the positions of the tombs within the landscape. Mortuary activity at Mochlos reflected, reinforced, and constantly recreated the social structure of a community based around socially differentiated family units. The tombs also provide evidence that Mochlos was a stratified society from approximately the Early Minoan (EM) II period (Soles 1988). This paper adds to the understanding of this social stratification by examining the use of the mortuary system and the natural layout of the land to communicate the ideology and social structure of the community and to give it an air of permanency. Social differentiation was stressed by the separate areas of mortuary deposition on the island, which differed in the levels of energy invested in their construction, rituals, and grave goods. Membership in these small-scale social units was the lasting identity of the individual in death, and social divisions were given an illusion of permanence (Fig. 2.2).

The cemetery on Mochlos consists of 28 excavated tombs (Soles 1992, 42). Most of these were roofed house tombs with three rock shelters (Tombs VII, VIII, and XVIII) and one pit burial (Tomb XIV) (Soles 1992, 41–42). The cemetery was first used in EM II and continued during EM III; only a few of the tombs were used in Middle Minoan (MM) IA (Soles 1992). Three distinctly defined spaces of deposition comprise the cemetery on Mochlos: the West Terrace, the South Slope, and the

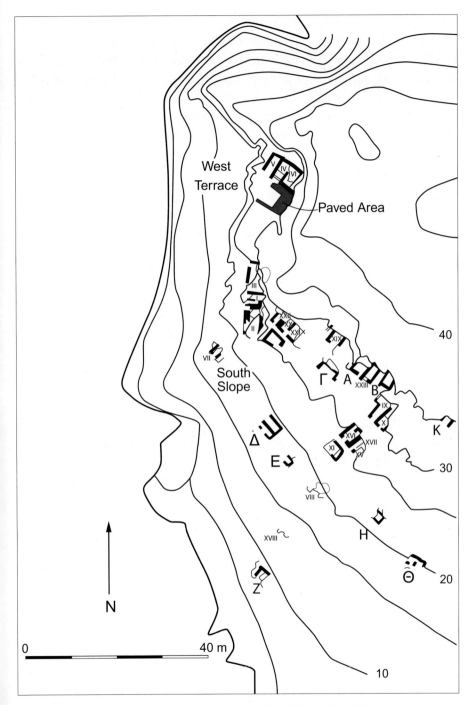

Figure 2.2. Plan of the Prepalatial cemetery at Mochlos (after Soles 1992).

area east of the South Slope (Soles 1988, 50; 1992). The two tombs on the West Terrace differ from the tombs in the other areas, as Seager (1912) and Soles (1988) have noted: they are architecturally wealthier and had more remnants of elite artifacts than the other tombs. There are 20 tombs in the South Slope cemetery, and, to date, four have been excavated in the area east of the South Slope.

SOCIAL UNIT OF BURIAL

The low rate of burial in the tombs on Mochlos suggests that the tombs were used by small family groups (Soles 1988, 59). From the relatively large number of tombs on the island (28 at present) and their skeletal evidence, it is possible to argue that hereditary nuclear family groups were the ones using the tombs. In his analysis of 30 skulls from Compartment I on the West Terrace in Tomb I/II/III, Soles suggested that 10–15 individuals were buried in the tombs every 100 years (Soles 1992, 254). Based on the size of the settlement and the catchment area of the coastal plain, the population of the island at any given time during the Prepalatial period is thought to have been around 300 people (Whitelaw 1983, 337–339; Soles 1988, 59). The number of tombs, combined with the estimated population figures and the number of dead in the tombs, suggests that there are two to three nuclear families in Compartment I, and they were not contemporary placements but successive generations of related nuclear families. As Soles (1988, 59) has pointed out, the use of the tombs by successive generations of families suggests that status was inherited.

ARTIFACTS

The distribution of artifacts in the tombs in the three cemeteries on Mochlos reflects social inequalities among the families using those tombs. The excavators found relatively few Prepalatial artifacts mainly due to the abandonment of the cemetery in MM IA and its reuse in MM III when the tombs were cleared out (Soles 1992, 58). The few remaining objects, however, evince superior wealth, and the tombs on the West Terrace contained a greater number of symbols of authority in contrast to other areas of the cemetery (Seager 1912; Davaras 1975; Soles 1992).

Although pottery was found on both the West Terrace and the South Slope, only small quantities were discovered in the former (Soles 1988, 59); in contrast, objects of intrinsic value were far more prevalent in the tombs on the West Terrace than elsewhere, although there were some exceptions on the South Slope and in the area east of the South Slope. Thirteen of the 15 gold diadems found at Mochlos were from the West Terrace (Soles 1992, 257); and Seager found some gold sheathing in Compartment V of Tomb IV/V/VI on the West Terrace (Seager 1912, 43, 63, fig. 41:V.K; Soles 1992, 258). Of the 129 artifacts found in Compartment II of Tomb I/II/III on the West Terrace, 85 were gold, 15 were stone vases, 13 were pieces of ivory, silver, or stone, nine were copper or bronze, four were lead, and three were clay. Seals were found both on the West Terrace and on the South Slope (Davaras 1975). Similarly, wealthy objects were found in small numbers in Tomb XIX on the South Slope, which was the richest of the smaller tombs. The distribution of artifacts and artifact types show that they were not limited to one section of the community but were available to both. This suggests, in turn, that the hierarchic division of the community was not tied to access to these objects, but that the quantities of the objects that were accessible to different segments of the population differed.

ARCHITECTURE OF THE TOMBS

Just as the distribution of objects of intrinsic value differentiates the tombs on the West Terrace from those in the other two areas of the cemetery, the West Terrace burial area also was distinguished architecturally by the building materials, numbers of rooms, size, and architectural details of its tombs, and by the elaboration of the area around those tombs. On the West Terrace, the tombs are constructed mostly of stone with monolithic slabs of purple and green schist incorporated into the structure. They have three and four rooms and are also substantially larger than tombs in other sections of the cemetery—twice as large as the largest and six times larger than the smallest—and they have a higher level of architectural sophistication, with internal doorways, recessed doorways, monumental rock slabs for orthostates, and upright slabs lining the inner and outer faces of some walls (Seager 1912; Soles 1988, 50; Soles 1992). The piers of green schist slabs on the outer doorway of the central compartment (Compartment 1) of Tomb I/II/III and in the stone slab threshold (Soles 1992, 53) in front of Compartment IV display externally the superior wealth of these tombs.

The architectural elaboration of the area outside the tombs on the West Terrace also visibly differentiates it from the other areas of the cemetery and reinforces its superiority as a mortuary area, thereby emphasizing the elite status of the people buried there. Although Seager had identified an open area in front of Tomb IV/V/VI, cleaning during the 1970s and 1980s revealed that the approach to the tombs on the West Terrace was much more complex than Seager had thought. Outside of Tomb IV/V/VI archaeologists uncovered a stepped, paved area using colored slabs of purple and green schist and blue-gray limestone for a mosaic effect and a paved terrace that runs along the side of the cliff face to the east (Soles 1992, 56–57). The remains of stone vases were found on a small platform discovered on the edge of this paved area near the southeast corner of Tomb IV/V/VI and against the cliff face (Soles 1992, 56). If this platform was an altar with religious significance, as Soles (1992, 56–57) suggests, it would have added to the social superiority of those using the West Terrace.

In contrast to the tombs on the West Terrace, the tombs on the South Slope are mostly rock shelters and one-room structures; there are, however, notable two-room exceptions—Tomb XIX and Tomb XX/XXI. Tomb XXIII, unlike the other tombs on the South Slope, had horizontal slabs in the walls. And, unlike the tombs on the West Terrace, the tomb walls on the South Slope make extensive use of the rock face in their construction. For example, Tomb XXII uses the rock face as a wall, and in Tomb XX/XXI the rock is incorporated into another wall. This use of naturally occurring rock faces would have decreased the energy expenditure in the construction of these South Slope tombs. Large slabs of purple schist are also used in Tombs XIII and XVI on the South Slope, but they are neither as large as the ones on the West Terrace nor as smooth (Soles 1992, 89). Most of the South Slope tombs had stone socles with mud-brick superstructures (Soles 1992, 207), although at least two tombs (Tombs IX and XVI) incorporated large limestone (*sideropetra*) orthostates into their construction (Soles 1992, 81, 88). There is also some adornment in the doorway of Tomb XXII. Thus, the tombs on the South Slope were generally smaller and less-elaborately built and decorated than those on the West Terrace, although some of them incorporated scaled-down versions of some of the embellishments found in the West Terrace tombs.

Access to the West Terrace was limited by topography, and the space could only be entered from the south. This limited access was used to control and direct the line of vision of a person entering that cemetery. Both the West Terrace and the South Slope have walkways in front of the tombs (Soles 1992, 56). However, the dead who were buried in the West Terrace would have been transported from the settlement on the south of the island along the South Slope and into the West Terrace; the ritual of the procession marked the dead being deposited on the West Terrace as separate from and superior to those on the South Slope. This separation is permanent and written in the landscape. The limited space on the West Terrace, combined with the limited access to it, communicates clearly that mere wealth, such as that evidenced by the tombs on the western side of the South Slope, did not confer access to the elite level of the West Terrace.

LANDSCAPE AND TOMB PLACEMENT

In terms of topography, the West Terrace is a small natural area situated on the western edge of the island. It is delineated by a sheer cliff drop to the sea on the west and by rising cliff walls to the north and east. It can only be entered from the south, and the area is separated naturally from the South Slope by the east cliff. The cemetery on the South Slope covers a much larger area than the West Terrace, and it is spread over several terraces. The most recently excavated area, to the east of the South Slope, is separated from the latter part of the cemetery by rock outcroppings with another rock outcrop running along its eastern side. This area is defined on the northwest side by a drop in bedrock that goes up to the West Terrace, and on the northeast by a rise in bedrock (Seager 1912; Soles 1992, 63). In each of these separate cemetery areas on the island, the wealth of the tombs is inversely proportional to the exposure of the terrain to erosion; nevertheless, the relatively large numbers of vases from the South Slope cemetery and the architectural differences among the areas of burial demonstrate that differential erosion has not caused the differences in excavated wealth from the tombs but instead reflects the selection of the most protected areas by the richest families.

The West Terrace, which contains the two wealthiest tomb complexes, is more protected from the elements and less prone to erosion than the other areas of the cemetery. The South Slope is steep and exposed to denudation and weathering, as is the area to its east. Seager (1912) commented on the degree of denudation due to the steep incline that destroyed many of the tombs on the South Slope, since he thought that there was room for double the number of tombs found there.

Even within the cemetery on the South Slope, the richer tombs occupy a geographically more favorable location; their position on the upper levels of the slope is less subject to the ravages of erosion than that of the poorer tombs below. Although the tombs on the South Slope were less grand than those on the West Terrace, there seems to be some clear hierarchy of wealth among these tombs. This hierarchy also is patterned in the cultural landscape. Two of the richest tombs, Tomb XIX and Tomb XXIII, are located on the highest terrace of the western side of the South Slope, and Tomb XX/XXI, another two-roomed structure, is located beside the West Terrace. From the privileged locations of these tombs, it would appear that certain families buried on the South Slope had access to some wealth, and positioned their tombs close to the still wealthier ones on the West Terrace; they were, however, unable to penetrate that location. These social divisions by their locations were further enforced through the mortuary system.

The landscape of Mochlos is thus encoded with the social ideology of the community, and it was incorporated into that ideology to highlight differences between different sections of the population. The topographical division between social groups in the landscape resonates with the divisions within the society, and the chronological persistence of that divided landscape endows the social system that mirrors it with the appearance of natural formation; the more protected West Terrace contrasts with the more easily denuded South Slope, reinforcing the permanence of the one against the transience of the other.

Lebena

The tombs in use during the Prepalatial and into the Protopalatial period at Lebena reveal a very different social paradigm from that found on

Mochlos; the evidence for this social ideology—the distributions of tombs in the landscape, the social unit of burial, the artifacts deposited in them, and the post-decompositional treatment of the bones and grave goods—overlaps with but is not identical to the categories of evidence for the social system at Mochlos. Exploration of the mortuary evidence from Lebena demonstrates that the landscape and the mortuary system were encoded with the dominant social ideologies of the related settlements, which emphasized the long-term unity of the society and its shared continuity, and they reflected the community's ideas of itself in the continuous creation of the social organization.

The distribution, number, architecture, and long-term use of the tombs that Alexiou excavated in three separate cemeteries in the area of Lebena on the south coast of the Asterousia Mountains is typical of the pattern of tombs in most of South-Central Crete (Halbherr 1905; Xanthoudides 1918, 1924; Banti 1930–1931; Stefani 1930–1931; Marinatos 1933; Paribeni 1913; Levi 1961–1962; Davaras 1964; Sakellarakis 1968; Branigan 1970, 1993, 1998; Blackman and Branigan 1973). The cemeteries consist of two pairs of adjoining tombs (Papoura and Gerokampos) and one single tomb (Zervou); these three burial areas range from 900 m to 3 km in distance from modern Lentas. Papoura and Gerokampos both have antechambers. Gerokampos II was built in EM I, while the other tombs—Papoura I and Ia, Gerokampos IIa, and Zervou—were constructed at different stages during EM II. The construction dates of these tombs and their development suggest that the social importance of the mortuary system was maintained, if not increased, during the Prepalatial period. Papoura I went out of use in EM II while Papoura Ia continued into MM IA. Both tombs at Gerokampos went out of use in MM IA; Zervou, however, shows some use into MM IB. The building of a second tomb at both Papoura and Gerokampos while the first tomb was still in use indicates the creation of a novel social division among both the living and the dead (Alexiou and Warren 2004, 191). This division was de-emphasized, however, by the position of the second tomb close to—indeed touching—the earlier one, and by their architectural similarity. In the pairs of tombs at Lebena, there are no overt differences to suggest that a hierarchy of power or status was associated with this long-lived social division, although this equality among tombs in a topographic cluster is not universal in South-Central Crete (Branigan 1991a). The pairs of tombs near Lebena thus create an image of equality among the social groups using them (Alexiou and Warren 2004, 11, 14, 15).

Structures at Aginaropapoura, whose presence has been confirmed by survey (Vasilakis 1989–1990), probably comprised the settlement associated with the nearby tombs at Papoura. And based on the close proximity of other known tombs and related settlements in South-Central Crete, the relatively large number of tombs in the area of Lebena, and their distances from each other, the tombs at Gerokampos and Zervou are likely to each have had their own adjacent settlements (contra Daux 1960, 846; Alexiou and Warren 2004, 14), which have not yet been identified. The clustering of the tombs within each cemetery would suggest a unity of the community that overrode the division into multiple burial groups. Even if all three groups of tombs near Lebena had been used by the inhabitants of the only known settlement at Aginaropapoura, the number of tombs, however, would still be quite small compared to the cemeteries at Mochlos. The relatively small number of tombs per settlement emphasized the small number of divisions within the society.

SOCIAL UNIT OF BURIAL

In contrast to the tombs at Mochlos, which are likely to have each held a nuclear family, related groups larger than a nuclear family were most probably using the tombs at Lebena. The number of tombs and the number of burials reported in each tomb, combined with ethnographic studies of population size of pre-industrial societies, demonstrate that the whole populations of the settlements were buried in the tombs. Early accounts of the excavation of the Lebena tombs reported skeletal remains from approximately 600 individuals (Daux 1960, 821); concrete numbers are currently available for Papoura I, where approximately 50 people were buried (Alexiou and Warren 2004, 12). This tomb was used only during EM II, which Alexiou dates to around two generations (Alexiou and Warren 2004, 12).

The methodology employed in studies carried out during the survey of the Hagio Farango Valley and the excavation of the tomb at Hagia Kyriaki (Blackman and Branigan 1977, 1982), which calculated that a nuclear family of five to six members would bury five people within a generation of 25 years (Blackman and Brangian 1977, 83–84), indicates that in order to account for 50 burials during two generations of use, five nuclear families would have used the tomb at Papoura I. Ethnographic parallels add a strong probability that these nuclear families were blood related and therefore are a kinship group (Forge 1972; see Branigan 1993 for a rebuttal of arguments against clan usage by Renfrew [1972] and Whitelaw [1983, 333]). Thus the number of burials combined with the tomb's span of use suggests that a related group of people larger than a nuclear family was making burials in this tomb. The appearance of the tomb in the landscape, therefore, memorialized neither the individual nor the nuclear family, but rather a larger kinship group that constituted the social unit of burial.

RANKING AT THE FUNERAL

The numbers, types, and positions of objects found in the tombs, together with the numbers of burials, suggest a dichotomy in the acknowledgment and display of social ranking. Initially, social status was displayed or claimed at the funeral through differential deposition of goods, but post-decompositional separation of the objects from the skeletons with which they had been deposited, and the disarticulation and separation of the bones of the skeletons themselves erased the evidence of ranking and identity. The evidence from the tombs at Lebena suggests that their communities, like many others in South-Central Crete, were predominantly egalitarian societies with low-level ranking developing in EM II (Branigan 1984; Murphy 2003, 281–283). This ranking was initially preserved or asserted in the burials of the dead.

The objects placed with the dead in the Lebena tombs vary in intrinsic value and rareness, and they range from pottery (albeit mostly fine ware) to seals, gold, and Egyptian scarabs. The number of objects in the Lebena tombs, combined with research from Hagia Kyriaki, suggests that all the dead were buried with some objects, but, since there are fewer items of high value and prestige such as the gold diadem, sealstones, stone vases, and Egyptian scarabs (Alexiou and Warren 2004, 57, 142, 151, 154; Blackman and Branigan 1982) than burials, these items could not have been equally distributed. It is likely that the individuals who were buried with objects of superior wealth had differential access to such wealth, and they probably had more elaborate burials than the other people in the tombs (O'Shea 1984; Barrett 1988).

The superior amounts of wealth both expended and invested in the funeral would have served to draw attention to the ideal or real position held by the individual in life (Huntington and Metcalf, eds., 1979; Pader 1982; O'Shea 1984). The selective deposition, therefore, of some high-status grave goods in the tombs indicates that the funeral following the death of an individual could be an opportunity to reinforce, claim, or create an elite status for the deceased and the surviving family (Hodder 1989, 89). Branigan (1970, 66, 112) has argued that the objects in the tombs in South-Central Crete were personal possessions important to the identity of the deceased, but analysis of status symbols suggests that the objects with the dead are most commonly placed there to stress the individual's wealth rather than any other aspect of their social persona (Binford 1972, 225–235). Like the apparent variety in the grave goods initially deposited with the dead, the bodies were also placed in the tombs in different positions, either contracted or extended (Daux 1959, 742; Alexiou 1960; 1967; Alexiou and Warren 2004, 12, 18, 189). The manner of the deposition of the body, especially in the later periods of use of the tombs, as well as the accompanying artifacts, might thus have enabled the identification of individual skeletons in the period immediately following the burial.

TREATMENT OF THE DEAD AFTER DECOMPOSITION

The post-depositional treatment of the artifacts and bodies demonstrates, however, that any ranking or individuality that was expressed in the burial was de-emphasized in the long-term social ideology of the community. Although the elevated position of an individual could have been stressed through the funeral rituals and his/her identity would have been preserved not only by the accompanying grave goods but also by a distinctive burial position, the enduring role of the individual as expressed through the landscape and mortuary system is one of equality and oneness with all other dead from that community. This conclusion is evidenced by the post-funerary and post-decompositional treatment of both the bones and grave goods within the tombs.

In addition to recent disturbance caused by the looting of the tombs at Lebena, the tombs had also been purposely disturbed by the people using them (Alexiou and Warren 2004, 12, 18, 21). Very few of the innumerable objects from the tombs can be associated with any particular skeleton; the artifacts had been brushed aside when the tombs were cleared. Thus, there was no lasting connection between the grave goods and the individual with whom they had been interred. Those objects, in fact, no longer marked either the identity or the rank of the individual with whose body they had originally been deposited.

The skeletons were likewise dissociated not only from their original assemblages of grave goods, but also from their burial containers (like the possible pithos burial in Zervou [Alexiou and Warren 2004, 189]) and their burial positions; indeed, they were routinely disassembled after they had decomposed. In some tombs the bones and objects were placed in annex rooms at the entrance to the tholos tomb (e.g., large deposits of bones in the entryway of Papoura I and in the ante-room in Gerokampos II have been interpreted as ossuaries) (Alexiou and Warren 2004, 12). In Papoura I and Gerokampos II, Alexiou reports that the bones were mixed throughout the fill of the tomb, and there were two piles of bones at the edges of the tomb. Some bones seemed to have been moved there, while others appeared to be in their original position (Alexiou and Warren 2004, 12, 16), indicating that not all bodies were moved after decomposition. The main chambers were therefore used both for primary burial and also, like the annex rooms, for the storage of the bones from older burials.

The signs of burning in the tombs suggest several sources of fire during their periods of use. In addition to torches used during burials and possibly for fumigation, Gerokampos IIa was cleaned out extensively (Alexiou 1958, 470; Alexiou and Warren 2004, 12, 16, 18) and a layer of sand or other white substance was then deposited over the burial stratum in the lower level of the circular chamber; this may have been done in preparation for new burials (Alexiou 1959, 371; Alexiou and Warren 2004, 18.) Such periodic clearing and burning within the tombs would have further removed any marks or memories of the identities of the decomposed dead. The periodic tomb cleanings and the post-decompositional manipulation of the remains (which separated both the grave goods from the skeletons with which they had been deposited and the bones of the skeletons from each other) had the effect of negating individual status in favor of a common identity among the dead or the ancestors. Despite the differential levels of wealth expended on the burials and the ethnographic parallels that suggest elites had the most expensive incorporation rites demonstrating recognition of their superior positions in society (Barrett 1988, 1990), the social ideology communicated by the mortuary system and by the cultural landscape was that the differences between members of the communities were transient while the similarities were lasting and enduring (Branigan 1987; Murphy, forthcoming). Signs of ranking and social distinctions were muted to stress the unity and continuity of the community. If death was not the great leveler in this society, decomposition certainly was.

In some cases, there is scant evidence that might preserve the identity of an individual or family. Possible instances of this occur in the areas at Papoura I and Gerokampos II where stones were laid out to form an apparent enclosure within the tomb (Alexiou and Warren 2004, 11, 15, 141). The example in Gerokampos II is better preserved; a burial was found within an enclosure with artifacts close in date to the EM I construction of the tomb. The objects in Papoura I were similarly early. These burials have been interpreted as the remains of the founders of the communities (Alexiou and Warren 2004, 141, 189); their retention in the communal tomb, as opposed to separate, more private tombs, would serve to elevate the common ancestors of the society. Furthermore, if the piles of bones reported in all of these tombs, but especially those of Papoura Ia (Alexiou and Warren 2004, 12), are evidence for a purposeful grouping of the dead rather than random individuals cleared to the side, they would indicate a continued post-mortem relationship between those people. Skeletal analysis, which could investigate the possibilities of a close blood relationship or a shared differential access to food resources, might elucidate relationships between the bones in the piles. Despite the possibility of at least one person's identity being preserved in both Papoura and Gerokampos and the possible subdivision of some bones into social units, it must be stressed that these divisions would only have been visible from inside the tomb. These five structures in the landscape memorialized a maximum of five subdivisions within the community or communities in the area of Lebena and a common identity for members of those five possible social groups.

The small number of tombs per settlement in South-Central Crete, the location of the tombs, the mortuary rituals, the use of those tombs for all known burials, and the post-interment treatment of the skeletal remains and the objects left with the dead demonstrate that the tombs were used by community groups that were larger than a nuclear family. The archaeological contexts of the skeletal material and grave goods evince, at minimum, a two-stage sequence of rituals following death through which different aspects of the social ideology of the community were expressed. First, during the deposition of the corpse in the tomb immediately following death, the personal identity and rank (either real or asserted) of the dead were displayed, but then, in the post-decompositional treatment of the skeleton and grave goods, evidence for individual or social identity was largely eradicated. Through the long-term deposition of bones and artifacts, the tombs in the landscape around Lebena emphasized the corporate identity of the community rather than the personal wealth or position of any individual or social sub-group, and this, in turn, muted aspects of individual or group social differentiation.

It was the ideology of the second stage of the funeral process that was visible in the landscape—a communal identity into which the individual and distinctions of rank were subsumed. The unity of the tombs within the landscape memorialized the long-term corporate identity of the anonymous dead, and this may have caused their ideologies of community cohesion and of the fleeting duration of rank in the mortal world to seem as natural and unchanging as the land itself.

Conclusion

As outlined in the anthropological studies discussed at the start of this chapter, the location of the tombs, the long-term use of the tombs, and the separation of different community groups in different topographical locations all help to socialize the members of (and visitors to) the local community to the hegemonic cultural narratives; people emotionally internalize what they see in the constructed environment on a daily basis (Basso 1996; Archibald 1999). The sensory impact of the environment on a person becomes deeply embedded in their psyche and worldview.

The present discussion of the mortuary evidence from Mochlos and Lebena demonstrates that social ideologies were communicated, reinforced, and created during the Prepalatial period on Crete through mortuary systems in conjunction with the landscape. Although the two societies discussed here had different social structures and organizations. Ranking in the tombs at Lebena and in other communities in South-Central Crete is muted in the long-term mortuary symbolism, and an egalitarian cluster of one, two, or a maximum of five large kinship groups is displayed in the tableau of the landscape. Although social ranking appears to have been acknowledged and displayed at the initial interment of a body within the tomb, in the enduring external appearance of the monument all were indistinguishable and equal; both the funerary and ethnographic evidence suggest that such unequivocal equality is unrealistic and only idealistic. The people of Lebena were clearly also well aware of this, as the distinctions of wealth through the grave goods interred during the initial deposition of the bodies demonstrates, and they used the mortuary system to present an idealized image of their society.

At Mochlos, in contrast, the social distinctions in rank were underlined and emphasized through the topographical placement of the tombs. The largest tombs, which have elaborate architecture and decoration displaying the greatest energy expenditure in construction and contain the largest number of intrinsically valuable artifacts, were in the most-protected and least-accessible area of the cemetery—the West Terrace. The South Slope also housed architecturally and artifactually rich tombs, although they are not as rich as those on the West Terrace, and their privileged locations set them apart from other tombs in the South Slope area of the cemetery. No one type of architectural elaboration or class of objects was exclusive to the tombs on the West Terrace, but it is clear that even the wealthier tombs on the South Slope were not part of the ultimate elite. The separation between the ranks of those living in this society was demonstrated, created, and emphasized through the different locations of the tombs of their families and ancestors. The permanence claimed for these social ranks at Mochlos was as unrealistic as the idealized egalitarian society projected at Lebena; in both communities the tombs in the landscape were encoded with the locally preferred social narrative.

The Prepalatial tombs of both Mochlos and Lebena are constructed elements in the landscapes of their communities that serve to promote the idealized social self-perceptions of those communities. The post-decompositional eradication of the individual and social identities of the dead at Lebena creates and portrays an ideology that valued community cohesion over social ranking. The small number of tombs per community, the clustering of those tombs together, and the absence of external distinctions in rank among the tombs advertised the same values in their visible presence in the landscape. The socio-economic distinctions distributed by families among the burials at Mochlos, in contrast, indicate that social rank—especially the rank of the nuclear family—was emphasized in death and beyond by that particular community. The social divisions at Mochlos were encoded in the landscape through architecture, decoration, placement, and protection against erosion. Thus, each of these communities manipulated the landscape to create, enforce, and maintain dominant social narratives. Their tombs made visible statements about constructed notions in the local ideologies and embodied long-term memories that supported them.

References

Alexiou, S. 1958. "Ἡ ἀρχαιολογικὴ κίνησις ἐν Κρήτῃ κατὰ τὸ ἔτος 1958," *CretChron* 12, pp. 459–483.

———. 1959. "Ἡ ἀρχαιολογικὴ κίνησις ἐν Κρήτῃ κατὰ τὸ ἔτος 1959," *CretChron* 13, pp. 359–379.

———. 1960. "New Light on Minoan Dating: Early Minoan Tombs at Lebena," *ILN* 237 (6 August 1960), pp. 225–227.

———. 1967. "Ἀρχαιοθέτες καὶ μνημεία κεντρικῆς καὶ ανατολ. Κρήτης-Ανασκαφαί," *ArchDelt* 22, pp. 482–484.

Alexiou, S., and P. Warren. 2004. *The Early Minoan Tombs of Lebena, Southern Crete* (*SIMA* 30), Sävedalen

Archibald, R. 1999. *A Place to Remember: Using History to Build Community*, London.

Ashmore, W., and A.B. Knapp, eds. 1999. *Archaeologies of Landscape: Contemporary Perspectives*, Malden.

Baker, A.R.H., and G. Biger, eds. 1992. *Ideology and Landscape in Historical Perspective*, Cambridge.

Banti, L. 1930–1931. "La grande tomba a tholos di Haghia Triada," *ASAtene* 13–14 [1933], pp. 155–257.

Barrett, J.C. 1988. "The Living, the Dead and the Ancestors: Neolithic and Early Bronze Age Mortuary Practices," in *The Archaeology of Context in the Neolithic and the Bronze Age: Recent Trends*, J.C. Barrett and A.I. Kinnes, eds., Sheffield, pp. 30–42.

————. 1990. "The Monumentality of Death: The Character of Early Bronze Age Mortuary Mounts in Southern Britain," *WorldArch* 22, pp. 179–189.

Basso, K. 1996. *Wisdom Sites in Places: Landscape and Language among the Western Apache*, Albuquerque.

Binford, L. 1972. *An Archaeological Perspective*, New York.

Blackman, D., and K. Branigan. 1973. "An Unusual Tholos Tomb at Kaminospelio, South Crete," *CretChron* 25, pp. 199–206.

————. 1977. "An Archaeological Survey of the Lower Catchment of the Ayiopharango Valley," *BSA* 72, pp. 13–84.

————. 1982. "The Excavations of an Early Minoan Tholos Tomb at Hagia Kyriaki, Ayio Farango, Southern Crete," *BSA* 77, pp. 1–57.

Bourdieu, P. 1977. *Outline of a Theory of Practice*, Cambridge.

Bradley, R. 1998. *The Significance of Monuments*, London.

————. 2000. *An Archaeology of Natural Places*, London.

Brady, J.E., and W. Ashmore. 1999. "Mountains, Caves, Water: Ideational Landscapes of the Ancient Maya," in Ashmore and Knapp, eds., 1999, pp. 124–145.

Branigan, K. 1970. *The Tombs of the Mesara: A Study of Funerary Architecture and Ritual in Southern Crete, 2800–1700 B.C.*, London.

————. 1984. "Early Minoan Society: The Evidence of the Mesara Tholoi Reviewed," in *Aux origines de l'hellénisme: La Crète et la Grèce. Hommage à Henri van Effenterre*, G. Glotz, ed., Paris, pp. 29–37.

————. 1987. "Ritual Inference with Human Bones in the Mesara Tholoi," in *THANATOS: Les coutumes funéraires en Egée à l'âge du Bronze. Actes du colloque de Liège, 21–23 avril 1986 (Aegaeum 1)*, R. Laffineur, ed., Liège, pp. 43–51.

————. 1991a. "Funerary Ritual and Social Cohesion in Early Bronze Age Crete," *Journal of Mediterranean Studies* 1, pp. 83–192.

————. 1991b "Mochlos—An Early Aegean 'Gateway Community'?" in *Thalassa: L'Égée préhistorique et la mer. Actes de la 3e Rencontre égéenne internationale de l'Université de Liège, Station de recherches sous-marines et océanographiques, Calvi, Corse, 23–25 avril 1990 (Aegaeum 7)*, R. Laffineur and L. Basch, eds., Liège, pp. 97–105.

————. 1993. *Dancing with Death: Life and Death in Southern Crete c. 3000–2000 B.C.*, Amsterdam.

————. 1998. "The Nearness of You: Proximity and Distance in Early Minoan Funerary Behaviour," in *Cemetery and Society in the Aegean Bronze Age*, K. Branigan, ed., Sheffield, pp. 13–26.

Cooney, G. 2000. *Landscapes of Neolithic Ireland*, London.

Daux, G. 1959. "Chronique des fouilles en 1958," *BCH* 83, pp. 731–754.

———. 1960. "Chronique des fouilles en 1959," *BCH* 84, pp. 819–853.

Davaras, K. 1964. "Ἀπεσοκάρι," *ArchDelt* 19, p. 441.

———. 1975. "Early Minoan Jewelry from Mochlos," *BSA* 70, pp. 101–114.

Earle, T.K. 1987. "Chiefdoms in Archaeological and Ethnohistorcial Perspectives," *Annual Review of Anthropology* 16, pp. 279–308.

Edmonds, M. 1999. *Ancestral Geographies of the Neolithic: Landscapes, Monuments and Memory*, London.

Forge, A. 1972. "Normative Factors in the Settlement Size of Neolithic Cultivators (New Guinea)," in *Man, Settlement and Urbanism. Proceedings of a Meeting of the Research Seminar in Archaeology and Related Subjects Held at the Institute of Archaeology, London University*, P.J. Ucko, R. Tringham, G.W. Dimbledy, eds., London, pp. 363–376.

Foucault, M. 1984. *The Foucault Reader*, P. Rabinow, ed., London.

Halbherr, F. 1905. "Rapporto sugli Scavi ad Haghia Triada ed a Festo, 1904," *Memorie del Reale Istituto Lombardo* 31, pp. 235–54.

Halbwachs, M. 1992. *On Collective Memory*, L. Coser, ed., trans., Chicago.

Hayden, B. 2003. *Shamans, Sorcerers, and Saints: The Prehistory of Religion*, Washington, D.C.

Hodder, I. 1989. *The Meaning of Things: Material Culture and Symbolic Expression*, London.

Huntington, R., and P. Metcalf, eds. 1979. *Celebrations of Death: The Anthropology of Mortuary Ritual*, Cambridge.

Izikowitz, K.G. 1951. *Lamet: Hill Peasants in French Indochina* (*Ethnologiska Studier* 17), Goteborg.

Kealhofer, L. 1999. "Creating Social Identity in the Landscape: Tidewater, Virginia, 1600–1750," in Ashmore and Knapp, eds., 1999, pp. 58–82.

Knapp, A.B., and W. Ashmore. 1999. "Archaeological Landscape: Constructed, Conceptualized, Ideational," in Ashmore and Knapp, eds., 1999, pp. 1–30.

Legarra Herrero, B. 2009. "The Minoan Fallacy: Cultural Diversity and Mortuary Behaviour on Crete at the Beginning of the Bronze Age," *WorldArch* 28 (1), pp. 21–57.

Levi, D. 1961–1962. "La tomba a tholos di Kamilari presso Festós," *ASAtene* 39–40, pp. 7–148.

Levy, J. 1999. "Gender Power and Heterarchy in Middle-Level Societies," in *Manifesting Power: Gender and the Interpretation of Power in Archaeology*, T.L. Sweely, ed., London, pp. 62–78.

Mann, M. 1986. *The Sources of Social Power: A History of Power from the Beginning to A.D. 1760*, Cambridge.

Marinatos, S. 1933. "Δυὸ πρώιμοι Μινωικοὶ τάφοι," *ArchDelt* 12–13, pp. 137–170.

Moore, S.F. 1977. "Political Meetings and the Simulation of Unanimity" in *Secular Ritual*, S.F. Moore and B.G. Myerhoff, eds., Amsterdam, pp. 151–172.

Murphy, J.M. 1998. "Ideology, Rites, and Rituals: A View of Prepalatial Minoan Tholoi," in *Cemetery and Society in the Aegean Bronze Age*, K. Branigan, ed., Sheffield, pp. 27–40.

———. 2003. *Changing Roles and Locations of Religious Practices in South-Central Crete during the Pre- and Proto-Palatial Periods*, Ph.D. diss., University of Cincinnati.

———. Forthcoming. "The Individual, the Household, and the Community after Death in South-Central Crete during the Pre- and Proto-Palatial Periods," in *STEGA: The Archaeology of Houses and Households in Ancient Crete* (*Hesperia Suppl.* 44), K. Glowacki and N. Vogeikoff-Brogan, eds., Princeton.

O'Shea, J.M. 1984. *Mortuary Variability: An Archaeological Investigation* (*Studies in Archaeology*), Orlando.

Pader, E.-J. 1982. *Symbolism, Social Relations and the Interpretation of Mortuary Remains* (*BAR-IS* 130), Oxford.

Paribeni, R. 1913. "Scavi nella necropoli preellenica di Festo: Tombe a tholos scoperte presso il villaggio di Siva," *Ausonia* 8, pp. 13–32.

Parker Pearson, M. 1982. Mortuary Practices, Society and Ideology: An Ethnoarchaeological Study," in *Symbolic and Structural Archaeology*, I. Hodder, ed., Cambridge, pp. 99–113.

Rabinowitz, D. 1997. *Overlooking Nazareth: The Ethnography of Exclusion in Galilee*, Cambridge.

Rappaport, R. A. 1999. *Ritual and Religion in the Making of Humanity* (*Cambridge Studies in Social and Cultural Anthropology* 110), Cambridge.

Reay, M. 1959. *The Kuma: Freedom and Conformity in the New Guinea Highland*, Melbourne.

Relaki, M. 2004. "Constructing a Region: The Contested Landscape of Prepalatial Mesara," in *The Emergence of Civilisation Revisited*, J.C. Barrett and P. Halstead, eds., Oxford, pp. 170–188.

Renfrew, C. 1972. *The Emergence of Civilisation: The Cyclades and the Aegean in the Third Millennium B.C.*, London.

Rowlands, M. 1993. "The Role of Memory in the Transmission of Culture," *WorldArch* 25, pp. 141–151.

Sakellarakis, I. 1968. "Excavations of Tholos Tomb at Hagios Kyrillos, Mesara," *AAA* 1, pp. 50–55.

Scarre, C., ed. 2002. *Monuments and Landscape in Atlantic Europe: Perception and Society during the Neolithic and Early Bronze Age*, London.

Seager, R. 1912. *Explorations in the Island of Mochlos*, New York.

Snead, J.E., and R.W. Preucel. 1999. "The Ideology of Settlement: Ancestral Keres Landscapes in the Northern Rio Grande," in Ashmore and Knapp, eds., 1999, pp. 169–197.

Soles, J. 1988. "Social Ranking in Prepalatial Cemeteries," in *Problems in Greek Prehistory. Papers Presented at the Centenary Conference of the British School of Archaeology at Athens, Manchester, April 1986*, E.B. French and K.A. Wardle, eds., Bristol, pp. 49–61.

———. 1992. *The Prepalatial Tombs at Mochlos and Gournia and the House Tombs of Bronze Age Crete (Hesperia Suppl. 24)*, Princeton.

Stefani, E. 1930–1931. "La grande tomba a tholos di Haghia Triada," *ASAtene* 13–14 [1933], pp. 147–154.

Taçon, P.S.C. 1994. "Socializing Landscapes: The Long-Term Implication of Signs, Symbols and the Marks on the Land," *Archaeology of Oceania* 29, pp. 117–129.

Tilley, C. 1994. *A Phenomenology of Landscape: Places, Paths, Monuments*, Oxford.

———. 1999. *Metaphor and Material Culture*, Oxford.

Vasilakis, A. 1989–1990. "Λεβήνα," *Κρητική Εστία* 3, p. 286.

Whitelaw, T.M. 1983. "The Settlement at Fournou Koriphi Myrtos and Aspects of Early Minoan Social Organization," in *Minoan Society. Proceedings of the Cambridge Colloquium, 1981*, O. Krzyszkowska and L. Nixon, eds., Bristol, pp. 323–345.

Wilson, D.E., and P.M. Day. 1994. "Ceramic Regionalism in Prepalatial Central Crete: The Mesara Imports at EM I to EM IIA Knossos," *BSA* 95, pp. 21–63.

Xanthoudides, S. 1918. "Παράρτημα Πρωτομινωικός Τάφος Μεσαράς," *ArchDelt* 4, pp. 15–23.

———. 1924. *The Vaulted Tombs of the Mesara*, trans. J. Droop, London.

3 | The Secret Lives of the Early and Middle Minoan Tholos Cemeteries: Koumasa and Platanos

BORJA LEGARRA HERRERO

Perhaps no other type of archaeological context has attracted so much interest in the study of the 3rd and early 2nd millennia B.C. on Crete as the tholos cemeteries. Tholos cemeteries are defined by the presence of tholos tombs, stone-built round tombs measuring approximately 3 m in diameter (e.g., Krasi: Marinatos 1929, 106) to 13.1 m (e.g., Platanos Tholos A: Xanthoudides 1924, 88), which were used collectively, sometimes for more than a millennium (e.g., Lebena Gerokampos: Alexiou and Warren 2004). Some of the Early Minoan (EM) and Middle Minoan (MM) tholoi may have been corbelled, although this possibility is still the subject of debate (Warren 1973; 2007; Pelon 1976; Belli 1984, 120–124; Branigan 1993, 41–56; 1994).

The large number of known tholos cemeteries (Fig. 3.1), most of them found in South-Central Crete, has allowed researchers to engage in the detailed study of the social, economic and ideological structure of the region (Branigan 1970, 1984; Blackman and Branigan 1977; Relaki 2004) to a degree that would be difficult to achieve in other parts of the island or using other types of data during the Early and Middle Bronze Age on Crete (but see Watrous, Hadzi-Vallianou, and Blitzer 2004).

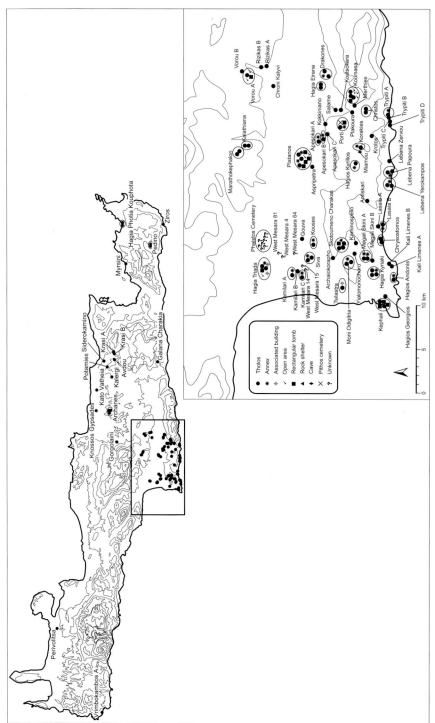

Figure 3.1. Tholos tombs in Crete and Pre- and Protopalatial cemeteries in South-Central Crete.

The long history of research on the tholos cemeteries (the first excavation of a tholos took place in 1903 at Hagia Triada; see Halbherr 1903; Paribeni 1903) resulted in the early establishment of a research agenda that included some assumptions that have become intrinsically linked to our views of these contexts without subsequent critical appraisal. A new wave of archaeologists is starting to show that the traditional approaches and explanations attached to the long history of research on the tholoi are inadequate and that new views based on new theoretical and methodological foundations are required (Papadatos 1999; Whitelaw 2000; Relaki 2003, 2004; Bardsley 2004; Watrous, Hadzi-Vallianou, and Blitzer 2004; Catapoti 2005; Campbell-Green 2006; Goodison 2006). This fresh perspective in the understanding of the tholos cemeteries has been based mainly on the new publications of tholos tombs from Archanes-Phourni (Maggidis 1994; Sakellarakis and Sapouna-Sakellaraki 1997; Panagiotopoulos 2002; Papadatos 2005), Lebena (Alexiou and Warren 2004), the re-excavation of Hagia Triada (Di Vita 1990–1991, 1996–1997, 1998–2000; La Rosa 1992–1993, 2001b; Cultraro 2000, 2004; Palio 2004; Todaro 2004), the re-evaluation of Kamilari (Girella 2003), and the publication of Moni Odigitria (Campbell-Green 2006; Branigan 2008; Vasilakis and Branigan 2010). Previously excavated and published tholos cemeteries have only been included in this reassessment of the subject to a very limited extent, even though they still offer important data that contribute to our attempts to create new theoretical models for the significant role of mortuary behavior in Early and Middle Bronze Age Crete.

This present study focuses on the reassessment and re-interpretation of two large tholos cemeteries, Platanos and Koumasa, which have been staples in discussions not only of tholos cemeteries, but also, and more importantly, in the creation of explanatory models about social, political, and economic organization on Crete in the 3rd and early 2nd millennium. It is argued here that a more detailed look at the evidence of these cemeteries that were excavated long ago, paired with a fresh approach free of the traditional assumptions, reveals a much more complex picture of a constantly changing heterogeneous region than has been assumed until now. Targeting these two important cemeteries not only challenges the weaknesses of traditional models at their core, but it also brings a key corpus of material back into the current discussion of interpretations of

tholos cemeteries and the more general discussion of Early and Middle
Bronze Age Cretan communities.

The Long Tradition and Some Outstanding Problems

The history of research on the tholos cemeteries is almost as old as that
of archaeological work on Crete; the assemblage of a probable tholos tomb
at Hagios Onouphrios in South-Central Crete was published as early as
1895 (Evans 1895; Branigan 1970, 1; for a detailed account of the history
of research, see Branigan 1993, 1–15). Unfortunately, the excavation of
tholos cemeteries was normally conducted under the restricted conditions
of rescue excavations, usually after the cemetery had been looted. And, in
fact, only a few excavated cemeteries have been published. At present, of
the more than 60 known tholos cemeteries, only the one at Archanes-
Phourni (Fig. 3.1) can be considered ideal from a research standpoint: it
was not looted, it was excavated using modern techniques, and it is extensively (though not yet completely) published (Maggidis 1994; Sakellarakis
and Sapouna-Sakellaraki 1997; Karytinos 2000; Lahanas 2000; Panagiotopoulos 2002; Papadatos 2005).

Besides the conditions of the archaeological deposits themselves, this
long history of research has added more problems to the study of the tholos cemeteries. If the communal use of the tombs for centuries created
highly disturbed deposits within the cemetery—a process that was exac-
erbated later by looting—then the early excavation of cemeteries, in
accordance with the standards of that time (usually in the form of rescue
excavation with limitations on time and resources) have precluded the
detailed application of archaeological techniques for the better understanding of the difficult depositional and post-depositional history of the
cemeteries. A clear example of this is the fact that the rapid rescue excavations usually only explored a small area around the tholos tombs and in
front of the entrance, ignoring the possibility of other buildings at the
back or sides of the tholos tombs.

The few cemeteries that were excavated extensively, such as Hagia
Triada (Banti 1930–1931; Stefani 1930–1931; Di Vita 1990–1991,
1996–1997, 1998–2000; La Rosa 1992–1993, 1999a, 1999b, 2001a),

show that other buildings related to the cemetery may be present in the immediate vicinity of the tholos tombs, and, in many cases, tholos cemeteries could have been larger than presently known. At present, the understanding of the cemeteries relies almost entirely on the study of the tholos tomb components in each cemetery. Other features, even when excavated, have been largely ignored, or, as in the case of the annexes, treated merely as subordinate to the tholoi. This is why this study prefers to call the sites tholos cemeteries, as all of them include features apart from the tholos tombs that need to be considered carefully as part of an architectural whole.

But our interest resides in another, more prominent problem that stems from the lack of chronological definition of the assemblages produced by the old excavations and the incomplete publication of the cemeteries. These two features of the scholarship have resulted in the creation of vague interpretative models in which the cemeteries have been considered. They are vague in two different ways: chronologically, because the tholos cemeteries have been viewed within a uniform model that has no detailed chronological framework for the changes occurred within the long history of use of the cemeteries (see, e.g., Branigan 1984; Murphy 1998); but also spatially, because every single tholos cemetery has been included in the same explanatory model, regardless of their particular location or characteristics (see, e.g., Cultraro 2001, 107–115; Belli 2003; Goodison 2006). Only variations based on inferred socioeconomic differences have been taken into consideration (Branigan 1984; Murphy 1998; Sbonias 1999; Cultraro 2001, 107–115), but this does not cover the whole range of variables that affect mortuary behavior (Ucko 1969; Hodder 1980, 1982; Pader 1982; Parker Pearson 1982), nor has this inferred general behavior been explained through a comprehensive consideration of the particular social dynamics in South-Central Crete. It has become clear that the traditional interpretations of the tholos cemeteries, with their disregard for variability, context, and lack of detailed analysis, are not sustainable (Papadatos 1999; Relaki 2004; Campbell-Green 2006). Tholos cemeteries not only changed through time, and with them their role as a social arena for Cretan communities, but at certain times they also show considerable differences that transcend any simple distinction between rich and poor cemeteries or communities.

At this point it is necessary to stand back and look at the tholos cemetery in a broader perspective. Cemeteries are not an object of study per
se, but their study can offer a very insightful approach to the study of the
societies that use them (Binford 1971; Parker Pearson 1982). The proposed shift of research toward variation (which here is defined as the
investigation of differences and similarities) is not only a simple methodological change, but it represents also a fundamental transformation in
the way we understand the relation between cemeteries and society.
Current approaches have viewed the tholos cemetery as a direct reflection
of the social structure of the community that used it (Blackman and
Branigan 1977; Whitelaw 1983; Branigan 1984; Watrous 1994; Murphy
1998; Sbonias 1999). Cemeteries reflect the kind of society that use them,
and, therefore, they can be used to understand Minoan society, particularly because they are placed within a stage of the social evolutionary
spectrum (i.e., chiefdoms, ranked societies). But modern archaeological
research views the cemetery in a very different light, as a complex social
arena where society is not reflected but actively constructed and reconstructed, and where direct links between society and cemetery are never
straightforward (Hodder 1980; Bartel 1982; Pader 1982; Parker Pearson
1982, 1999; Wason 1994; Carr 1995; Pearson 1998; Charles 2005).
    The cemetery is such a powerful social arena for interaction and nego-
tiation of social relationships because it has unique ideological, religious,
and sentimental characteristics created by the traumatic event of death.
Such characteristics empower the cemetery as a social arena, but they
also contort and restructure the social canvas of the everyday life of the
community that is not directly reflected in the mortuary arena. Society
transforms itself in the cemeteries through dealing with the reality of
death and the changes it brings to the composition and social organization
of a community. Such interruptions in the normal life of the community
are ideal for the transformation of social relationships (transformations
involving efforts to change it, but also efforts to maintain it unchanged,
as both dynamics need to be deployed actively). For archaeologists
this means that the social structure deployed in the cemeteries does not
necessarily match the social structure through which everyday life was
organized, but at the same time it does offer an excellent window for its
study, as well as for the study of interaction and the processes involved in
social stability and transformation.

Under these circumstances the understanding of a cemetery must rely on the study of variability, defined as the study of both differences and similarities that can be achieved through a contextual approach (Carr 1995, 193–194; Hodder and Hutson 2003, 183–187). We need to understand the characteristics that are common to the human groups that occupy a certain region in terms of how they deal with death and the deceased. The location of a community in a culturally similar region (for a discussion of the definition of region in South-Central Crete, see Relaki 2004) with extensive social, economic, and ideological links means that there are regularities in the way they employed cemeteries as social arenas. At the same time, each community is unique, and the way they use their cemeteries changes because they adapt the common rules to their specific needs. Studying variability permits us to interpret regularities in the use of cemeteries that will facilitate the discovery of patterns in the way mortuary behavior relates to the social, ideological, and economic relationships within and between communities of South-Central Crete. Moreover, it allows the identification of the individualities of each community's mortuary behavior and an interpretation of their meaning.

This paper suggests that such a detailed study of variability is possible through the study of newly excavated material and a reconsideration of old published material, both of which are necessary for a comprehensive understanding of the record and the fullest contextualization of new data. It is time to reclaim the old data and use it to identify variations among sites and the changes that occurred in these cemeteries. The identification of changes that occurred in the 1,000-year history of use of the old excavated cemeteries, and hence their social role, can be achieved through a careful and integrated look at both the assemblages and their associated architectural features. Also, more attention needs to be paid to variation between contemporaneous cemeteries. Differences normally have been explained in a simple hierarchical model, where larger cemeteries or the ones with more high-value items (both Koumasa and Platanos have been thought to belong in these categories) were considered to reflect communities that functioned as local centers and were developing toward a clearly defined regional hierarchical structure (Branigan 1984; Watrous 1994, 730–731; Murphy 1998, 38; Sbonias 1999; Cultraro 2001, 107–115; Watrous, Hadzi-Vallianou, and Blitzer 2004, 244–269). But such a simple interpretation has many problems.

The position of a community in synchronous or longer-term developmental contexts cannot be based on the simple reading of the cemetery assemblages in terms of rich against poor; instead, it requires a contextual approach to the commonalities and differences in mortuary behavior among the South-Central Cretan communities. If we are to begin to understand variations and patterns in the record, we first need to understand the meanings and ways in which architecture and assemblages were deployed as a social means of interaction in South-Central Crete. A detailed investigation of the data provides us with a much better idea of the mechanisms used for the negotiation of social position and status, and, therefore, we can then better understand key traits in the social structure of South-Central Cretan communities.

While recent studies have explored the potential of a more flexible approach to the tholos cemetery record (Papadatos 1999; Relaki 2004; Campbell-Green 2006), we still have a limited data base for the application of such new perspectives, since the largest part of the record continues to be handicapped by old assumptions and the descriptive orientation of previous studies. As an illustration, this study focuses on two of the classic sites that feature in most of the studies of Early Bronze Age Crete—Koumasa and Platanos. The aim is to show that it is possible and necessary to re-visit cemeteries that were excavated in the distant past in order to challenge some of our misconceptions about tholos tombs, particularly in terms of socioeconomic issues and the history of the region. Furthermore, it aims to show that old data can still be useful for the creation of new models for South-Central Crete. Koumasa and Platanos are perfect examples; both are key sites for our understanding of the EM and MM periods, they are usually considered to be comparable sites with similar local and regional roles and developmental histories (Branigan 1984; Murphy 1998; Watrous, Hadzi-Vallianou, and Blitzer 2004, 245), and they both provide examples of how problematic data can still be relevant for current studies.

Koumasa

The Koumasa cemetery (Fig. 3.2) was excavated by Xanthoudides in 1904 and 1906 and published a few years later (Xanthoudides 1924,

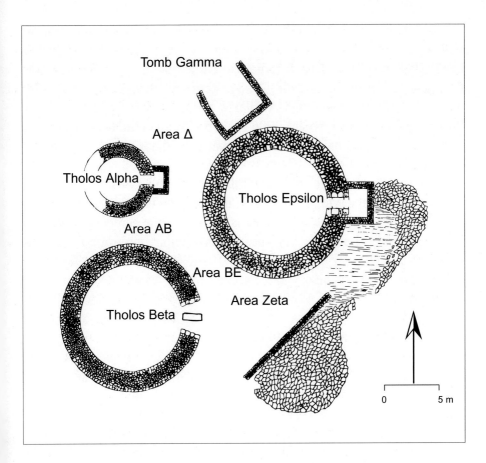

Tomb Gamma

Area Δ

Tholos Alpha

Area AB

Tholos Epsilon

Area BE

Area Zeta

Tholos Beta

0   5 m

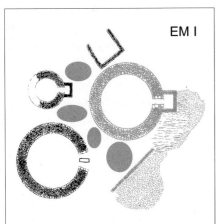

EM I

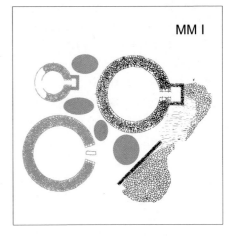

MM I

Figure 3.2. Koumasa cemetery (after Xanthoudides 1924). Gray shading indicates areas without clear dating.

1–50). The cemetery has never been re-excavated, and although we must rely on Xanthoudides' publication, some of the material recovered has been re-assessed in different studies (to name only a few examples, see: Branigan 1968a, 63; Zois 1968, 73–81; Renfrew 1969; Karagianni 1984, 63, 70, 77, 91; Sbonias 1995; Vasilakis 1996, 84–86; Papadatos 2003b; Pieler 2004, 111, 114; Koehl 2006, 71, 75–76) and is now better understood, allowing a reconsideration of the patterns of use for the cemetery as a whole.

The cemetery is located on a low hill at the boundary of the Asterousia Mountains and the Mesara Valley. Xanthoudides reported that a settlement was located on the hill immediately above the cemetery, although limited investigations have yet to establish occupation during the period of use of the cemetery (Xanthoudides 1924, 49; Rutkowski 1989). The presence of a MM sanctuary in the community is debated (Xanthoudides 1924, 49–50; Rutkowski 1989; Georgoulaki 1990). The cemetery is composed of three tholos tombs—Alpha, Beta, and Epsilon—two of which are larger than average (Beta [9.5 m] and Epsilon [9.3 m]; compare with other tholos tomb measurements in Belli 1984; Goodison and Guarita 2005), and another two features—rectangular Tomb Gamma and the paved area southeast of Tholos Epsilon that is known as Area Zeta. Another three areas—AB, BE, and Delta—have not been defined by any features, but rather by the deposits of material found within them. It is therefore unclear whether the objects were deposited in these areas purposefully or whether they represent material re-deposited (in the past or the present) from other contexts.

But what is the chronology and history of all these features? Were they all constructed and used simultaneously (Branigan 1993, 111–114)? If not, what is the story of the cemetery? To answer these questions, two different aspects need to be addressed: the architectural features and the character, distribution, and association of the material assemblage.

The Koumasa cemetery can be defined by the simplicity of its layout. Tholoi Alpha and Epsilon have only an anteroom at the entrance of the tomb, and a similar layout was suggested for Tholos Beta (Xanthoudides 1924, 8); no annexes or other related buildings are known for the cemetery, with the exception of Tomb Gamma and some rooms outside Tholos Epsilon together with paved Area Zeta. Xanthoudides suggested that such annexes and associated buildings may have existed, given the debris found in the areas between the tholoi (Xanthoudides 1924, 33). This, however, does not seem to be the case: the tholoi and Tomb Gamma were in a very good state of preservation (at Tholos Epsilon, even the closing slab was found in place; Xanthoudides 1924, 33), and it seems strange that only the annexes would have perished. The debris mentioned by Xanthoudides may have come from the tholos tombs. Moreover, the details provided by Xanthoudides regarding the areas outside the tholos do not seem to fit our understanding of annexes. The excavated ante-rooms outside the tholoi are clearly contained and were probably never embedded in larger annex complexes. The small area between Tholos Epsilon and the paved area outside it is quite small to house a significant annex complex, whereas the interments and burn marks outside Tholos Beta (Xanthoudides 1924, 33) do not have parallels in any other known annex. It seems that annexes at Koumasa, if they ever existed, may not have had significant architectural features in terms of size and quality of construction, as is seen in other cemeteries.

Simple layouts are typical of EM I–II tholos cemeteries. The well-understood tholos cemeteries at Lebena Gerokampos (Alexiou and Warren 2004), Hagia Triada (Carinci 2004; Todaro 2004), Hagia Kyriaki (Blackman and Branigan 1982), and Moni Odigitria (Vasilakis 1992; Vasilakis and Branigan 2010) show that tholos tombs constructed in EM I–II had, at most, one or two anterooms (Branigan 1993, 63; Murphy 1998, 37–38); only in later periods were these expanded into large annex complexes. Even newly established MM tholos tombs were being con-structed with large annexes at Apesokari and Kamilari (Apesokari Alpha: Schörgendorfer 1951; Kamilari Alpha: Levi 1961–1962). At Koumasa, only Tomb Gamma disrupts the simplicity of the layout, but only EM II material has been published from this context (Xanthoudides 1924, 34–50); the simplicity of its plan contrasts with the rectangular buildings found in EM III and MM I tholos cemeteries such as Hagia Triada (Banti 1930–1931; La Rosa 1999b; Cultraro 2000; Di Vita 1998–2000), thus sug-gesting an EM IIA date for the construction of this building. The architec-tural features of the Koumasa cemetery resemble EM I–II layouts rather than later ones. Also, it is worth noting that although Koumasa underwent important archaeological changes in EM III and MM I, it adapted archi-tecturally to the common EM III–MM I funerary architecture in a very restricted way (perhaps only with the construction of paved Area Zeta), and the cemetery retained a uniquely simple layout during its MM I phase of use.

The material assemblage of the cemetery is harder to assess as we know that only a very limited part was published, probably the most outstanding and complete material. However, since it was excavated by the same excavator as Platanos and the sites were published together, the publication of both cemeteries should be biased by the same interests, thus permitting a preliminary comparison of the assemblages at the two cemeteries. The Koumasa assemblage, as it was published, differs significantly from that of Platanos and from assemblages in other tholos cemeteries.

Although Xanthoudides mentions EM I ceramics (Xanthoudides 1924, 9), none of the illustrated material from the Koumasa cemetery can be dated earlier than the EM IIA period (Zois 1968, 71–96; Pelon 1976, 90; Wilson and Day 1994, 14; contra Branigan 1993, 146). EM IIA material has been found in Tholoi Alpha and Beta, Tomb Gamma, and Areas AB and Delta (Xanthoudides 1924, 9–11, 33; Zois 1968, 73–81). Only one EM II ceramic vessel from Tholos Epsilon was published, and it comes from the soil on top of the tomb (HM 4992; Xanthoudides 1924, 39). Only one kernos from this tomb could be dated earlier than MM I (HM 4999; Zois 1967, 720; Karagianni 1984, 70), and other material from this tomb dates to MM I (Platon 1969 [*CMS* II, 1 no. 156]; Walberg 1983, 102; Sbonias 1995, 119).

While the published ceramic vessels are too few in number for a comprehensible characterization of the assemblage, there are a few items that seem to date to EM IIA, which indicate an exceptional assemblage. In Tomb Gamma, three silver daggers were found in a probable EM II closed deposit (Xanthoudides 1924, 47; Soles 1992, 157–158). These are a very rare type of object, found elsewhere only in the (possible) funerary deposit at Teke-Knossos (together with typical EM IIA folded-arm figurines; Marinatos 1933, 298–304; Alexiou 1975; Vasilakis 1996, 82–84; Papadatos 2003a; 2003b), at Galana Charakia (Branigan 1968a, 63; Vasilakis 1996, 82–87), and at Mochlos (T. Tselios, pers. comm.). Silver is a very rare imported material on the island, particularly in the Mesara, and it may have been imbued with high social value (Branigan 1968b; Davaras 1975, 107; Legarra Herrero 2004, 43–45). Six folded-arm figurines were found at Koumasa, a significant number that has only been surmounted at Archanes-Phourni, although the latter were all found in one tholos (Gamma) and in the area surrounding it (Sakellarakis and Sapouna-Sakellaraki 1997, 236; Papadatos 2005, 29–32); one or perhaps two of those from Tholos Beta at Koumasa are actual imports from the Cyclades, an even rarer occurrence (inv. nos. HM 125, HM 127; Xanthoudides 1924, 21–22; Renfrew 1969, 19; Pieler 2004, 110). Folded-arm figurines are also rare in Cretan cemeteries and were probably deposited only during EM IIA (Papadatos 1999, 223; 2003a). They may represent a type of object with a high value attached to its symbolic meaning (Papadatos 2003b), an idea that is reinforced by the actual presence of imports from the Cyclades. Other possible valuable objects at Koumasa are gold items in Tholos Beta, but most of these seem to come from the upper levels (Xanthoudides 1924, 8), which may be MM I as indicated by the presence of numerous stone vessels (see below). Zoomorphic and anthropomorphic vases in Koumasa ware, typically EM IIA in date, are found in numbers larger than in any other known cemetery (Xanthoudides 1924, 39–41; Branigan 1970, 133; Warren 1977, 138; Miller 1984, 28–31, 557–558; Krause 1992, 224–227; Koehl 2006, 71, 75–76, 78).

Sixteen seals were recovered from Tholos Alpha and 19 from Tholos Beta, including EM III–MM I examples (Platon 1969, nos. 138–169; Platon, Pini, and Salies 1977, no. 26; Sbonias 1995, 88 nn. 94, 103); these are fairly low quantities when compared to the examples recovered from Hagia Triada Tholos Alpha (108 seals) and Platanos Tholos Beta (80 seals). Finally, not many stone vessels were found at the cemetery, with the exception of Tholos Beta, which produced 80 (Xanthoudides 1924, 17). Following Xanthoudides' description that places most of the material in the upper layers of Tholos Beta (Xanthoudides 1924, 8), combined with the presence of a substantial quantity of bird's-nest bowls (44 bird's-nest bowls; Warren 1969, 120) that can be most securely dated to the MM I period onward (Warren 1969, 8; Bevan 2007), it can be suggested that the majority of stone vessels in Tholos Beta was deposited in the MM I period; the same probably holds true for the nine gold items found in the upper stratum.

It seems that Tholoi Alpha and Beta and rectangular Tomb Gamma were constructed in the EM IIA period, and the discovery of contemporary material in Areas Delta and AB shows intensive use of the cemetery during this period. Area Zeta and Tholos Epsilon may have been constructed as early as EM IIA, although the evidence here is far from conclusive. The presence of EM IIA objects in Area AB and Tomb Gamma may also indicate that much of the material that was originally deposited in the tholos during this period was cleared away, and that the EM IIA picture of the tholos cemetery may be obscured by secondary re-deposition. Items such as the folded-arm figurines or silver daggers, had they been found together in one of the tholoi, would have marked an exceptional burial group. While it is difficult to create a detailed chronology for each context in the Koumasa cemetery, the general impression seems to be that the architectural layout and the material assemblage recovered provides us with a snapshot of the life of this cemetery during the early EM II period. Our understanding of the cemetery's use in EM III and MM I is restricted to the upper stratum of Tholos Beta and the little evidence found around Tholos Epsilon.

In the process of trying to establish a chronology for Koumasa, we have stumbled upon the fact that Koumasa does not represent a typical EM IIA tholos cemetery. Architecturally, it is larger than average, with two tholoi—one uncommonly large (Tholos Beta) and one associated rectangular tomb (Tomb Gamma). A two-tholos cemetery in EM IIA is not a unique phenomenon; other examples are known, such as Lebena Papoura (Alexiou and Warren 2004), but it is by no means a general pattern: at Hagia Triada a second tholos tomb was added in MM I (Carinci 1999, 115 n. 2; 2004, 99). Moreover, the assemblage is quite peculiar, as it includes an exceptionally large number of typically high-value objects (silver daggers and folded-arm figurines), which, together with the anthropomorphic vases, set Koumasa apart from other contemporaneous sites. Unfortunately, it is not possible to ascertain the internal structure of the cemetery in EM IIA; as we have noted, only a small part of the material was published and some of it may have been found in secondary deposits. Furthermore, it is not possible at present to establish whether the exceptional material originated from only one tholos tomb or whether it was deposited in various tombs, which would dramatically change the way we understand the internal socioeconomic dynamics of the cemetery and the burial groups within the community.

After the EM IIA period, the Koumasa cemetery seems to have undergone significant changes: Tholos Alpha and Tomb Gamma may have been abandoned, and Tholos Epsilon was constructed or, if it had already been built, acquired more significance within the cemetery. Other evidence for the MM I period is difficult to assess. It does not seem that the architecture of the site was transformed in EM III and MM IA to match the features appearing in the rest of the tholos cemeteries in the region in the form of large annexes and associated buildings. Even small cemeteries in the Asterousia Mountains were adapting their architecture to create complex annexes and associated spaces (e.g., at Hagia Kyriaki; see Blackman and Branigan 1982). At the same time, two large tholoi seem to have been in use—Beta and Epsilon. The deposition in Tholos Beta, including the gold objects and a large number of stone vessels, indicates that the Koumasa cemetery was still an important social arena. The swap from EM II Tholos Alpha and Tomb Gamma to Tholoi Epsilon and Beta in MM I may indicate profound changes in the social organization of the community, perhaps related to the establishment of a new settlement nearby (Xanthoudides 1924, 49; Rutkowski 1989). Unfortunately, without being able to assess Tholos Epsilon, it is difficult to identify changes in the internal dynamics of the cemetery and relate them to the changes in Koumasa's mortuary behavior in MM I. In any case, Koumasa's history suggests something quite different from the straightforward evolution toward socioeconomic complexity that has normally been suggested (Whitelaw 1983; Branigan 1984; Murphy 1998).

Platanos

The Platanos cemetery is located on the outskirts of modern Platanos village, not far from Koumasa, inside the Mesara Valley. This site was also excavated by Xanthoudides in 1914 and 1915 (Xanthoudides 1915; 1924, 2), and he published it together with Koumasa and other tholos cemeteries a few years later (Fig. 3.3; Xanthoudides 1924, 88–125). Our understanding of the cemetery has been limited by nearby modern buildings, but in this case the comprehensive excavation by Xanthoudides was complemented by small trials in later periods that brought some important deposits to light that have helped to date the cemetery more accurately (Platon 1953; 1955; Alexiou 1973a, 462–463; 1973b, 562–563; Ioannidou 1973; Gerontakou 2003, 303). As in the case of Koumasa, new studies of the older published material have also helped to clarify the

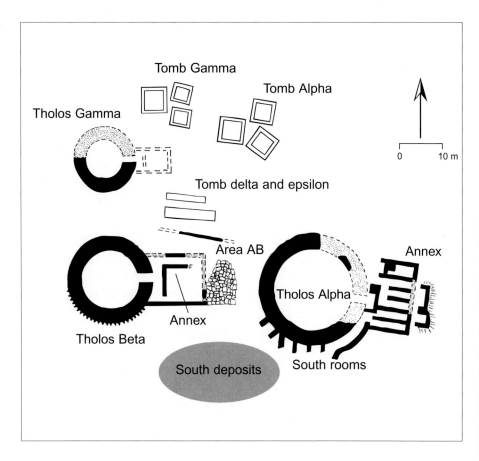

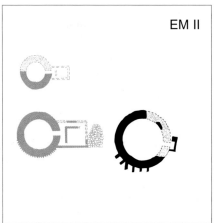
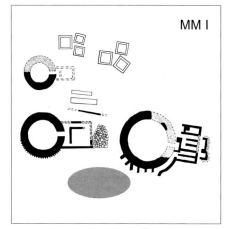

Figure 3.3. Platanos cemetery (after Branigan 1970). Gray shading indicates areas without clear dating.

nature and history of the cemetery (e.g., see: Branigan 1965; Kenna 1968; Warren 1969; Ward 1981; Sbonias 1995; Pini 2000, 107; Bevan 2001; Phillips 2004; Koehl 2006, 75–76).

As in the case at Koumasa, the cemetery consists of three tholos tombs: Alpha, Beta, and Gamma. However, there are also important architectural differences. Platanos has a much more complicated layout with at least nine other spaces, most of them defined by built architecture. Xanthoudides reported two rectangular tombs, alpha and gamma (non-capitalization of the rectangular tomb names follow Xanthoudides' original publication), but it is unclear whether each of these corresponds to three different small buildings (Xanthoudides 1924, 93; Branigan 1970, 12, fig. 2) or two large rectangular tombs with three rooms (Georgoulaki 1996, ill. 25:b). Tombs delta and epsilon were described as long trenches, half-constructed with built walls; they were considered ossuaries by Xanthoudides (1924, 93), although they could also represent rectangular tombs. The three tholoi had annexes, and the ones preserved near Tholoi Alpha and Beta were quite large. Tholos Alpha had various rooms abutting its south side, which may relate to deposits that had been excavated in the 1950s and 1970s near this area (for the south deposits, see: Platon 1953; 1955; Orlandou 1972; Alexiou 1973a, 462–463; 1973b, 562–563; Ioannidou 1973; Gerontakou 2003). Lastly, outside the annex of Tholos Beta there is a small paved area named Area AB. Traces of walls were also reported, which may have marked further divisions within the cemetery (Xanthoudides 1924, pl. LXII).

The architectural features of Platanos, with the large annexes and its complicated layout combining various rectangular tombs and other deposits, make it very different from Koumasa. It does, however, have clear parallels with EM III and MM I tholos cemeteries such as Lebena Gerokampos (Alexiou and Warren 2004) and Hagia Triada (Carinci 2004). Indeed, the Tholos Beta annexes are very similar in plan to those at Apesokari, which were constructed in MM I (Schörgendorfer 1951; Branigan 1998, 20, fig. 1.5; Catapoti 2005). This is not to say that the Platanos cemetery was constructed in MM I–EM II material was found in the cemetery, indicating that the first burials were made in this period. Nevertheless, given the architectural traits and the fact that the few published EM II items originate exclusively from Tholoi Alpha (Zois 1998, 155) and Beta (Warren 1965, 13; although he considers it a possible survival that could place the construction of Tholos Beta in EM III or MM I), most architectural features may have been constructed in EM III or MM I.

Taking a more detailed look at the assemblage, it is surprising how little EM II material has been published, particularly because Xanthoudides took great interest in the EM IIA material from Koumasa. Only one ceramic EM II vessel was reported from Tholos Alpha (HM 6892; Zois 1998, 155), but Xanthoudides reported an even lower layer (Xanthoudides 1924, 89), which may suggest an EM II construction for the tomb (clearly defined lower strata in tholoi normally date to that period; e.g., Lebena Gerokampos Tholoi II and IIa: Alexiou and Warren 2004, 145, fig. 33; Archanes-Phourni Tholos Gamma: Papadatos 2005, 52). On the basis of the descriptions given by Xanthoudides, most of the non-ceramic material published from Tholos Alpha came from the upper level. Considering that the small number of ceramic vessels published can be dated to EM III–MM I (Xanthoudides 1924, 89, 95; Walberg 1983, 99), it can be suggested that the upper layer and the material within it also dates to this period. Xanthoudides proposed that Tholos Beta is later than Tholos Alpha, perhaps constructed at the end of EM III (Xanthoudides 1924, 92). Apart from an incised pyxis (HM 1904a; Warren [1965, 13] suggests that is probably a survival) and the possibility that some of the seals date to EM II–III (Sbonias 1995, 80 n. 49, 83 n. 62; see also Kenna 1968, 327 n. 61 for a different view), the assemblage has been dated to EM III and MM I (Warren 1969, 196; Walberg 1983, 99). Tholos Gamma may have been in use in EM II (vessel HM 6873 was dated to EM II by Xanthoudides [1924, 94] and Warren [1969, 196]), but it seems that the other published material can be dated to EM III and MM I (Koehl 2006, 76).

Very little pottery was published from the Tholos Alpha annex, but the presence of a large number of bird's-nest stone vases indicates a MM I–II date (Xanthoudides 1924, 99–100; Warren 1969, 8–9; Bevan 2007). No material was published from the rooms south of Tholos Alpha, but the assemblage from the south deposits is clearly MM IB–II (Gerontakou 2003). Rectangular tombs alpha and gamma seem to have contained MM I and Late Minoan material (Xanthoudides 1924, 93; Soles 1992, 193). The annex to Tholos Beta and other walls shown in the original plan are not datable because no material was reported from them. In Area AB various bird's-nest stone vessels and an imitation Egyptian stone vessel point to a MM I date (Warren 1969, 8–9; Bevan 2001). The folded-arm figurine found in the area (Xanthoudides 1924, 121) may indicate an EM IIA use of the area, although it may have been moved from Tholos Beta and not be representative of the period of construction or use of the pavement.

It seems that a major building phase occurred at Platanos during EM III and MM I that resulted in a complex cemetery that has few known parallels; at Hagia Triada various associated buildings were constructed in MM I around Tholos A, but the two tholoi were used simultaneously only for a short period of time (Carinci 2004). This does not seem to be the case at Platanos, where both seem to have been in use for much or all of the MM I period. Similarly, other cemeteries such as Kamilari (Levi 1961–1962) or Apesokari (Schörgendorfer 1951), while having large and complex annexes in MM I, had only one tholos in use and no other known directly associated buildings.

The material assemblage of the Platanos cemetery requires detailed analysis, as its interpretation is more complicated than the first glance might suggest, particularly in Tholos Alpha, where the assemblage presents some peculiarities. Xanthoudides' report on the deposits locates the gold and daggers in the upper stratum, and these should be dated to the EM III and MM I use of the tomb. This is also suggested strongly by the large annex filled with MM I material, together with the parallels in stratigraphy from other known tholos tombs (for Archanes-Phourni, Tholoi Gamma and Epsilon, see Panagiotopoulos 2002; Papadatos 2005; for Lebena Gerokampos, see Alexiou and Warren 2004). However, the composition of the assemblage is strange for a MM I funerary deposit and resembles EM II funerary assemblages more closely. The comprehensive study of tholos cemetery assemblages is beyond the scope of this article and has been done elsewhere (Legarra Herrero 2004, 34, 43; 2007), and those studies show that while there is no clear chronological break in the composition of assemblages, there are some clear distinctions between EM I–II and MM I assemblages, as defined by the deposits at Archanes-Phourni Tholoi Epsilon (Panagiotopoulos 2002) and Gamma (Papadatos 2005) and Krasi's lower levels (Marinatos 1929).

EM I–II assemblages (lower strata at Krasi and Archanes-Phourni Tholoi Gamma and Epsilon) were defined by significant amounts of gold and silver objects, objects with Aegean connections, and a small number of seals and stone vessels (Fig. 3.4). EM III–MM I deposits are

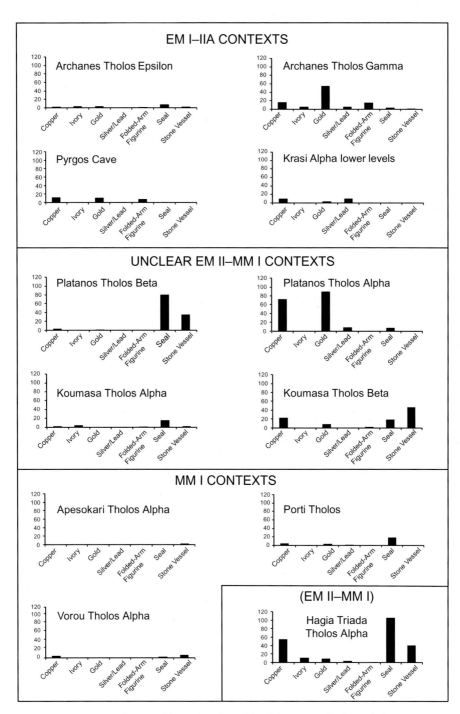

Figure 3.4. Non-ceramic assemblages in selected burial contexts in Central Crete.

better characterized by smaller numbers of copper-based objects, silver and gold, orientalia, and significant numbers of seals and stone vessels (upper strata at Tholoi Gamma and Epsilon at Archanes-Phourni, upper stratum at Koumasa Tholos Beta, Apesokari Tholos Alpha). The composition of the assemblage from Platanos Tholos Alpha seems to follow the first pattern rather than the second (Fig. 3.4). The large amount of gold found in the upper stratum of Tholos Alpha (Xanthoudides 1924, 89) is uncommon in MM I burial deposits, even in those without evidence of looting (Fig. 3.4). Even more uncommon is the significant number of silver objects. Extremely large numbers of stone vases were found in the annexes (around 300; Xanthoudides 1924, 98) and in the south deposits (64 vessels; Gerontakou 2003), but not in the tholos chamber, as in the cases of Platanos Tholos Beta, Koumasa Tholos Beta, and Hagia Triada Tholos Alpha. Around 60 daggers come from the upper stratum of Tholos Alpha, as opposed to the 14 found in the lower level (Xanthoudides 1924, 106–107); this is an unusually large number. At Hagia Triada Tholos Alpha, where the second largest concentration of daggers in a tholos was found, 48 daggers were found in both strata dating to EM II–MM I (Banti 1930–1931; Cultraro 2004). Only six seals were recovered inside Platanos Tholos Alpha, and no material with off-island connections was found. If we accept that this assemblage dates to the MM I period, we are obliged to suggest that Platanos is abnormal not only in terms of rich metal depositions, but also because it represents an abnormal assemblage by the mortuary behavior standards of this period. Moreover, the conspicuous lack of stone vessels and seals in Tholos Alpha contrasts with the assemblages of the annex and the south deposits. In the latter, more than 300 stone vessels were found along with approximately 15 seals, some of them described by Xanthoudides as the most important ivory seals (Xanthoudides 1924, 111). No metal object is described as coming from the annex or the south deposits.

The Tholos Beta assemblage at Platanos also contained large quantities of non-ceramic objects, which this time were dominated by the presence of seals (80) and stone vessels (33), as well as a Babylonian cylinder seal (Kenna 1968, 324–328; Platon 1969, no. 306; Ward 1971, 75) and three Egyptian-style scarabs (Platon 1969, nos. 267, 283, 332; Warren 1980, 494–497; Ward 1981; Yule 1983, 363 nn. 12, 22; Pini 2000, 107; Phillips 2004, 164; Ben-Tor 2006). Only one gold object was found in the tomb, but Xanthoudides suggested that this tomb may have been looted in pre-historic times, in contrast to Tholos Alpha (Xanthoudides 1924, 89, 92), and many of the gold objects may have been removed. It seems that Tholos Beta also contained an exceptional assemblage. Material with Egyptian parallels has been found in other tholos cemeteries in the form of stone vessels (e.g., Hagia Triada; see Warren 1969, 105–111; Bevan 2004) and scarabs (Pini 2000; Phillips 2004, 2006; Ben-Tor 2006), but never in such large quantities as in the case of Platanos Tholos Beta. This together with the significant number of stone vessels (33) and seals (80), is sufficient to indicate that the assemblage of the tomb was quite exceptional, but with a very different composition from Tholos Alpha that was more in line with the kind of assemblages found in MM I cemeteries, and with close parallels with Hagia Triada Tholos Alpha's EM II–MM I assemblage (Fig. 3.4).

Platanos clearly stands out in the funerary record of MM I South-Central Crete, given its layout and the assemblages in Tholos Alpha and Tholos Beta. Interestingly, there seem to be different choices made in regard to the types of items determined for deposition in Tholos Alpha (gold, daggers) and in Tholos Beta (seals, orientalia, stone vessels) as well as how these assemblages relate to those in their respective annexes. As Xanthoudides warned, this pattern may have been produced in part by differential looting of metal objects in the two tholoi, but this cannot account for the differences in stone vessel and seal deposition within the tholoi. We can, however, suggest a couple of scenarios to explain these patterns. The first is based on the more traditional approach that suggests similar extended kin groups were interred in each tholos. The differences in the assemblages may express a choice by the two groups in the way they display their social status, as this may have relied on different social roles (e.g., administrators, traders, warriors, priests). This, however, does not explain the differences in the structure of the assemblages between the two tholoi and their annexes. In a second scenario, the tholoi may not be differentiated on the basis of kinship but rather in terms of social status. The majority of the population would be interred in one tholos, and particular individuals with a privileged social position (e.g., chief, big-man, priest) would be interred in the other. Daggers have been suggested to be important representations of status and power in South-Central Crete (Whitelaw 1983; Nakou 1995), and their number in Tholos Alpha may reinforce the idea that only persons of certain status were being interred in this tholos. This model better explains the depositional pattern in Tholos Alpha and its annex, as the different status could be accompanied by a distinct ritual. Similar scenarios are indicated at MM I Archanes-Phourni and Malia, where a focal building was created in EM III or MM I times (the Tholos Beta complex and Chrysolakos, respectively). Unfortunately, we do not know the compositions of the MM I assemblages from those contexts, so we cannot compare them with the Tholos Alpha deposition pattern.

I would like to return to the large number of stone vessels found around Tholos Alpha, as it is an exceptional feature that has no parallels in any other cemetery on the island and requires some explanation. It should be noted that the stone vessels are found in the same contexts in which we would normally find large deposits of conical cups: in rooms within annexes, sometimes concentrated in one specific room, as in the case of the stone vessels in Room alpha in the Platanos Tholos Alpha annex (other examples include: Room Mu at Lebena Gerokampos [Alexiou and Warren 2004, 159–160]; Room Lambda at Hagia Triada Tholos Alpha [Banti 1930–1931, 160, 178, fig. 4]); or in non-burial contexts near the tholoi, as in the south deposits outside Tholos Beta at Archanes-Phourni, which contained jugs and other types of vessels (Sakellarakis and Sapouna-Sakellaraki 1997, 204–205). It is possible that this represents a qualitative leap from the ritual activities in other tholos cemeteries; for example, at Platanos Tholos Alpha, ceramic conical cups were replaced by more valuable stone vessels.

The rituals performed around Tholos Alpha were profoundly different from any that may have been performed in contemporaneous cemeteries. The large annexes indicate new ways of performing ritual across South-Central Crete. The annexes (for a catalog of annexes, see Petit 1987), the open areas (e.g., Hagia Kyriaki [Blackman and Branigan 1982]; Kamilari [Levi 1961–1962]; and Moni Odigitria [Vasilakis 1992]), and the large deposition of vessels (e.g., West Camarette at Hagia Triada [Banti 1930–1931; La Rosa 2001b]; and the North Deposit at Vorou [Marinatos 1931]) suggest that group ritual becomes one of the main foci of burial activity in MM I South-Central Crete and that it was spatially controlled by the new architecture and probably clearly defined, as the recurrent patterns in the funerary architecture document. At Platanos, it is this new focal activity that was qualitatively exaggerated around Tholos Alpha that shows how the community started to adapt and manipulate the key features of the new ritual on their own terms. In other words, it highlights what kind of activities and dynamics were socially important for MM I communities.

It is difficult to assess Platanos before the MM I period, because significant modifications and large-scale deposition may have obliterated the earlier deposits. We have enough early material to confirm that the cemetery was first used in EM II and that it was composed of Tholos Alpha and perhaps Tholoi Beta and Gamma. Despite the fact that negative evidence has only a limited value given the history of use of the cemetery, it is true that even when it was excavated by the same archaeologist as Koumasa, the published EM IIA material was very limited and may suggest that Platanos did not match Koumasa's exceptional character in the EM IIA period.

When Appearances Deceive

Koumasa and Platanos look similar at a first glance and are often treated together. They are, however, two very different cemeteries with varying mortuary behavior trajectories that provide evidence for two significantly different communities in diverse periods. The Koumasa evidence seems to illustrate better the EM IIA situation, while Platanos better illustrates the MM I. These disparities cannot but relate to diverse ways in which each community used its cemetery in each period. Both funerary contexts show that very different strategies were used to negotiate the particular social, ideological, and economic aspects of each period. The common feature is that the cemetery always represented a powerful social arena regardless of its period of use and the changes it experienced.

In general, we could suggest that MM I mortuary behavior is a more complicated affair, with various spaces delimiting and focusing the ritual in a way that is difficult to appreciate at Koumasa. The architecture shows a more complex separation of spaces that frames more involved ritual processes. Mortuary behavior and ritual activities were more focused on the deposition of the body and the accompanying material in EM IIA, and on group participation in MM I. This is not to say that one pattern completely replaces the other, but rather that the balance in MM I seems to have tilted toward the group participating in the burial ritual and their performances in differentiated spaces. This could have possibly involved the differential participation of different social groups within and beyond the burial group, in varied activities separated in space and potentially in time. While the EM IIA Koumasa community seems more focused on marking the status and position of certain individuals with grave goods, the Platanos community is more concerned about the participation of the living. This is a very significant difference, and it may indicate the very different ways in which the two communities were structured and represent very different mechanisms for the management of the social relationships both within and between burial groups. Koumasa may have been organized around clear and strongly marked social positions (i.e., heads of family [Whitelaw 1983; Karytinos 1998] or religious figures), perhaps because these individuals were key decision makers in the atomized groups around which everyday life was organized (Whitelaw 2000; Relaki 2004). The MM I Platanos community may have been structured around social arenas and the participation of the whole community (and indeed others) in public events. It is possible that this much more inclusive strategy was used by a community living together in a settlement (as opposed to the more fragmented EM II settlement pattern) because they could easily and frequently engage in ritual practice in the cemetery.

The different social structure between the two periods becomes clearer when we think of the way in which both cemeteries express their exceptionality in the funerary landscape of Crete. Koumasa has clear Aegean connections, as illustrated in the community members' choice of material, but, more importantly, this is displayed mainly inside the tomb through material objects that are intimately linked to the deceased. This material, while not necessarily owned by the deceased in life, established a connection with the individual when it was deposited in the tomb, thus helping to mark their status. As a result, the ritual seems not to have been staged in front of a large group of people—only a small group could attend the interment within the chamber of the tomb. While it is very probable that rituals took place outside the tholoi, the lack of clear evidence in the form of material deposits outside the tombs or architectural features may indicate that formal, large communal rites did not feature prominently in the sequence of ritual activities that marked the burial.

The focus for the display may have been within the community, affecting mainly relationships within and between the groups buried in the different tholoi in the cemetery. Small groups living dispersed in the landscape (Whitelaw 2000; Relaki 2004) may have found it necessary to affirm their position within the extended kin networks that were entitled to use the tholos cemeteries. Perhaps some of the small groups managed to acquire a privileged status, as possibly indicated by some of the material at Koumasa; but, given the limited patterning in the material record, this is far from clear.

At Platanos, potentially high-value material is deposited in the tombs and is probably linked to the deceased. However, that the architecture, particularly the annexes, indicates a more complex ritual, suggests that the ritual was longer and better choreographed for the active involvement of a larger group outside the tombs and for public display to an audience. I would suggest that a longer sequence of rituals allowed an expansion of the radius of influence of the mortuary ritual (Keswani 2004, 82; Oestigaard and Goldhahn 2006). A series of rituals that lasts days, weeks, even years, allows people from more distant areas to attend and to deliver the messages conveyed by the ritual to a larger population that comes from a wider geographical area. Also it permits elaboration of the ritual, and it gives more time to prepare the material means of marking differences (Keswani 2004, 15). Significantly, at Platanos the public aspects of the ritual show exceptional elaboration, with a greater effort in constructing different spaces and the large-scale deposition of stone vessels outside Tholos Alpha. It seems that group ritual was modified to mark or define some sort of privileged status. The mortuary behavior is better designed here for the display of distinction by one group to another. The architectural and depositional elaborations associated with Tholos Alpha may indicate a strong community where the interest resided in displaying and asserting their power of the whole community at a regional level. This is not surprising; it has been suggested by various authors that there is a clear and strong regional competition dynamic in South-Central Crete by MM I (Sbonias 1999; Relaki 2004).

What nobody has been able to define until now is how the Platanos cemetery managed to engage in this competition and express its dominant position. The simple deposition of rich material is not a particularly effective mechanism, as we have seen at Koumasa. It has to be reinforced and modified to permit it to communicate at a larger social and regional scale, and to relate more efficiently to the high status marked by the burial ritual to the burial group and community that performed it. However, we cannot forget Tholos Beta, with its significant assemblage, and the other contexts in the cemetery, which show that there were also some internal divisions within the Platanos community that needed to be taken into consideration. The community may be a central social context for its members, but kinship relationships and other intra-community relationships were negotiated at a local level.

Conclusion

This article has outlined some of the clearest and more important traits in the use of two tholos cemeteries in South-Central Crete, which are usually treated as directly equivalent sites. It is intended to serve as a first step toward the understanding of the material record of this area, encouraging new studies of the old material. Even under adverse circumstances, a new approach to old data can yield interesting results that validate the construction of new and more complex explanatory models. A more detailed look at the data is possible, particularly if armed with approaches that pay more attention to variation and the active role of each cemetery in the human landscape of South-Central Crete. While the identification of particularities—both temporally and spatially—raises new questions, these are more relevant for our discussion, and they push our knowledge forward toward a much more detailed assessment of the societies that inhabited EM and MM Crete. In the end, it is clear that addressing old and new questions about socioeconomic organization in EM and MM Crete requires both new research with open-ended models and a more accurate look at the archaeological record.

Acknowledgments

This article is largely based on my doctoral research, and I would like to thank Todd Whitelaw for his supervision, encouragement, and useful comments on different drafts of this paper. I would also like to thank the organizer of the session on mortuary customs of prehistoric Crete at the 108th Annual Meeting of the Archaeological Institute of America in 2007, Joanne Murphy, for providing me the opportunity to present my research in such an interesting forum and inviting me to publish my ideas in the resulting volume. I am also indebted to her and the anonymous referees for their useful comments on earlier drafts of this paper. Finally, I would like to thank Anna Stellatou for her support and helpful discussions of the different drafts and her dedicated revision of my English. The research included in this paper was undertaken with the help of a Grant for the Formation of Researchers, type AK, from the Government of the Basque Country, and the Post-Doctoral Research Fellowship from the Institute for Aegean Prehistory (INSTAP).

References

Alexiou, S. 1973a. "Αι αρχαιότητες Ηράκλειου κατά το 1972," *CretChron* 25, pp. 457–478.

———. 1973b. "Αρχαιότητες και μνημεία κεντρικής και ανατολικής Κρήτης," *ArchDelt* 28 (Β΄, 2 Chronika) [1977], pp. 559–564.

———. 1975. "Cleansing of Silver Objects in the New Laboratory in the Heraklion Museum," *AAA* 8 (2), pp. 138–139.

Alexiou, S., and P. Warren. 2004. *The Early Minoan Tombs of Lebena, Southern Crete* (*SIMA* 30), Sävedalen.

Banti, L. 1930–1931. "La grande tombe a tholos di Haghia Triadha," *ASAtene* 13–14, pp. 155–241.

Bardsley, C.S. 2004. "Cognitive and Cultural Evolutionary Perspectives on Religion: A Socio-Communicative Approach to the Archaeology of the Mesaran Tholos Tombs," in *Belief in the Past. The Proceedings of the 2002 Manchester Conference on Archaeology and Religion* (*BAR-IS* 1212), T. Insoll, ed., Oxford, pp. 17–26.

Bartel, A. 1982. "A Historical Review of Ethnological and Archaeological Analyses of Mortuary Practices," *JAnthArch* 1, pp. 32–58.

Belli, P. 1984. "Nuovi documenti per lo studio delle tombe circolari cretesi," *SMEA* 25, pp. 91–142.

———. 2003. "On Measuring Tholoi in the Aegean Bronze Age," in *METRON: Measuring the Aegean Bronze Age. Proceedings of the 9th International Aegean Conference, New Haven, Yale University, 18–21 April 2002* (*Aegaeum* 24), K.P. Foster and R. Laffineur, eds., Liège, pp. 403–409.

Ben-Tor, D. 2006. "Chronological and Historical Implications of the Early Egyptian Scarabs on Crete," in *Timelines: Studies in Honour of Manfred Bietak* (*Orientalia Lovaniensia Analecta* 149), E. Czerny, I. Hein, H. Hunger, D. Melman, and A. Schwab, eds., vol. 2, Leuven, pp. 77–86.

Bevan, A. 2001. *Value Regimes in the Eastern Mediterranean Bronze Age: A Study through Stone Vessels*, Ph.D. diss., University College London.

————. 2004. "Emerging Civilized Values? The Consumption and Imitation of Egyptian Stone Vessels in EMII–MMI Crete and Its Wider Eastern Mediterranean Context," in *The Emergence of Civilisation Revisited* (*Sheffield Studies in Aegean Archaeology* 6), J.C. Barrett and P. Halstead, eds., Oxford, pp. 107–126.

————. 2007. *Stone Vessels and Values in the Bronze Age Eastern Mediterranean*, Cambridge.

Binford, L.R. 1971. "Mortuary Practices: Their Study and Their Potential," in *Approaches to the Social Dimensions of Mortuary Practices* (*Memoirs of the Society for American Archaeology* 25), J.A. Brown, ed., Washington, D.C., pp. 6–29.

Blackman, D.J., and K. Branigan. 1977. "An Archaeological Survey of the Lower Catchment of the Ayiofarango Valley," *BSA* 72, pp. 13–84.

————. 1982. "The Excavation of an Early Minoan Tholos Tomb at Ayia Kiriaki, Ayiofarango," *BSA* 77, pp. 1–57.

Branigan, K. 1965. "Four 'Miniature Sickles' of Middle Minoan Crete," *CretChron* 19, pp. 179–182.

————. 1968a. *Copper and Bronze Working in Early Bronze Age Crete* (*SIMA* 19), Lund.

————. 1968b. "Silver and Lead in Prepalatial Crete," *AJA* 72, pp. 219–229.

————. 1970. *The Tombs of Mesara: A Study of Funerary Architecture and Ritual in Southern Crete, 2800–1700 B.C.*, London.

————. 1984. "Early Minoan Society: The Evidence of the Mesara Tholoi Reviewed," in *Aux origines de l'hellénisme: La Crète et la Grèce. Hommage à Henri van Effenterre*, G. Glotz, ed., Paris, pp. 29–37.

————. 1993. *Dancing with Death: Life And Death in Southern Crete c. 3000–2000 B.C.*, Amsterdam.

————. 1994. "The Corbelling Controversy: Another Contribution," *Cretan Studies* 4, pp. 65–70.

————. 1998. "The Nearness of You: Proximity and Distance in Early Minoan Funerary Behaviour," in *Cemetery and Society in the Aegean Bronze Age*, K. Branigan, ed., Sheffield, pp. 13–26.

———. 2008. "Communal ceremonies in an Early Minoan Tholos Cemetery," in *Dioskouri: Studies Presented to W.G. Cavanagh and C.B. Mee on the Anniversary of Their 30-Year Joint Contribution to Aegean Archaeology*, C. Gallou, M. Georgiadis, and G. Muskett, eds., Oxford, pp. 15–22.

Campbell-Green, T. 2006. *Cemetery, Ceramics and Space: An Analysis of the Pottery Assemblage from the Early Minoan Cemetery of Moni Odigitria, South-Central Crete, with Specific Reference to Its Function*, Ph.D. diss., University of Sheffield.

Carinci, F.M. 1999. "Haghia Triada nel periodo dei primi palazzi: I nuovi dati sulle produzioni ceramiche," in *Επί πόντον πλαζομένοι: Simposio italiano di Studi Egei, dedicato a Luigi Bernabó Brea e Giovanni Pugliese*, V. La Rosa, D. Palermo, and L. Vagnetti, eds., Rome, pp. 115–132.

———. 2004. "Haghia Triada nel periodo Medio Minoico," *Creta Antica* 4, pp. 97–144.

Carr, C. 1995. "Mortuary Practices: Their Social, Philosophical-Religious, Circumstantial, and Physical Determinants," *Journal of Archaeological Method and Theory* 2, pp. 105–200.

Catapoti, D. 2005. *From Power to Paradigm: Rethinking the Emergence of the "Palatial Phenomenon" in Bronze Age Crete*, Ph.D. diss., University of Sheffield.

Charles, D.K. 2005. "The Archaeology of Death as Anthropology," in *Interacting with the Dead: Perspectives on Mortuary Archaeology for the New Millennium*, G.F.M. Rakita, J.E. Buikstra, L.A. Beck, and S.R. Williams, eds., Gainesville, pp. 15–24.

Cultraro, M. 2000. "La brocchetta dei vivi per la sete dei morti: Riconsiderazione delle Camerette a Sud della Grande Tholos di Haghia Triada," in *Πεπραγμένα Η' Διεθνούς Κρητολογικού Συνεδρίου, Ηράκλειο, 9–14 Σεπτεμβρίου 1996*, A' (1), Herakleion, pp. 309–326.

———. 2001. *L'Anello di Minosse: Archeologia della regalità nell'Egeo Minoico*, Milano.

———. 2004. "La Grande Tholos di Haghia Triada: Nuovi dati per un vecchio complesso," *Creta Antica* 4, pp. 103–130.

Davaras, C. 1975. "Early Minoan Jewelry from Mochlos," *BSA* 70, pp. 101–114.

Di Vita, A. 1990–1991. "Atti Della Scuola 1990–1991. Haghia Triada," *ASAtene* 68–69, pp. 428–432.

———. 1996–1997. "Atti Della Scuola 1996–1997. Haghia Triada," *ASAtene* 74–75, pp. 478–484.

———. 1998–2000. "Atti Della Scuola 1998–2000. Haghia Triada 1998–1999," *ASAtene* 76–78, pp. 390–397.

Evans, A.J. 1895. *Cretan Pictographs and the Mycenaean Script*, London.

Georgoulaki, E. 1990. "The Minoan Sanctuary at Koumasa: The Evidence of the Material," in *Aegaeum* 6, pp. 5–23.

———. 1996. *Burial Evidence and Its Religious Connotations in Prepalatial and Old Palace Minoan Crete*, Ph.D. diss., University of Liège.

Gerontakou, E. 2003. "Δύο Μεσομινωικοί αποθέτες στο νεκροταφείο του Πλάτανου," in *ΑΡΓΟΝΑΥΤΗΣ: Τιμητικός τόμος για τον καθηγητή Χρίστο Γ. Ντούμα από τους μαθητές του στο Πανεπιστήμιο Αθήνων (1980–2000)*, A. Vlachopoulos and K. Birtacha, eds., Athens, pp. 303–330.

Girella, L. 2003. "La morte ineguale: Per una lettura delle evidenze funerarie nel Medio Minoico III a Creta," *ASAtene* 81, pp. 251–300.

Goodison, L. 2006. "Re-constructing Dialogues with the Dead," in *Πεπραγμένα Θ´ Διεθνούς Κρητολογικού Συνεδρίου, Ελούντα, 1–6 Οκτωβρίου 2001* A´ (3), Herakleion, pp. 325–340.

Goodison, L., and C. Guarita. 2005. "A New Catalogue of the Mesara-Type Tombs," *SMEA* 47, pp. 171–212.

Halbherr, F. 1903. "Resti dell'età Micenea scoperti Ad Haghia Triada presso Phaestos," *MontAnt* 13, col. 5.

Hodder, I. 1980. "Social Structure and Cemeteries: A Critical Appraisal," in *Anglo-Saxon Cemeteries, 1979: The Fourth Anglo-Saxon Symposium at Oxford (BAR-BS 82)*, P. Rahtz, T. Dickinson, and L. Watts, eds., Oxford, pp. 161–169.

———. 1982. *Symbols in Action: Ethnoarchaeological Studies of Material Culture*, Cambridge.

Hodder, I., and S. Hutson. 2003. *Reading the Past: Current Approaches to Interpretation in Archaeology*, 3rd ed., Cambridge.

Ioannidou, A. 1973. "Περισυλλογή αρχαίων τυχαία ευρήματα," *ArchDelt* 28 (Β´, 2 Chronika) [1977], pp. 569–574.

Karagianni, E. 1984. *Μινωικά σύνθετα σκεύη (Κέρνοι?)*, Athens.

Karytinos, A. 1998. "Sealstones in Cemeteries: A Display of Social Status?" in *Cemetery and Society in the Aegean Bronze Age*, K. Branigan, ed., Sheffield, pp. 78–88.

———. 2000. "The Stylistic Development of Seals from Archanes-Phourni throughout the Prepalatial Period—Style and Social Meaning," in *Minoisch–Mikenische Glyptik: Stil, Ikonographie, Funktion. V. Internationales Siegel-Symposium, Marburg, 23.–25. September 1999 (CMS Beiheft 6)*, W. Müller, ed., Berlin, pp. 124–134.

Kenna, V.E.G. 1968. "Ancient Crete and the Use of the Cylinder Seal," *AJA* 72, pp. 321–336.

Keswani, P.S. 2004. *Mortuary Ritual and Society in Bronze Age Cyprus* (*Monographs in Mediterranean Archaeology*), London.

Koehl, R.B. 2006. *Aegean Bronze Age Rhyta* (*Prehistory Monographs* 19), Philadelphia.

Krause, S. 1992. *Die Typologie der frühminoischen Idole: Versuch einer evolutionären Typologie*, Hamburg.

La Rosa, V. 1992–1993. "La c.d. tomba degli Ori e il nuovo settore nord-est," *ASAtene* 70–71, pp. 121–174.

———. 1999a. "Nuovi dati sulla tomba del sarcofago dipinto di H. Triada," in *Eπί πόντον πλαζομένοι. Simposio italiano di Studi Egei dedicato a Luigi Bernabò Brea e Giovanni Pugliese*, V. La Rosa, D. Palermo, and L. Vagnetti, eds., Rome, pp. 177–188.

———. 1999b. "Άγια Τριάδα," *ArchDelt* 54 (B΄, 2 Chronika) [2006], p. 857.

———. 2001a. "Festos 2001," *ASAtene* 79, pp. 357–369.

———. 2001b. "Minoan Baetyls: Between Funerary Rituals and Epiphanies," in *POTNIA: Deities and Religion in the Aegean Bronze Age. Proceedings of the 8th International Aegean Conference, Göteborg, Göteborg University, 12–15 April 2000* (*Aegaeum* 22), R. Laffineur and R. Hägg, eds., Liège, pp. 221–227.

Lahanas, A. 2000. "Συνοπτική παρουσίαση της στιλιστικής εξέλιξης της κεραμικής των Αρχανών από την ΠΜ έως την ΜΜ ΙΒ περίοδο," in *Πεπραγμένα Η΄ Διεθνούς Κρητολογικού Συνεδρίου, Ηράκλειο, 9–14 Σεπτεμβρίου 1996* Α' (2), Herakleion, pp. 155–169.

Legarra Herrero, B. 2004. "About the Distribution of Metal Objects in Prepalatial Crete," *Papers of the Institute of Archaeology* 15, pp. 29–51.

———. 2007. *Mortuary Behaviour and Social Organisation in Pre- and Protopalatial Crete*, Ph.D .diss., University College London.

Levi, D. 1961–1962. "La Tomba a Tholos Di Kamilari Presso a Festos," *ASAtene* 39–40, pp. 7–148.

Maggidis, C. 1994. *Burial Building 19 at Archanes: A Study of Prepalatial and Early Protopalatial Funerary Architecture and Ritual*, Ph.D. diss., University of Pennsylvania.

Marinatos, S. 1929. "Πρωτομινωικός θολωτός τάφος πάρα το χορίων Κρασί Πεδιάδα," *ArchDelt* 12 [1932], pp. 102–141.

———. 1931. "Δύο πρώιμοι τάφοι εκ Βόρου Μεσαράς," *ArchDelt* 13 [1933], pp. 137–170.

———. 1933. "Funde und Forschungen auf Kreta," *AA* 1933, cols. 287–314.

Miller, E.B. 1984. *Zoomorphic Vases in the Bronze Age Aegean*, Ph.D. diss., New York University.

Murphy, J.M. 1998. "Ideologies, Rites and Rituals: A View of Prepalatial Minoan Tholoi," in *Cemetery and Society in the Aegean Bronze Age*, K. Branigan, ed., Sheffield, pp. 27–41.

Nakou, G. 1995. "The Cutting Edge: A New Look at Early Aegean Metallurgy," *JMA* 8 (2), pp. 1–32.

Oestigaard, T., and J. Goldhahn. 2006. "From the Dead to the Living: Death as Transactions and Re-Negotiations," *Norwegian Archaeological Review* 39, pp. 27–48.

Orlandou, A.K. 1972. "Κρήτη (περισυλλογή αρχαίων)," *Ergon* 1972, pp. 125–130.

Pader, E.-J. 1982. *Symbolism, Social Relation and the Interpretation of Mortuary Remains* (*BAR-IS* 130), Oxford.

Palio, O. 2004. "Vasi in pietra dai livelli MM II del 'Settore Nord-Est' di Haghia Triada," *Creta Antica* 4, pp. 329–342.

Panagiotopoulos, D. 2002. *Das Tholosgrab E von Phourni bei Archanes: Studien zu einem frühkretischen Grabfund und seinem kulturellen Kontext* (*BAR-IS* 1014), Oxford.

Papadatos, Y. 1999. *Mortuary Practices and Their Importance for the Reconstruction of Society and Life in Prepalatial Crete: The Evidence from Tholos Tomb Gamma in Archanes-Phourni*, Ph.D. diss., University of Sheffield.

———. 2003a. "The 'International Spirit' and Interregional Interaction in the EBA Southern Aegean: The Evidence from Pre-Palatial Crete (Abstract)," *BICS* 46, pp. 232–233.

———. 2003b. " Ένα παλίμψηστο λοιπόν . . ." in *ΑΡΓΟΝΑΥΤΗΣ: Τιμητικός τόμος για τον καθηγητή Χρίστο Γ. Ντούμα από τους μαθητές του στο Πανεπιστήμιο Αθήνων (1980–2000)*, A. Vlachopoulos and K. Birtacha, eds., Athens, pp. 277–291.

———. 2005. *Tholos Tomb Gamma: A Prepalatial Tholos Tomb at Phourni, Archanes* (*Prehistory Monographs* 17), Philadelphia.

Paribeni, R. 1903. "Lavori eseguiti dalla missione archeologica Italiana nel palazzo e nella necropoli di Haghia Triada Dal 23 febbraio Al 15 luglio 1903," *Rendiconti della Reale Accademia dei Lincei Classe di Scienze Morali, Storiche e Filologiche* ser. 5, 12, pp. 317–351.

Parker Pearson, M. 1982. "Mortuary Practices, Society and Ideology: An Ethno-archaeological Study," in *Symbolic and Structural Archaeology*, I. Hodder, ed., Cambridge, pp. 99–113.

———. 1999. *The Archaeology of Death and Burial*, Stroud.

Pearson, M. 1998. "Performance as Valuation: Early Bronze Age Burial as Theatrical Complexity," in *The Archaeology of Value: Essays on Prestige and the Processes of Valuation* (*BAR-IS* 730), D. Bailey, ed., Oxford, pp. 32–41.

Pelon, O. 1976. *Tholoi, tumuli et circles funéraires: Recherches sur les monuments funéraires de plan circulaire dans l'Égée de l'Âge du Bronze (IIIe et IIe millénaires av. J.-C.)*, Athens.

Petit, F. 1987. "Les tombes circulaires de la Messara: Problèmes d'interprètation des pièces annexes," in *Thanatos: Les coutumes funéraires en Egée a l'âge du Bronze. Actes du colloque de Liège, 21–23 avril 1986 (Aegaeum* 1), R. Laffineur, ed., Liège, pp. 35–43.

Phillips, J. S. 2004. "The Odd Man Out: Minoan Scarabs and *Scaraboids,"* in *Scarabs of the Second Millennium B.C. from Egypt, Nubia, Crete and the Levant: Chronological and Historical Implications. Papers of a Symposium, Vienna, 10th–13th of January 2002*, M. Bietak and E. Czerny, eds., Vienna, pp. 161–170.

———. 2006. "Why? . . . And Why Not? Minoan Reception and Perceptions of Egyptian Influence," in *Timelines: Studies in Honour of Manfred Bietak (Orientalia Lovaniensia Analecta* 149), E. Czerny, I. Hein, H. Hunger, D. Melman, and A. Schwab, eds., vol. 2, Leuven, pp. 293–300.

Pieler, E.C. 2004. "Kykladische und 'kykladisierende' Idole Auf Kreta und im helladischen Raum in der Frühbronzezeit—Eine Klassifizierung," *SMEA* 46 (1), pp. 79–119.

Pini, I. 2000. "Eleven Early Cretan Scarabs," in *Κρήτη—Αίγυπτος. Πολιτισμικοί δεσμοί τριών χιλιετιών*, A. Karetsou, ed., Athens, pp. 107–113.

Platon, N. 1953. "Η αρχαιολογική κίνησις εν Κρήτη κατά το έτος 1953," *CretChron* 7, pp. 479–492.

———. 1955. "Η αρχαιολογική κίνησις εν Κρήτη κατά το έτος 1955," *CretChron* 9, pp. 553–569.

———. 1969. *Iraklion Archäologisches Museum 1: Die Siegel der Vorpalastzeit (CMS* II, 1), Berlin.

Platon, N., I. Pini, and G. Salies. 1977. *Iraklion Archäologisches Museum 2: Die Siegel der Altpalastzeit (CMS* II, 2), Berlin.

Relaki, M. 2003. *Social arenas in Minoan Crete: A Regional History of the Mesara in South-Central Crete from the Final Neolithic to the End of the Protopalatial Period*, Ph.D. diss., University of Sheffield.

———. 2004. "Constructing a Region: The Contested Landscapes of Prepalatial Mesara," in *The Emergence of Civilisation Revisited (Sheffield Studies in Aegean Archaeology* 6), J.C. Barrett and P. Halstead, eds., Oxford, pp. 170–188.

Renfrew, C. 1969. "The Development and Chronology of the Early Cycladic Figurines," *AJA* 73, pp. 1–32.

Rutkowski, B. 1989. "Minoan Sanctuaries at Christos and Koumasa, Crete: New Field Research," *ArchKorrBl* 19, pp. 47–51.

Sakellarakis, J.A., and E. Sapouna-Sakellaraki. 1997. *Archanes: Minoan Crete in a New Light*, 2 vols., Athens.

Sbonias, K. 1995. *Frühkretische Siegel. Ansätze für eine Interpretation der sozial-politischen Entwincklung auf Kreta während der Frühbronzezeit* (*BAR-IS* 620), Oxford.

———. 1999. "Social Development Management of Production and Symbolic Representation in Prepalatial Crete," in *From Minoan Farmers to Roman Traders: Sidelights on the Economy of Ancient Crete*, A. Chaniotis, ed., Stuttgart, pp. 25–51.

Schörgendorfer, A.S. 1951. "Ein mittelminoisches Tholosgrab bei Apesokari," in *Forschungen auf Kreta 1942*, F. Matz, ed., Berlin, pp. 13–22.

Soles, J.S. 1992. *The Prepalatial Cemeteries at Mochlos and Gournia and the House Tombs of Bronze Age Crete* (*Hesperia Suppl.* 24), Princeton.

Stefani, E. 1930–1931. "La Grande Tomba a tholos di Haghia Triadha," *ASAtene* 13–14, pp. 147–154.

Todaro, S. 2004. "Haghia Triada nel periodo Antico Minoico," *Creta Antica* 4, pp. 73–96.

Ucko, P. 1969. "Ethnography and Archaeological Interpretation of Funerary Remains," *WordArch* 1, pp. 262–280.

Vasilakis, A. 1992. "Odigitria," in *The Aerial Atlas of Ancient Crete*, E.E. Myers, J.W. Myers, and G. Cadogan, eds., Berkeley, pp. 213–215.

———. 1996. *Ο χρυσός και ο αργυρός στην Κρήτη κατά την Πρώιπη Περίοδο του Χαλκού*, Herakleion.

Vasilakis, A., and K. Branigan. 2010. *Moni Odigitria: A Prepalatial Cemetery and Its Environs in the Asterousia, Southern Crete* (*Prehistory Monographs* 30), Philadelphia.

Walberg, G. 1983. *Provincial Middle Minoan Pottery*, Mainz am Rhein.

Ward, W.A. 1971. *Egypt and the East Mediterranean World, 2200–1900 B.C.: Studies in Egyptian Foreign Relations during the First Intermediate Period*, Beirut.

———. 1981. "The Scarabs from Tholos B at Platanos," *AJA* 85, pp. 70–75.

Warren, P. 1965. "The First Minoan Stone Vases and EM Chronology," *CretChron* 19, pp. 7–43.

———. 1969. *Minoan Stone Vases*, Cambridge.

———. 1973. "The Mitata of Nidha and Early Minoan Tholos Tombs," *AAA* 6, pp. 449–456.

———. 1977. "The Beginnings of Minoan Religion," in *Antichità Cretesi: Studi in onore di Doro Levi* (*Cronache di Archeologia* 12), Catania, pp. 137–147.

———. 1980. "Problems of Chronology in Crete and the Aegean in the Third and Earlier Second Millennium B.C.," *AJA* 84, pp. 487–499.

———. 2007. "The Roofing of Early Minoan Round Tombs: The Evidence of Lebena Tomb II (Gerokampos) and of Cretan Mitata," in *Krinoi kai Limenes: Studies in Honor of Joseph and Maria Shaw* (*Prehistory Monographs* 22), P.P. Betancourt, M.C. Nelson and H. Williams, eds., Philadelphia, pp. 9–16.

Wason, P.K. 1994. *The Archaeology of Rank*, Cambridge.

Watrous, L.V. 1994. "Crete from Earliest Prehistory through the Protopalatial Period," *AJA* 98, pp. 698–753.

Watrous, L.V., D. Hadzi-Vallianou, and H. Blitzer. 2004. *The Plain of Phaistos: Cycles of Social Complexity in the Mesara Region of Crete* (*Monumenta Archaeologica* 23), Los Angeles.

Whitelaw, T.M. 1983. "The Settlement at Fournou Korifi, Myrtos and Aspects of Early Minoan Social Organization," in *Minoan Society. Proceedings of the Cambridge Colloquium, 1981*, O. Krzyszkowska and L. Nixon, eds., Bristol, pp. 323–345.

———. 2000. "Settlement Instability and Landscape Degradation in the Southern Aegean in the Third Millennium," in *Landscape and Land Use in Postglacial Greece* (*Sheffield Studies in Aegean Archaeology* 3), P. Halstead and C. Frederick, eds., Sheffield, pp. 135–161.

Wilson, D.E., and P.M. Day. 1994. "Ceramic Regionalism in Prepalatial Central Crete: The Messara Imports at EM I to EM IIA Knossos," *BSA* 89, pp. 1–87.

Xanthoudides, S. 1915. "Ἡ ἀρχαιολογικὴ περιφέρεια.—Περὶ ἀνασκαφῆς μεγάλου θολωτοῦ τάφου Πρωτομινωϊκῆς ἐποχῆς ἐν Πλατάνῳ Κρήτης," *ArchDelt* 1 [1916], pp. 60–62.

———. 1924. *The Vaulted Tombs of the Mesara*, London.

Yule, P. 1983. "Notes in Scarabs and Aegean Chronology," *BSA* 78, pp. 359–368.

Zois, A. 1967. "Ἔρευνα περὶ τῆς μινωικῆς κεραμεικῆς," *Ἐπετηρὶς Ἐπιστημονικῶν Ἐρευνῶν* 1967–1968, pp. 703–732.

———. 1968. *Der Kamares-Stil: Werden und Wesen*, Tübingen.

———. 1998. *Κρήτη: Η πρώιμή εποχή του χαλκού. Αρχαιολογία και ιστορία σχεδόν όλων των θέσεων της νήσου από τις πιο ανατολικές ως τις πιο δυτικές περιοχές. 5: Μεσαρά Κρήτης και Νότια Κεντρική Κρήτη*, Athens.

4 | Tomb 4 at Pseira: Evidence for Minoan Social Practices

PHILIP P. BETANCOURT

A number of archaeologists have commented on the presence of open courts and enclosed or partly enclosed spaces in front of Minoan tombs, with the frequent suggestion that they were used for ceremonies and special cult activities (see, among others, Evans 1921–1935, IV, 1000–1001; Soles 1992, 224; Branigan 1993, 131–136; 1998, 21). Tomb 4 at Pseira had a court in front of its entrance, and its importance in regard to these discussions stems from the fact that excavation provided a firm date for the court's construction in Middle Minoan (MM) II, many centuries after the first use of the location as a sepulcher. Thus, the use of this special space can be fixed within the life of the cemetery, and some of the details of its nature can be explained from the corpus of vessels of stone and clay that were buried as offerings within its soil. Because Tomb 4 was one of the most modest rock shelters in the Pseiran cemetery, its evidence shows that the veneration accorded ancient graves by the Minoans was by no means limited to the more monumental places used for burial.

The Pseiran Cemetery

The island of Pseira, located in the Gulf of Mirabello in northeastern Crete (Fig. 4.1), was settled during the Final Neolithic (FN) period

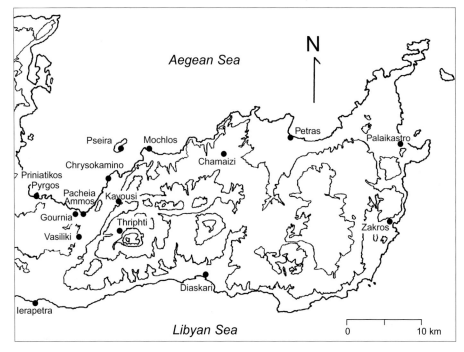

Figure 4.1. Map of East Crete.

(for the excavation, see Seager 1910; Betancourt and Davaras, eds., 1995, 1998a, 1998b, 1999, 2001, 2002, 2003, 2009; Betancourt, Davaras, and Hope Simpson, eds., 2004, 2005). Houses were built on a rocky peninsula that afforded easy anchorage on its western side next to a small beach where boats could be drawn up on shore. The town was on the southeast side of the tiny offshore island, and the mass of the island provided protection from northern and northwestern winds. Seafaring and trade were always important components of the settlement's livelihood.

The town's cemetery (Fig. 4.2) was located on the lower slope of a hill 310 m southwest of the small beach (Onyshkevych et al. 2002). It was not visible from the town. The earliest tombs were constructed when the town was founded in the FN period, and the same location for burial was used continuously until MM II (Betancourt and Davaras, eds., 2002, 2003). Pseira's cemetery differed from some of the other Minoan cemeteries in that it included several different types of architecture for burial purposes. Tombs consisted of small graves built from vertical slabs, cists made of

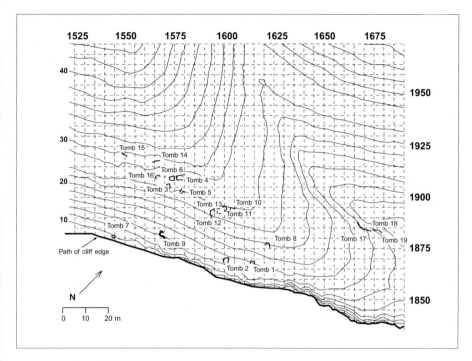

Figure 4.2. Plan of the Pseira cemetery.

fieldstones, larger house tombs, man-made caves called rock shelters, and a few burials inside clay jars.

Tomb 4

Tomb 4 is one of the rock shelters (Fig. 4.3). It is located near the northern limits of the cemetery, carved into a soft rock formation called calcrete. Pseira's exposed bedrock consists primarily of two types of rock: a hard, dark gray limestone named Plattenkalk, which is part of the African tectonic plate, and a softer and more friable phyllite forma- tion that is part of the European tectonic plate. The phyllite lies over the limestone because tectonic movements pushed in south over the other plate. At the interface between these two rock formations, the upper part of the Plattenkalk is compressed and partly metamorphosed to form a sub-category of the limestone called metacarbonate. Smaller

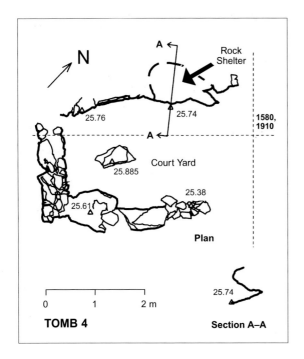

A

N

Rock
Shelter

25.76

A

25.74

1580,
1910

Court Yard

25.885

25.38

25.61

Plan

0   1   2 m

25.74

TOMB 4

Section A–A

Figure 4.3. Plan of Tomb 4 and its courtyard.

and geologically more-recent exposures include poorly consolidated aeolian sandstone and a calcareous formation named calcrete. One of the calcrete exposures occurs as a low shelf or cliff at the northern edge of the cemetery.

This calcrete cliff rests on hard metacarbonate, and the Minoans took advantage of its topographic situation and carved several small rock shelters into the soft bedrock. The harder metacarbonate was left as the floor of the resulting chambers. Walls were added across the front to close off the small caverns after they were used for burial, but the underground rooms were looted long ago, and only traces of the blocking walls were present when Pseira was excavated by the modern project.

Tomb 4 was the smallest rock shelter in the cemetery. Its entrance was about 1 m wide by 0.6 m high. It extended 0.73 m into the cliff. The tiny rock shelter was carved in the FN period, making it a member of the first group of tombs on Pseira. Rock shelters that were suitable for only a single burial at a time also occur elsewhere in eastern Crete (Soles 1992, 105–106). In spite of its diminutive size, Tomb 4 must have held a significant position at Pseira because it was the focus of long-standing ceremonial activity lasting into MM II, the last period before the entire cemetery was abandoned.

Excavations at Pseira investigated both inside the tombs and in the spaces near them. The small burial chambers were all communal, and they were used repeatedly by successive generations. To make room for the new burials, the underground chambers were periodically cleaned out, and excavating the area near them yielded fragments of pottery from the long history of a location's use. Tomb 4 was so small that it is hard to imagine more than one burial at a time in it unless the bones were deposited here after an earlier burial elsewhere.

For Tomb 4, complete clay vases and fragments could be recognized from the following periods:

Date of Pottery	Number of Pieces
FN/EM I	7
EM I	2
EM I–II	13
EM IIA	1
EM IIB	10
EM II–MM I	1
EM II–MM II	2
EM III–MM II	1
MM IA–B	2
EM–MM II	1
MM I–IIA	3
MM I–IIB	12
MM IIA–B	4

This evidence demonstrates periodic use for well over a thousand years from the end of the Neolithic to MM II. The only complete vessel found inside the small disturbed tomb was a cup made of Vasiliki Ware, one of the definitive classes for the Early Minoan (EM) IIB period (Fig. 4.4:A; Betancourt and Dierckx 2003, 41, no. 4.1). The objects cleaned out of the cave and spread across the area downhill from its mouth provide a very incomplete history because only fragments survived. Erosion was severe on this hillside, and most pieces were surely lost down the slope. For most early periods, we have only a glimpse of what might have been originally placed in the tomb.

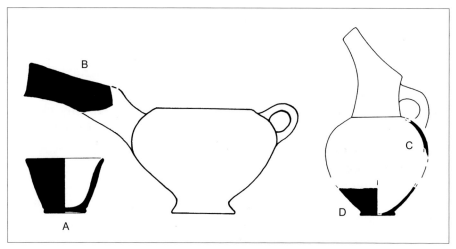

Figure 4.4. Vasiliki Ware pottery found inside and near Tomb 4 (after Betancourt and Dierckx 2003, 41–42, nos. 4.1, 4.3–4.5).

Only a few sherds come from the earliest period of Tomb 4. The FN to EM I fragments are made of dark, heavily burnished, thick clay fabrics. Small pieces of plant stems (perhaps chaff) as well as rock fragments are used as temper for some of the vases from this period. Sherds come from cups, open vessels that could have been either cups or bowls, and one closed vessel. These fragments show that, as is usual in Minoan tombs, beverage appears to have been an important offering at the time of burial. In this case, of course, no evidence survives to suggest whether the beverage was offered inside the tomb, consumed by the mourners, or deposited later.

A similar picture can be reconstructed for the Early Bronze Age, although a few other shapes survive as well. In addition to cups and pouring vessels, a sherd from a pyxis (Betancourt and Dierckx 2003, 41, no. 4.2) and a small lid (Betancourt and Dierckx 2003, 43, no. 4.13) provide evidence for other types of grave goods. For EM IIB, the pouring and drinking vases in Figure 4.4 again show that liquids were either involved in the burial ceremony or were presented as grave goods for the deceased. The presence of a spout sherd from a large teapot (Fig. 4.4:B; Betancourt and Dierckx 2003, 42, no. 4.3), one of the premier vessels for this period, shows that the tomb included some of the community's finest pottery. Jugs and a cup were also present.

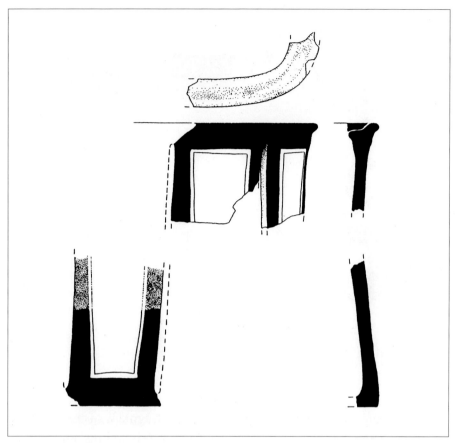

Figure 4.5. Fragmentary fenestrated stand found at Tomb 4 (after Betancourt and Dierckx 2003, 46, no. 4.57).

The fragments from the later periods of the cemetery suggest continued use until the hillside was abandoned in MM II. Among the pieces found within the soil of the terrace are the ones illustrated in Figures 4.5 and 4.6. A handmade perforated stand, a rare vessel from this period, is unique to the cemetery (Fig. 4.5; Betancourt and Dierckx 2003, 46, no. 4.57). Many sherds survive from the object, which must have been a cylindrical stand open at both top and bottom. With an elliptical base and possibly an elliptical upper opening as well, it will have been an unusual object. Rectangular perforations in the sides and thin white lines painted on vertical black stripes add modest decoration. A ledge inside the rim would have supported some other object, perhaps a bowl for offerings.

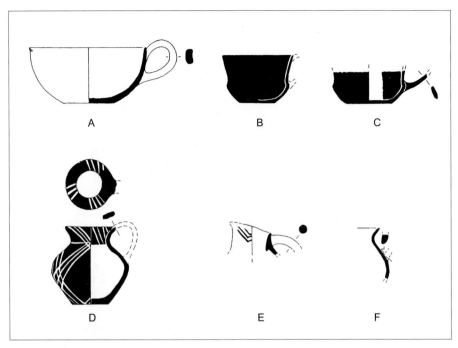

Figure 4.6. Incomplete pottery vessels found inside the terrace in front of Tomb 4 (after Betancourt and Dierckx 2003, 45, 46, nos. 4.50, 4.52–4.54, 4.61, 4.62).

Another unusual piece from this period is a fragment of the rim from an open vessel with a S-shaped profile (Fig. 4.6:F). The sherd may be part of a kantharos (Betancourt and Dierckx 2003, 45, no. 4.50). Kantharoi, which are goblets with two large opposed handles, are not unknown in eastern Crete, and another example comes from Pseira itself (Betancourt 1999a, 114), but they are unusual for Crete as a whole. They sometimes have undulating rims and very thin walls, suggesting they may reflect metallic antecedents. An analysis of the fabric of this example indicates it was probably a local vessel from a nearby part of Crete (Vaughan 2002, 147).

Changes were made to the topographic setting of this tomb in MM II. By this time Tomb 6 had been constructed just west of the entrance to the small rock shelter. The MM II builders added a wall that extended east from the southeast corner of Tomb 6 to make a terrace wall across the landscape in front of Tomb 4 (Fig. 4.3). The eastern part of the new wall was laid on soil rather than bedrock, indicating that it was a late construction in this part of the cemetery. Several finds of MM II pottery within the soil established the date for its construction (Fig. 4.6).

The terrace wall was built rather informally. Stones were unworked fieldstones gathered from nearby on the slope of the hill. They were too irregular to make a tall wall, and they were probably set no more than one or two courses high to form a small terrace. Sherds in this terrace show that it was packed with soil during MM II. The result was a flat space in front of the entrance to Tomb 4. A calcrete boulder was allowed to stick up above the soil in the terrace, near its western end. It lies on bedrock, but whether it was already present when the terrace was constructed or whether it was moved here from some other location when the terrace was built is unclear.

THE OFFERINGS

Several vases made of clay and stone were buried in the soil in Tomb 4's terrace. They were all set upright in the soil, so they may have been buried for their contents. The vessels were all from MM II, so they were new offerings (rather than items from early burials removed from this tomb or some other location).

The investigation of this terrace collected a substantial amount of information. It involved careful excavation, dry sieving of all the soil, the retrieval of microscopic remains by using a water separation machine (for the technique, see French 1971; Peterson 2009), and the collection of soil samples for micromorphological analysis. From this detailed inspection, several activities could be ruled out in regard to what was done on the terrace. The micromorphology showed that the soil and its contents were natural for this hillside (Goldberg 2003, 48). Neither charcoal nor ash was present, and human or animal bones were not found in the soil (for evidence of burning from elsewhere in the Pseiran cemetery, see Schoch 2003). From this negative evidence, it is safe to assume that no cooking or burning played any role in the activities here. This conclusion is important for the interpretation of the open court because burning does occasionally occur at other cemetery sites (Branigan 1970a, 171–172; 1970b, 108–109; Murphy 1998, 35).

The pottery came from a broad period of time, from FN to MM IIB (Betancourt and Dierckx 2003). It was mostly in small fragments that represented material that had been spread outside the mouth of the small tomb before the terrace was constructed, probably in periodic cleaning operations to make room for new burials. The corpus included 26 closed vessels designed for pouring (teapots, jugs, jars, and side-spouted vessels) and 19 cups, including four carinated cups that were contemporary with the MM IIB construction of the terrace. Other fragments included fragments from a pyxis and a pyxis lid and a sherd from a goblet. The small number of cups in contrast with cult areas at cemeteries in the Mesara (Branigan 1970b, 99–102, 119–120) indicates that toasting with large numbers of cups was not an activity conducted here.

Ceremonies involving lighting fires, cooking, and feasting can be excluded because they would have left positive traces (at least at the microscopic level). Possible ceremonies involving the exposed rock or activities like singing, chanting, praying, or dancing might have occurred, but they cannot be documented by the archaeological record. Cult ceremonies involving natural stones like the one in this terrace are illustrated on Minoan seals (Warren 1988, 1990), but no archaeological evidence survives for activities here. The only activity on the open terrace that we can be certain about involved the burial of offerings within the soil. The objects in Figure 4.7 all come from this activity. The offerings include small stone jars, clay vases, and smooth pebbles (the pebbles are not illustrated). The datable items are all from MM II, but their style does not allow enough precision in dating to know if they were buried as a single event or placed in the soil over a period of time. Specific conclusions are not possible, but certainly the activities must have involved some type of reverence or commemoration of earlier generations associated with the small rock shelter.

The practice of MM II commemoration at a tomb with a long earlier history has been documented from one other location on Pseira. Small caches of MM II objects were also buried near Tomb 2 (Betancourt, Reese, and Schoch 2003, 29). They included objects of metal as well as vessels of clay and stone, suggesting that perhaps other items (such as perishable goods) may also have been involved in ceremonies of this type.

The entire Pseira cemetery was abandoned near the end of MM II. The settlement was destroyed at this time, and it may not have been rebuilt immediately. Very little MM III pottery is present from Pseira. The new settlement had a different plan from the Neolithic to MM II town, in that

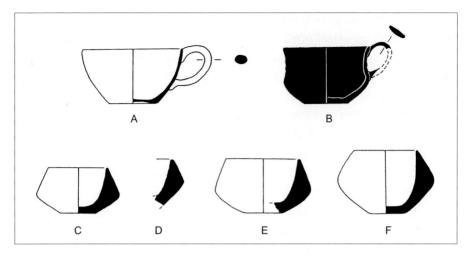

Figure 4.7. Complete vessels of clay and stone found buried upright in the terrace in front of Tomb 4 (after Betancourt and Dierckx 2003, 43–44, nos. 4.18, 4.19, 4.21–4.24).

houses were now built on the slope west of the small beach. The road system was also changed, and clearly attitudes toward both public and private architectural space were now very different from what they were before the town's destruction. The location where the people who inhabited the Pseiran MM III to Late Minoan (LM) I town buried their dead has not yet been discovered.

DISCUSSION

The cemetery at Pseira presents several interesting characteristics. In spite of the fine techniques of stone construction visible in the town, the tombs are small, and they are sometimes poorly built. Even the house tombs are among the smallest examples of the class (Soles 1992, 114–201). Ostentatious display is not a custom at this cemetery, either in architecture or in the objects buried in the tombs. Gold and fine jewelry are rare, daggers are not common, stone seals, pendants, beads, and other fine small items are not numerous, and neither animal effigy nor human effigy vessels are present at all. No large stores of pottery are found in the cemetery.

Within the strict confines of a limited and modest set of tombs, however, the residents of Pseira had a surprising diversity of individual tomb designs. Small cist graves could be built of either fieldstones or large vertically placed metacarbonate slabs. Some of the cist graves were large enough to be classed as house tombs while others were smaller. Graves were entered either from the side or from above. Rock shelters varied in size from under a meter across to several meters in width. A few individuals were buried in jars instead of in stone tombs or caves.

Little evidence survived for most aspects of the actual burials inside Tomb 4. The tomb was looted before the modern period, and only a few sherds and a single complete vase survived inside it. By analogy with other Pseiran tombs, the burials inside would have been cleared out of the tomb periodically to make room for newer ones, which explains the discovery of so many fragments of objects just downhill from the tomb's mouth. This practice has been associated with a belief that the Minoans conceived of the dead as departing from the world of the living in stages (Murphy 1998, 32–35). In this view, after the body has decayed and the flesh is no longer present, the individual characteristics of the deceased (like facial features) are no longer visible, and the departed member of the community has become a member of the collective group of ancestors (Branigan 1987; 1998, 23–25; Hamilakis 1998). It is at this stage that the remains can be removed from the tomb because they are no longer closely associated with a particular individual.

If this reasonable view is accepted, then the later commemoration that focuses on the tomb itself might be associated not so much with an individual as with a group of ancestors. It suggests that the reverence for a specific tomb refers to a family's or clan's past members, with the added implication that a tomb was used exclusively by a particular family or household. Can we assume that each household at Pseira used its own tomb?

If this were true, then the total number of tombs used in one period might equal the total number of actively used houses in the Pseiran town. Unfortunately, one cannot be certain of the numbers because neither the number of MM houses nor the number of MM tombs is known. Seager reported finding 33 tombs, but he probably did not count the six rock shelters (Seager 1910). In addition, the spread of sherds across the cemetery at Pseira proves the existence of additional tombs that have not been located or are completely destroyed through erosion (Betancourt 2002). A little over 50 houses were present during LM I in the part of the town where the MM settlement had once existed, and this is perhaps the upper limit for what would have been there during the Middle Bronze Age. One can probably estimate between 40 and 50 tombs and houses for the EM to MM periods.

Tomb 4 was not the only location in the Pseiran cemetery that received new offerings during MM II. Tomb 2 was a simple cist grave made from unworked fieldstones. It was partly below ground, but its upper part extended above the shallow soil of the cemetery's slope. It was an almost-rectangular small chamber that was too narrow for a body to be laid out in an extended position. An unexcavated section of the small tomb was found at the northwest corner of the room, and its excavation recovered fragments of human bones and several artifacts. Like all the other burials on this hillside, Tomb 2 was communal. It was used by many successive generations. When the small burial chamber ran out of room, its contents were apparently simply swept outside the small compartment onto the side of the hill. The offerings from Tomb 2 were buried at the west of the sepulcher and covered with a slab of stone.

The creation of a flat terrace in front of a rock shelter is not unique to Pseira. Rock shelters in eastern Crete were often built so that a natural open space was already in front of them (Soles 1992, 98, 100), and such a space could be built or enhanced if more room was required. The small FN–MM cemetery located in a gorge uphill from Zakros included one small cave with "traces of a rectangular structure" in front of it (Hogarth 1900–1901, 142–143). The cemetery of Hagios Nikolaos near Palaikastro also had a rock shelter with an adjacent court (Tod 1902–1903, 340). A terrace supported by boulders was found in front of a rock shelter at Hagios Antonios on the Cretan coast not far from Pseira (Haggis 1993, 13). In all of these cases, a flat surface was evidently needed for whatever was done in commemoration of the deceased. Because these terraces were not excavated, we do not know if objects were buried in them as was the case at Pseira.

Burying objects near the entrance to a tomb is very different from placing items inside the tomb itself at the time of burial. The act of placing an object inside a tomb involves a direct association with the deceased. Placement in the soil of a terrace has less connection to a specific individual and involves a different set of beliefs. Whether the gift is presented a short time or many years after the individual's death, the gift is to a spirit, an ancestor, or some other conceptual focus. The separation of the offering from the body of a specific individual involves later commemoration rather than something for the deceased to possess shortly after the time of death.

The use of the terrace in front of the entrance to Tomb 4 and the open area near Tomb 2 represented a new custom that appeared at Pseira during MM II. Small offerings of stone vases and clay containers were buried in the ground near these graves, and they were then covered with soil or a stone slab to protect them. These vases, all of them small containers from about the same period, represent a custom that was not unique to Pseira. Although MM II offerings have not been discovered at other tombs at Pseira, the extremely eroded condition of the steep hillside of the Pseiran cemetery suggests that other instances could have been present at one time.

Comments and Speculations

The archaeological situation in Tomb 4 is straightforward and easy to describe, but the social explanation that lies behind it is more difficult to discover. A small man-made cave was carved out of the calcrete cliff and used for burials, and it was apparently reused a number of times over many centuries. Finally, in MM IIB, it received its own terrace and new, though rather modest, offerings.

What was different about the social situation at Pseira in MM II that could have inspired a new wave of veneration of early burials? Changes in the affirmation of traditional practices in regard to belief-systems associated with life and death often occur in times of crisis or when new beliefs rise to challenge established traditions (Betancourt 1999b; Driessen 2001). Does evidence exist for either of these situations at the transition between MM IIB and MM III?

The answer to this question is "yes." In fact, substantial evidence survives for both of these situations. The end of the Middle Bronze Age was a transitional period in Minoan Crete when the older palaces were destroyed and new ones took their place. Many people think this was the time when Knossos extended its political power over all of Crete. The crisis within the region of the Gulf of Mirabello is well illustrated by a tiny refuge settlement at Monastiraki Katalimata, perched on lofty ledges high above the Cha Gorge (Nowicki 2001). The MM IIB pottery from this remote and easily defended refuge has the same style as the latest pottery from Tomb 4.

This was a time of rapidly changing social patterns. Religious beliefs and their associated ceremonies were taking new directions. Special ceremonial locations on mountains (called "peak sanctuaries") had been important in East Crete for many centuries. The peak sanctuaries declined in popularity at the end of the Middle Bronze Age (Rutkowski 1986, 95), and they were replaced by new cult practices that were connected with the increasingly important palaces (Rutkowski 1986, 94–95; Driessen 2001, 366). The new institutionalized ceremonies required different types of focal points, and they used dynamic visual symbols like the women handling snakes and the many other objects buried in the Temple Repositories at Knossos (Panagiotaki 1999) and the expansion of iconography in the cult activities at Hagia Triada (Militello 2001).

Changes in attitudes toward treatment of the dead were also challenging the customs that stood behind the use of rock shelters like Tomb 4. In place of the traditional grave types, increasing numbers of people in East Crete were choosing individual interment inside jars and larnakes buried within the soil or under the sand of a beach in preference to the traditional communal burial that had been in vogue since the FN period. The new custom was already expanding toward the end of the Middle Bronze Age (Pini 1968, 12–13), and it would reach its peak in East Cretan jar cemeteries like those at Sphoungaras (Hall 1912) and Pacheia Ammos (Seager 1916). We know the new custom was already present at Pseira because the intensive surface survey of the cemetery discovered a few fragments that must come from burial jars. All of the parallels for jars like the one from the Pseiran cemetery published here (Fig. 4.8; Betancourt et al. 2002, 59, no. 121) come from East Cretan jar burials.

Could the terrace at Tomb 4 be a conservative affirmation of regard for the long-standing tradition of communal burial in small graves in the face of new challenges to the old beliefs? The fact that jar burials did not replace traditional practices immediately must mean that a segment of the population resisted the new custom and refused to accept it. Veneration of the older beliefs and what they stood for is what may lie behind the new activity at some of these traditional burial places.

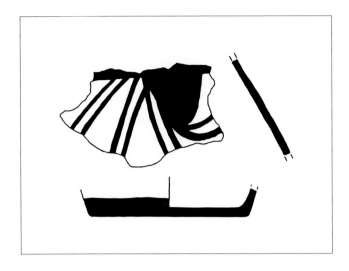

Figure 4.8. Fragments of a burial jar from the Pseiran cemetery (after Betancourt et al. 2002, 59, no. 121).

References

Betancourt, P.P. 1999a. "Area BN West: 1. Introduction and History of the Excavations," in Betancourt and Davaras, eds., 1999, pp. 113–114.

———. 1999b. "Discontinuity in the Minoan-Mycenaean Religions: Smooth Development or Disruptions and War?" in *POLEMOS: Le context guerrier en Egée à l'âge du Bronze. Actes de la 7e Rencontre égéenne international, Université de Liège, 14–17 avril 1998* (*Aegaeum* 19), ed. R. Laffineur, Liège, pp. 219–225.

———. 2002. "The Size of the Cemetery," in Betancourt and Davaras, eds., 2002, pp. 122–124.

Betancourt, P.P., and C. Davaras, eds. 1995. *Pseira* I: *The Minoan Buildings on the West Side of Area A*, Philadelphia.

———. 1998a. *Pseira* II: *Building AC (the "Shrine") and Other Buildings in Area A*, Philadelphia.

———. 1998b. *Pseira* III: *The Plateia Building* (*University Museum Monograph* 102), by C.R. Floyd, Philadelphia.

———. 1999. *Pseira* IV: *Minoan Buildings in Areas B, C, D, and F* (*University Museum Monograph* 105), Philadelphia.

———. 2001. *Pseira* V: *The Architecture of Pseira* (*University Museum Monograph* 109), by J.C. McEnroe, Philadelphia.

———. 2002. *Pseira* VI: *The Pseira Cemetery. 1: The Surface Survey* (*Prehistory Monographs* 5), Philadelphia.

————. 2003. *Pseira* VII: *The Pseira Cemetery.* 2: *Excavation of the Tombs (Prehistory Monographs* 6), Philadelphia.

————. 2009. *Pseira* X: *The Excavation of Block AF (Prehistory Monographs* 28), by P.P. Betancourt, Philadelphia.

Betancourt, P.P., C. Davaras, and R. Hope Simpson, eds. 2004. *Pseira* VIII: *The Archaeological Survey of Pseira Island.* 1 (*Prehistory Monographs* 11), Philadelphia.

————. 2005. *Pseira* IX: *The Archaeological Survey of Pseira Island.* 2: *The Intensive Surface Survey* (*Prehistory Monographs* 12), Philadelphia.

Betancourt, P.P., and H.M.C. Dierckx. 2003. "Tomb 4: Catalog of Objects," in Betancourt and Davaras, eds. 2003, pp. 41–48.

Betancourt, P.P., H.M.C. Dierckx, N. Poulou-Papadimitriou, D.S. Reese, W.H. Schoch, and F. Zervaki. 2002. "Data from the Intensive Surface Survey," in Betancourt and Davaras, eds., 2002, pp. 25–100.

Betancourt, PP., D.S. Reese, and W.H. Schoch. 2003. "Tomb 2: Catalog of Objects," in Betancourt and Davaras, eds., 2003, pp. 23–30.

Branigan, K. 1970a. *The Foundations of Palatial Crete*, London.

————. 1970b. *The Tombs of the Mesara*, London.

————. 1987. "Ritual Interference with Human Bones in the Mesara Tholoi," in *THANATOS: Les coutumes funéraires en Egée à l'âge du Bronze (Aegaeum* 1), R. Laffineur, ed., Liège, pp. 43–51.

————. 1993. *Dancing with Death: Life and Death in Southern Crete, c. 3000–2000 B.C.*, Amsterdam.

————. 1998. "The Nearness of You—Proximity and Distance in Early Minoan Funerary Landscapes," in *Cemetery and Society in the Aegean Bronze Age*, K. Branigan, ed., Sheffield, pp. 13–26.

Driessen, J. 2001. "Crisis Cults on Minoan Crete?" in *POTNIA: Deities and Religion in the Aegean Bronze Age. Proceedings of the 8th International Aegean Conference Göteborg, Göteborg University, 12–15 April 2000 (Aegaeum* 22), R. Laffineur and R. Hägg, eds., Liège, pp. 361–369.

Evans, A.J. 1921–1935. *The Palace of Minos at Knossos*, 4 vols., London.

French, D.H. 1971. "An Experiment in Water Sieving," *AnatSt* 21, pp. 59–64.

Goldberg, P. 2003. "Tomb 4, Micromorphology Analysis," in Betancourt and Davaras, eds., 2003, p. 48.

Haggis, D.C. 1993. "The Early Minoan Burial Cave at Ayios Antonios and Some Problems in Early Bronze Age Chronology," *SMEA* 31, pp. 7–32.

Hall, E.H. 1912. *Excavations in Eastern Crete: Sphoungaras*, Philadelphia.

Hamilakis, Y. 1998. "Eating the Dead: Mortuary Feasting and the Politics of Memory in the Aegean Bronze Age Societies," in *Cemetery and Society in the Aegean Bronze Age*, K. Branigan, ed., Sheffield, pp. 115–132.

Hogarth, D.G. 1900–1901. "Excavations at Zakro, Crete," *BSA* 7, pp. 121–149.

Militello, P. 2001. "Archeologia, iconografia e culti ad Haghia Triada in età TM I," in *POTNIA: Deities and Religion in the Aegean Bronze Age. Proceedings of the 8th International Aegean Conference, Göteborg, Göteborg University, 12–15 April 2000*, R. Laffineur and R. Hägg, eds., Liège, pp. 159–167.

Murphy, J.M. 1998. "Ideologies, Rites and Rituals: A View of Prepalatial Minoan Tholoi," in *Cemetery and Society in the Aegean Bronze Age*, K. Branigan, ed., Sheffield, pp. 27–40.

Nowicki, K. 2001. "A Middle Minoan II Deposit at the Refuge Site of Monastiraki Katalimata (East Crete)," *Aegean Archaeology* 5, pp. 27–45.

Onyshkevych, L., K.E. May, W.B. Hafford, and H. Eiteljorg II. 2002. "The Topography of the Pseira Cemetery," in Betancourt and Davaras, eds., 2002, p. 17.

Panagiotaki, M. 1999. *The Central Palace Sanctuary at Knossos* (*BSA Suppl.* 31), London.

Peterson, S.E. 2009. *Retrieval of Materials with Water Separation Machines* (*INSTAP Archaeological Excavation Manual* 1), Philadelphia.

Pini, I. 1968. *Beiträge zur minoischen Gräberkunde*, Wiesbaden.

Rutkowski, B. 1986. *The Cult Places of the Aegean*, New Haven and London.

Schoch, W.H. 2003. "Tomb 2: The Charcoal Remains," in Betancourt and Davaras, eds., 2003, pp. 32–33.

Seager, R.B. 1910. *Excavations on the Island of Pseira, Crete*, Philadelphia.

———. 1916. *The Cemetery of Pachyammos, Crete*, Philadelphia.

Soles, J.S. 1992. *The Prepalatial Cemeteries at Mochlos and Gournia and the House Tombs of Bronze Age Crete*, Princeton.

Tod, M.N. 1902–1903. "Excavations at Palaikastro II: 10, Hagios Nikolaos," *BSA* 9, pp. 336–341.

Vaughan, S.J. 2002. "Appendix C: Petrographic Analysis of Ceramics from the Pseira Cemetery," in Betancourt and Davaras, eds., 2002, pp. 147–165.

Warren, P.M. 1988. *Minoan Religion as Ritual Action*, Gothenburg.

———. 1990. "Of Baetyls," *OpAth* 18, pp. 193–206.

5 | A Power House of the Dead: The Functions and Long Life of the Tomb at Myrtos-Pyrgos

GERALD CADOGAN

The Tomb at Myrtos-Pyrgos (Ovenden 1976; Cadogan 1977–1978, 1992, 2006, forthcoming a, forthcoming c; Hankey 1986) was in use for much of the long life of the Minoan settlement.* This paper reviews what we know or opine at present about the Tomb but, since study continues, is only provisional: we shall publish the Tomb as a whole in the first volume of *Myrtos-Pyrgos* reports. In calling it a power house, I am following the architectural and social historian Mark Girouard (1978, 2), who applied the term to English country houses, stating that "essentially they were power houses—the houses of a ruling class." It is a useful, if perhaps unexpected, analogy.

The Tomb is located in East-Central Crete at the edge of the Minoan settlement on the hill of Pyrgos, which is a low but steep and prominent

*I thank the British School at Athens for permission to present this paper here, the 23rd and 24th Ephoreias of Prehistoric and Classsical Antiquities in Crete for their constant support of the project, and the Institute for Aegean Prehistory (INSTAP), without whom any advances in completing Pyrgos would be impossible. I also thank INSTAP and the Kress Foundation for enabling my attendance at the meeting, Joanne Murphy for the invitation to attend, Piraye Hacigüzeller for the plans (that are based on those of the late David Smyth), and Eleni Hatzaki, Carl Knappett, and Jonathan Musgrave (who is studying the human remains for publication) for advice and information. This paper is presented very much as it was given, with a minimum of references.

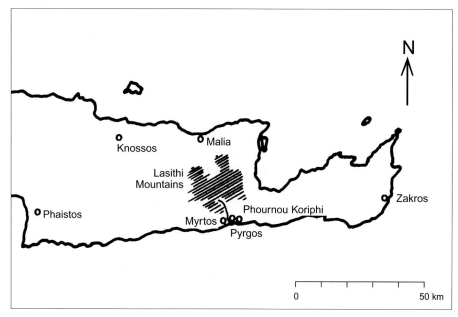

Fig. 5.1. The region of East-Central Crete.

hill on the east side of the mouth of the river Myrtos, opposite Myrtos village and now located in the *demos* of Ierapetra (Figs. 5.1, 5.2). The settlement enjoyed good farmland in the valley below and an excellent position on major lines of communication—by sea along the south coast, and by land on a, or, more likely, *the* main route from North- and South-Central Crete to the east of the island, as well as the route up the valley into Lasithi. Until the mid-20th century, the broad valley was one of the island's natural boundaries. This was probably also the case in antiquity, when its fluctuating allegiances in ceramic and other cultural terms—at times looking toward Knossos (in Middle Minoan [MM] I and Late Minoan [LM] I), and at other times toward Malia and Lasithi/ Mirabello (Early Minoan [EM] III–MM II)—suggest an important liminal location on the edge of different regions. (Likewise, it hosted a Hellenistic shrine that was probably a frontier sanctuary for Hierapytna.)

The first recognizable major occupation phase was in EM II, when Pyrgos (period I) seems to have been larger, and probably more important, than nearby Myrtos-Phournou Koriphi (Cadogan, forthcoming a; forthcoming c). Both sites burned down in EM IIB, and Phournou

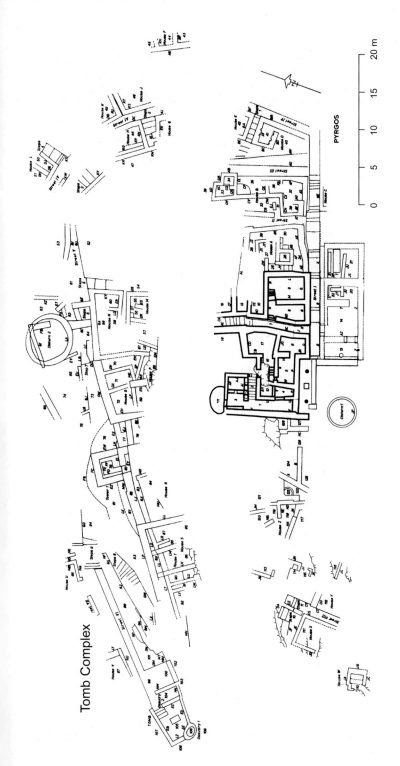

Fig. 5.2. Myrtos-Pyrgos: general plan.

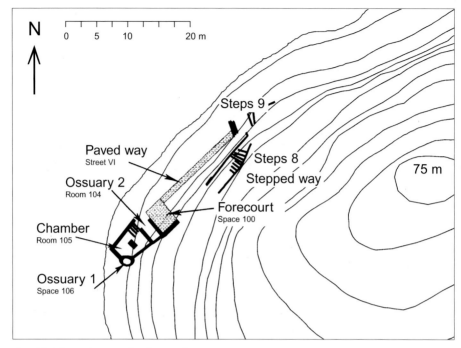

Fig. 5.3. Myrtos-Pyrgos: Tomb complex.

Koriphi was abandoned. Pyrgos, however, was re-occupied as a (probably) newly nucleated settlement (Pyrgos II), perhaps including former
villagers of Phournou Koriphi, and a monumental mortuary complex
was established at the west corner of the settlement (Fig. 5.3). The
complex, composed of a tomb chamber, two ossuaries, and a paved
forecourt, was reached by a paved processional way, which was itself
approached by a stepped way descending the west slope of the hill.

The Tomb complex was built on and into a terrace formed from lev-
elled debris of the EM II destruction. The Tomb is of the house type,
having a polygonal or irregularly shaped chamber (Room 105) measuring 5 x 3 m, with a central pier that supported an upper floor in LM I—
as it did almost certainly from the start. This upper floor would have
been a low mezzanine in relation to the Forecourt (Space 100), which
is 2 m above the chamber floor. The design with a pier, and perhaps
also the long, narrow space of Ossuary 2 (Room 104), derives, I
believe, from the largest and latest houses of Phournou Koriphi (cf.
Whitelaw 1983, 2007), and it has other EM II domestic analogues

(Cadogan, forthcoming c). In other words, the form of a domestic house was transposed into a ritual house.

The ossuaries, both of Pyrgos II date, appear to be integral parts of the scheme. Ossuary 1 (Space 106) is an oval pit crammed with bones (men, women, children, neonates, and fetuses) and a standing pithos (Fig. 5.4). Approximately 51 skulls were set along the wall of the pit or against the pithos. Other bones were packed so tightly in the middle that it is hard to imagine that they were deposited with flesh still adhering. The pithos itself contained more bones, with the long bones placed vertically

Fig. 5.4. Ossuary 1
(Space 106).

(like a crown of lamb) above five skulls. A stone was placed in the mouth of the pithos to keep all in their place. Since the ossuary is small and the bones were so carefully arranged within it with clear signs of skull veneration, we may see here a probable single secondary deposition after a clearing out of the tomb chamber. It is unknown if there was a conscious choice in deciding whose bones went into the pithos (in line with suggested individualistic uses of pithoi and larnakes from EM III). Ossuary 2 is a rectangular room between the chamber and the forecourt, with up to 12 dead, which are almost certainly secondary burials.

The Forecourt (Space 100), measuring about 4 x 3 m, had a kernos and what may have been a bench or an altar. Close to a large paving stone was a deposit, perhaps a foundation deposit, of a dove rhyton, a jug, and four cups (in both white-on-dark and polychrome styles), suggesting a fairly restricted group of imbibers (Figs. 5.5, 5.6). Other cups were found nearby.

Leading to the Forecourt, and aligned northeast–southwest to the door of the tomb, is probably the earliest Minoan processional walk (Street VI),

Fig. 5.5. Forecourt (Space 100) and dove rhyton group.

15 m long, and 20 m to the tomb door (Fig. 5.7). This paved way and the Forecourt rest on the terrace of EM II destruction material, with retaining walls behind. A stepped way (Steps 8 and 9; see Fig. 5.8) coming down to join it started presumably on the hilltop, where we may imagine a central building and/or gathering place (which may have existed already in EM II). The courtyard on the hilltop was certainly in use in Pyrgos III, and it is not unreasonable to see it as already there in Pyrgos II, or even Pyrgos I.

A

B

0   5 cm

Fig. 5.6. Dove rhyton group.

Fig. 5.7. Street VI, leading to the Forecourt and Tomb.

How soon after the EM II destruction the Tomb complex was built, or—to put it another way—how long the break was before re-occupation, needs more study. While we have pottery of Betancourt's early phase of East Cretan EM III (Betancourt, ed., 1984), both the use levels of the paved way and the dove rhyton deposit include MM IA polychrome.

Later in Pyrgos II, the paved way seems to have gone out of use and been covered by gravel spreads (yards), with one or two hearths, presumably cooking places, assigned to Pyrgos IIc and IId. It is hard to know the significance of the eventual disuse of the paved way; whether it was neglected on purpose or if storms washed down so much mud that it was deemed a pointless endeavor to clean it up. Whatever happened, the gravel yards suggest continued use of the terrace as the approach/assembly place for the Tomb, and the hearths could be connected with use of the

Tomb since, at some moment during these phases, or possibly in Pyrgos III, a new paved forecourt was put down 30 cm above the original one. Probably also of Pyrgos IIc/d date, and (in Knossian terms) going into MM IB, are a group of pedestalled lamps and a mass of bowls stacked on plaster(ed) shelving beside, or in, Ossuary 2.

For the use of the Tomb in Pyrgos III (mainly or solely MM IIB) and IV (in the case of the Tomb, solely LM IA), the evidence comes from the chamber, where two layers held six men in semi-extended burial in the lower layer and four men similarly in the upper layer. The lower, Pyrgos III burials had pottery placed with them, notably some jars made at Malia (C. Knappett, pers. comm.). Between the two layers was rain-washed mud, measuring 3–12 cm thick. Given the intensity of downpours on the steep hill, it is not possible to tell how many, or how few, seasons of not using the tomb this mud deposit represents. Flecks of charcoal and white lime plaster suggest fumigation and whitewashing or burying in lime.

The burials in the upper layer were in three depositions, over which a phenomenal amount of goods had cascaded down from the upper floor (Fig. 5.9); indeed, it is problematic if any items at all were specifically

Fig. 5.8. Steps 8 and 9 (foreground).

Fig. 5.9. Fallen objects in the tomb chamber over the upper burial layer.

placed beside the burials. These fallen goods include over 1,050 pots, which are currently being studied by Eleni Hatzaki. Of LM IA date, they are similar to the Minoan pottery of the volcanic destruction level at Akrotiri, which includes some pieces probably made at Pyrgos (pers. obs.). Nothing appears to date from the MM III period. If use of the Tomb lasted into LM IB—that is, up until the time of destruction of the Country House (and the end of period Pyrgos IV)—there seems no pottery assignable to that phase; but we need to examine further whether, or to what extent, LM IA styles at Pyrgos continued into LM IB.

Almost half the pots are cups, and a quarter are conical cups. Besides jugs and a rhyton, the main type among the rest was bridge-spouted jars (around 14%) for pouring. Many of these jars, particularly the plain versions, seem brand new, suggesting perhaps one ritual use (of a shape that is rare in settlement levels) before deposition. The same would hold for various mint coarse ware and cooking pot ware vessels, which indicate eating as well as drinking during the rites and visitations at the Tomb. There were also bronze knives and daggers, and triton shells. Stone drill guides (Fig. 5.10) suggest a link, symbolic or actual, with the stone vessel industry of Pyrgos. Around 50 stone vases include serpentine cups, some in sets, and two antique small bowls—a reminder, perhaps, of the antiquity of this funerary establishment.

The dead in the two burial layers were all male, and they represent a select social group. Indeed by LM I, given the general absence in Crete of archaeologically visible burials (and almost total lack of ordinary, modest burials), to have a burial at all—let alone a conspicuous one— must have marked out the elite. But there are odd features in the depositions, including signs of manipulation. One man received an extra long bone; another inivdual, fairly young, was given the skull of a mature man in lieu of his own. What family or community ideology— or violence—was behind these practices? The Tomb certainly gives scope to investigate social relations in a small group, through family or clan, or social ranking, or both, and it would make an excellent case

0   5 cm

Fig. 5.10. Stone drill guides.

study for DNA analysis, to determine kinship histories, if the Pyrgos Ten are descendants of the ossuary dead, and if the same families enjoy privileged access for centuries. Several males have unusually prominent chins (J. Musgrave, pers. comm.), and it would be interesting to see what kinship analysis could tell us about these individuals.

How then may we interpret this long-lived burial complex? Its construction was an aggressive statement within—and from—the probably newly nucleated settlement. Its liminal location at the west corner of the living area positions it as a gateway to the next world. Its design was probably based on existing house plans. Its ideological purposes include: (1) uniting the living and the dead by creating a ceremonial way through the living area to the house of the dead, and (2) to legitimize the elite who controlled the settlement and invested such labor, such intent, and such use of existing and ancestral/traditional norms in these works. If the forecourt could not hold many people and was intended for the elite and/or immediate family, it is easy to imagine other people, from the settlement and surrounding territory, watching the rites along the paved way or looking down from the stepped way once the cortege had passed.

The complex can also be viewed as a regional marker of authority. Being highly visible from the valley or the hills opposite (where the road from Knossos, Archanes, and the Mesara drops to sea level), it was explicit in asserting control of the rich valley, and perhaps a wider local territory. Regardless of limited, but significant, occurrences in other parts of the islands, this house tomb would have been immediately recognisable to visitors from the center of the island as typical of East-Central Crete (cf. Cadogan, forthcoming b). It is interesting too that kernos stones in funerary contexts—like the one found here in the forecourt—have been noted as confined to the Malia-Lasithi region (Whittaker 2002, 79). But since the Pyrgos II ceramic links were fairly soon (if not from the start of the period) with both Central Crete and East Crete, it is likely that Pyrgos was some sort of frontier post, where zones of regional cultures met. One may even envisage cross-regional marriages.

The Tomb, then, seems to have been in use, perhaps intermittently, through Pyrgos II and into Pyrgos III. In the archaeological record of the settlement it stands unique—or as a unique survivor—as a monumental building and gathering place in Pyrgos II; but it is easy to imagine another such building or gathering place up on the top of the hill as the starting point, with perhaps a cosmological authority from its elevated position, for the processions and memorial visitations. By Pyrgos III there is plenty of evidence for such a central building on the site of the later Country House—when it was one of an extraordinary collection of monuments in a small settlement, together with the Tomb, a large cistern (Cistern 2) with adjacent tower-bastion (Tower 1) and defensive walling, and a smaller cistern (Cistern 1) in the courtyard next to the central building.

The final use of the Tomb came in LM I. Tombs are extremely rare in this period, especially when the tomb is part of a small settlement (ca. 0.5 ha) and closely connected to a new central building, in this case, the magnificent Country House. We may mention two specific links between the Tomb and the Country House: the cross-in-a-circle motif painted on the House drains occurs also on some of the Tomb's bridge-spouted jars, and both the Tomb and the House contained triton shells (as either real shells or representations in other media), albeit that the Tomb's shells are datable to LM IA, while those in the Country House, and the depictions of them, belong generally to LM IB.

The strength of the ideology that the Tomb manifested over centuries from later Prepalatial to Neopalatial is most impressive. It began by uniting the living and the dead in an assertion of power in the re-established settlement on the Pyrgos hill, in a monumentally planned processional route that led through the settlement to the principal structure—a grand example of a familiar regional type, of domestic origins—the house of burial. In effect, by denying differences between the living and the dead and by being so visible from the valley below and from far away, the Tomb became a focus—or *the* focus—of the New Order at Pyrgos, harnessing ritual to maintain the community and its systems of authority. Subsequently, the Tomb continued to provide—and manipulate—the power of memory, place, region, tradition, and connection, and validate the elites of Pyrgos, into late Protopalatial and Neopalatial times. What could be more prestigious for those ten males (and their survivors) than for them to enter this ancient dwelling upon death? If Pyrgos emulated MM II Malia (Knappett 1999), it is fitting that the first extended burials that survive received Malia jars. By LM I an array of Pyrgos-made goods was deemed essential for the few leaders of the community lying in the chamber—and/or yet more for their survivors.

Indeed, we can see a tradition of drinking, pouring, and eating vessels—from the few early cups with the dove vase, through the MM IB bowls for *stifado* or *fasoulada*, to the many LM I bridge-spouted jars and cups—for the benefit of members of an elite group as they congregated in the forecourt, some perhaps entering the chamber or leaving items on the upper floor—all the while aware that everybody else at Pyrgos knew and could see what was happening and who was in charge.

Last but not least, this Tomb is important for the engendered exercise of power in Protopalatial and Neopalatial Crete (Cadogan 2009). The earlier depositions in the ossuaries or scattered outside the Tomb are composed of men, women, children, neonates, and fetuses, while the extended burials in the chamber were all men.

In short, the Myrtos-Pyrgos Tomb was a power house of the dead empowering the living and asserting their identity at local, regional and inter-regional levels for a good half millennium.

References

Betancourt, P.P., ed. 1984. *East Cretan White-on-Dark Ware: Studies on a Handmade Pottery of the Early to Middle Minoan Periods* (*University Museum Monograph* 51), Philadelphia.

Cadogan, G. 1977–1978. "Pyrgos, Crete, 1970–77," *AR* 24 (1977–1978), pp. 70–84.

———. 1992. "Myrtos-Pyrgos," in *The Aerial Atlas of Ancient Crete*, J.W. Myers, E.E. Myers, and G. Cadogan, eds., Berkeley, pp. 202–209.

———. 2006. "A Long-Lived South Coast Community," in *Πεπραγμένα Θ' Διεθνούς Κρητολογικού Συνεδρίου* A' (2), Herakleion, pp. 161–166.

———. 2009. "Gender Metaphors of Social Stratigraphy in Pre-Linear B Crete or "Is 'Minoan Gynaecocracy' (Still) Credible?" in *FYLO: Engendering Prehistoric "Stratigraphies" in the Aegean and the Mediterranean. Proceedings of an International Conference, University of Crete, Rethymnon 2–5 June 2005* (*Aegaeum* 30), K. Kopaka, ed., Austin and Liège, pp. 225–232.

———. Forthcoming a. "Ανθρώπινες δραστηριότητες στον μινωικό οικισμό του Μύρτου-Πύργου," in *Ανθρώπινες δράσεις στο προϊστορικό Αιγαίο: Ένας διάλογος με τους μεταπτυχιακούς φοιτητές του Πανεπιστημίου Κρήτης*, K. Kopaka, ed., Herakleion.

————. Forthcoming b. "Behind the Façade: What Social and Political Realities are Behind the Cultural Regionalities of Middle Minoan Crete?" in *Πεπραγμένα Ι' Διεθνούς Κρητολογικού Συνεδρίου*.

————. Forthcoming c. "Myrtos: From Phournou Koryphi to Pyrgos," in *STEGA: The Archaeology of Houses and Households in Ancient Crete from the Neolithic Period through the Roman Era* (*Hesperia Suppl.* 44), K. Glowacki and N. Vogeikoff-Brogan, eds., Princeton.

Girouard, M. 1978. *Life in the English Country House: A Social and Architectural History*, New Haven and London.

Hankey, V. 1986. "Pyrgos: The Communal Tomb in Pyrgos IV (Late Minoan I)," *BICS* 33, pp. 135–137.

Knappett, C. 1999. "Assessing a Polity in Protopalatial Crete: The Malia-Lasithi State," *AJA* 103, pp. 615–639.

Ovenden, D.M. 1976. "An Anthropological Expedition to Crete," *Radiography* 42, pp. 132–136.

Whitelaw, T.M. 1983. "The Settlement at Fournou Korifi Myrtos and Aspects of Early Minoan Social Organization," in *Minoan Society*, O. Krzyszkowska and L. Nixon, eds., Bristol, pp. 323–345.

————. 2007. "House, Household and Community at Early Minoan Fournou Korifi: Methods and Models for Interpretation," in *Building Communities: House, Settlement and Society in the Aegean and Beyond* (*BSA Studies* 15), R. Westgate, N. Fisher, and J. Whitley, eds., London, pp. 65–76.

Whittaker, H. 2002. "Minoan Board Games: The Function and Meaning of Stones with Depressions (So-Called Kernoi) from Bronze Age Crete," *Aegean Archaeology* 6, pp. 73–87.

6 LM IIIC Burial Culture in Crete: A Socioeconomic Perspective

KATIA PERNA

The aim of this paper is to analyze the Cretan burial customs during the Late Minoan (LM) IIIC period and to try to connect the changes attested in the mortuary practice to the political and economical transformations of the island. After the collapse of a consolidated political system at the end of the Bronze Age, between LM IIIC (12th to mid-11th century B.C.) and the Subminoan (SM) period (mid-11th to the beginning of the 10th century B.C.), Crete showed new political and economical patterns that involved the various regions of the island in different ways. Several politically important centers disappeared, and a great number of new ones arose. The production and exchange system changed radically, and even religion was influenced by different tendencies. The centrifugal force to which the island was subjected inevitably also modified the burial customs: new tomb architectures, methods of interments, and burial assemblages were introduced, but they also coexisted with more traditional ones.

Since many important previous works have considered transformations in burial customs as the result of external influence, I have chosen to explain these changes on an intra-island level. Although I agree that it is import to insert Crete into a wider geographic perspective, especially in a period of great mobility in the Aegean area, this paper focuses on relating the transformations in the mortuary habits to the new political and economic geography of the island.

Burial Customs and Social Strategies

Funerary data has often been used to identify ethnic groups, to try to understand the beliefs of ancient people, or—through the perspective of processual and social archaeology—to reconstruct the social structure of a community. Debate on the value of funerary data remains ongoing (see Morris 1987; 1992; Jones 1997; Dickinson 2006, 174–195), but old normative axioms have been partially exceeded by new methodological approaches—in particular by post-processual theory (Hodder 1986). These new approaches have been useful in underlining the symbolic value of the relationships between the community of the living and the community of the dead and their ideological implications (see Cuozzo 2003).

Nevertheless, decoding the many meanings of burial customs remains a difficult process, not exempt from the dangers of arbitrary interpretations. Many elements come into play just after the death of an individual. When someone dies and leaves his community, the living have to refer to an eschatological system and accept the passage of the deceased to a new condition. The living have to respect rigid rules in order to deliver the dead to the underworld, and they have to organize a funeral, which must be suitable to their social role and approved by the community. Through the funeral they can communicate specific messages concerning their social aspirations. Death becomes an important occasion in which social strategy and economic potential, as well as the desire for self-representation, significantly influence the funerary performance.

In this perspective, tombs could reveal the existence of mechanisms of social competition and of hierarchies in the social body or point out the relationship between groups of different sites or regions. The data offered by mortuary analysis can be used in a wider context by comparing them to the results obtained by other fields of archaeological research.

The meaningful changes that happened in Crete between the end of the Bronze Age and the start of the Iron Age as a consequence of the change in Aegean political geography offer an interesting ground for this type of research (Snodgrass 1971; Desbourough 1972; Coulson 1990; Dickinson 2006). The radical transformations in settlement patterns (Whitley 1991; Haggis 1993, 2001; Nowicki 2000), the variety of the religious expressions (see D'Agata 2001), and the profound differences between the various regions of the island are consistent with the lack of uniformity that characterized the necropoleis. Furthermore, some differences are also visible within a single cemetery in the tomb architecture, the treatment of the corpses buried in the same tomb, and the composition of grave goods. The overall picture is moreover complicated by the presence of elements of discontinuity with the past as well as a constant reference to "tradition." It is evident that the LM IIIC and SM funerary customs are so complex that they cannot be easily interpreted in a univocal manner. Some difficulties are also linked to the impossibility in some cases of establishing the phases in the use of the tombs and in the associations of goods and burials. Moreover, it is often not possible to link necropoleis and settlements and to insert some isolated tombs into a funerary system; it is to be said that the latter could be part of an undisclosed cemetery. The lack of osteological analysis adds to the difficulty in identifying the sex and age of the dead. Ultimately, only a small percentage of the tombs that have been excavated are useful for archaeological research.

Some important works (Kanta 1980; Löwe 1996) provide a picture both of the distribution and of the phases of use of the LM III necropolis; more specific studies about LM IIIC and SM burial customs (Catling 1995; Kanta 2003; Tsipopoulou 2005) focus instead on either the analysis of high-status burials or the understanding of the interconnections between Crete and other Aegean areas, often from an ethnic perspective. On the other hand, some interesting information has been obtained by taking mortuary evidence into consideration in a wider context (Borgna 2003b).

The identification of ethnic groups through the analysis of the tombs is certainly possible (Jones 1997). Some funerary habits in LM IIIC Crete have been attributed to the presence of Mycenaean people, who were on the island at that time as rulers (Tsipopoulou 2005, 327–329), or to the relationship with the Cypriot world (Catling 1996c, 648; Kanta 2003). On Crete, the interaction between Minoan and Mycenaean people and the exchange of goods and ideas with Cyprus were not a novelty, and in some fields there was a high grade of cultural syncretism between these Aegean groups. A novelty in this period is instead the manner in which old and

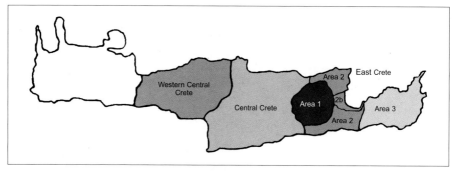

Figure 6.1. LM IIIC/SM mortuary areas on Crete.

new ideas and local and external traditions were used by newborn communities. For this reason, I will attempt to interpret the funerary customs of LM IIIC Crete and their lack of homogeneity by considering different cultural areas (Fig. 6.1) with specific characteristics and collating cemeteries, settlement, and cult places.

CHRONOLOGICAL FRAMEWORK

The debate on the LM IIIC Cretan mortuary evidence cannot leave out the definition of the chronological phases of the period, which is actually very problematic. The lack of stratigraphical sequences in many new-founded sites does not allow us to establish a relative chronology; additionally, it is difficult to relate the Cretan pottery production to the mainland chronological sequences. Among the scholars who have contributed to the definition of LM IIIC phases (Kanta 1980, 1997b; D'Agata 1999a, 2003; Hallager 2000; Borgna 2003a; Warren 2007), D'Agata has recently distinguished two moments of LM IIIC (early and late), and two phases of the Subminoan (SM I and SM II) (D'Agata 2007). This proposal denies the existence of the middle LM III, which some scholars have singled out in the stratigraphical sequences of the settlements or in the pottery production (Mook and Coulson 1997, 357; Rethemiotakis 1997). Nevertheless, the debate is still open and in some cases controversial (Borgna 2007; Warren 2007). Because of the difficulty in making subtle chronological distinctions in the funerary contexts, I will refer in this work to the chronological proposal of D'Agata.

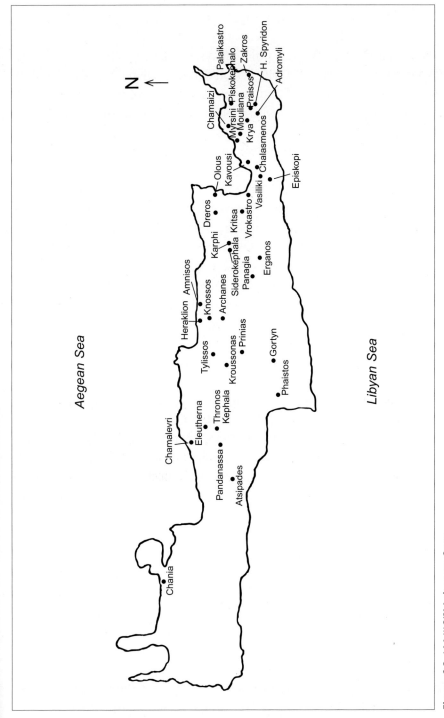

Figure 6.2. LM IIIC/SM sites on Crete.

Cretan Political Geography in LM IIIC

The collapse of the Aegean political system between the end of the LM IIIB and the start of the LM IIIC period determined in Crete the abandonment of many coastal sites and the establishment of new centers, especially on hills (Fig. 6.2); but these phenomena, often interpreted as the consequence of dangers by the coasts, do not occur simultaneously or with the same intensity in the different areas of the island.

At the beginning of the period several settlements (Praisos, Kavousi Kastro, and Thronos Kephala) were built on the mountains, some on low hills not far from the sea (Chamalevri), and others on the coast (Palaikastro Kastri and Elias to Nisi); but lowland centers and coastal stations already occupied in previous periods continued to exist: Phaistos in the Mesara Plain, Knossos, Tylissos, and Amnisos near the northern coast, and Chania on the eponymous gulf. During LM IIIC, instead, some of these settlements were abandoned (Palaikastro Kastri, Chamalevri, Chania), whereas some upland sites (Vrokastro, Kavousi Vronda, Chalasmenos, Vasiliki Kephala, Karphi, Prinias, and Gortyn) were founded. The territories of Phaistos and Knossos continued to be inhabited for the whole of LM IIIC and into the SM period, even if the former declined while the latter underwent some important changes and developments.

It is evident that the traditional idea—that a general threat suddenly urged residents of coastal towns to flee to the inland areas seeking refuge—is not sufficient to explain the profound changes in the settlement system. Besides the defense needs, which explain the choice of naturally fortified sites, the occupation of internal areas has to be read following other parameters (Perna 2009, 38). It is, in fact, part of a general political and economic transformation of the island that produced a system characterized by "unstable" political and social structures (Whitley 1991) and mainly centered on the primary economic activities (Watrous 1977; Borgna 2003b; Wallace 2003a). Even if the influx of people, goods, and ideas from the Aegean was still lively at the start of LM IIIC, overseas trade underwent a strong resizing. Some centers were still involved in Aegean trade (as the presence of mainland pottery at Chania, Chamalevri, Phaistos, and Knossos shows) and were important referents both for Aegean centers and for the upland Cretan ones, which were the main suppliers of textiles, livestock, and agricultural products (Borgna 2003b, 160–161, 163).

Such equilibrium remained throughout the first half of LM IIIC, after which, as noted above, the settlement landscape changed again. The growth of some mountain sites during the late phase of LM IIIC is shown by the presence of prominent buildings with storage facilities and rooms suitable for ceremonial activities, such as the Great House at Karphi (Pendlebury, Pendlebury, and Money-Coutts 1937–1937, 77–79; Day and Snyder 2004), Building A-B at Kavousi Vronda (Day and Snyder 2004, with previous bibliography), and the megara at Chalasmenos (Tsipopoulou 2005, 317–326). It is also accompanied, though, by their involvement in trade, which is attested to by the influx of imported goods (Bouzek 1985, 143–144; Borgna 2003b, 166–168). This clearly indicates the existence of a flow of communication between Crete and the Aegean, but also a change in the relationship between Cretan centers; the upland settlements seem at this stage more independent from the lowland ones, which used to manage the overseas trade.

The passage to the SM period saw further change to the Cretan settlement system. After this moment, in fact, only the centers that had created "stable" political structures, such as Knossos (Whitley 1991), emerged, whereas most of the others were abandoned.

Religious Expressions

LM IIIC religion is crossed by different trends. The many works on this subject (Gesell 1985; 2000; D'Agata 2001; Prent 2005; Kanta 2006; Perna 2009, 38–39; forthcoming a) show that even the organization was influenced by the dynamism of a society in formation.

The cult of the Goddess with Up-Raised Arms (Gesell 1985, 41–46; D'Agata 2001, 348–350; Prent 2005, 174–184, 616–620), already attested in LM IIIA–B lowland centers and linked to Minoan religious practices, is certainly the most impressive. In LM IIIC it is characteristic of the upland settlements, many of which (Kavousi Vronda, Karphi, Chalasmenos, Vasiliki Kephala, Prinias) had an independent "bench-sanctuary" consecrated to the Goddess. Her cult had a "popular" character (Gesell 2000), but in some contexts, such as that at Vasiliki

Kephala (Eliopoulos 1998) and Karphi (Pendlebury, Pendlebury, and Money-Coutts 1937–1938), it has been associated with elaborate rituals and subject to elitist interpretations (Perna, forthcoming a).

In addition to the traditional cults located in sacred caves (e.g., Psychro, Patsos) or in "regional" sanctuaries (e.g., Kato Symi) across the island, a new cult was experienced at Hagia Triada and perhaps at Tylissos. Both were open-air sanctuaries where, alongside the traditional cult items (e.g., horns of consecration), new iconographic elements were introduced—the fantastic animals being among the most impressive. Neither precious nor personal goods or weapons—traditional symbols of wealth—were offered in these cult places; according to D'Agata, this was a consequence of strong control over the sanctuary by a local authority, settled at Phaistos, which was able to maintain a low degree of competition between different groups and to conciliate old and new religious symbols (D'Agata 2001, 351–352). Finally, a ritual deposition of pottery and animal bones is attested at Thronos Kephala. This phenomenon was probably the final act of ceremonial activity focusing on the communal consumption of food (D'Agata 1997–2000).

LM IIIC Cemetery Distribution

Only a few of the known LM IIIC/SM cemeteries can be associated with a specific settlement; many extensive necropoleis of the LM IIIC–SM period are not securely related to any center at present (Fig. 6.3). There are also numerous isolated tombs in various parts of the island, and, in some cases, these were probably part of a necropolis while others seem to be the result of occasional deposition. This makes it difficult to distinguish homogeneous mortuary areas and also, when possible, many variables have to be considered.

Traditionally, three main areas are distinguished: East Crete, Central Crete, and the western area of Central Crete (Fig. 6.1). Within each, micro-areas were identified by peculiarities in the funerary architecture, in the depositional practices, or in the composition of the assemblages. Most of the known LM IIIC/SM cemeteries are located in the eastern area of the island where the prevailing pattern is that of the large-scale

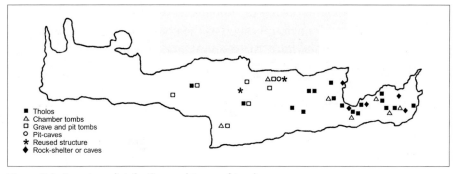

Figure 6.3. Cemetery distribution and types of tombs.

adoption of the tholos tomb with widespread use of inhumation. The burial customs here are subject to experimentation, which occasionally produced phenomena of bi-ritualism, such as the coexistence of inhumed and cremated corpses.

In Central Crete a distinction should be made between upland and lowland sites, which were evolving mostly in different directions. In the first half of LM IIIC the coastal sites maintained funerary customs that were partly in line with local tradition or exploited the necropoleis (which were used during the previous period). At the end of the period, however, some groups emerged that followed different burial customs; they adopted new tombs and introduced cremation. At the highland sites, instead, after the early LM IIIC period, the tholos tomb was the most widespread form of burial architecture, but at the end of the period new types of tombs and cremations were attested.

The scanty data concerning the western area of Central Crete does not allow us to establish the boundaries of specific mortuary areas, but they testify that the region between the western and central part of the island (the farther western-central area) shows different tendencies from the other parts of Crete until the SM period.

EAST CRETE

As mentioned previously, East Crete (Fig. 6.1) was the region most affected by the *ex-novo* occupation after the disintegration of the Post-palatial political organization. During LM IIIA–B this area, which seemed to be peripheral during the apogee of the last Palace of Knossos, recorded interesting innovations such as the construction of the tholos of Achladia and the appearance of weapons and precious objects among the grave goods (Perna 2001, 133–134).

In LM IIIC, the rise of many small settlements in the mountainous and hilly areas and the occupation of the island's interior areas led to the creation of new cemeteries, which were composed of tholos tombs. Tholoi of modest size, usually 2–3 x 1.5–2 m (although the tholos at Praisos Photoula measured 4.3 x 3.4 m), were carefully built, some-times with a dromos. The tholoi had a non-functional stomion, which in many cases made it necessary to remove the vault's capstone in order to introduce the dead to the chamber. The plan was often circular, but more frequently square—an architectural change already experienced in various parts of the island during the LM IIIA–B period (Belli 1991, 439; Kanta 1997a, 245). Some of these tholoi, however, display signif-icant variations, which I will describe below.

As mentioned above, other types of tombs were sporadically attested in this area. Chamber tombs, for example, became less popular in LM IIIC and continued to be adopted at those sites that had already been inhabit-ed during LM IIIB, such as Episkopi, Kritsa Katharos, and Kata Lakkoi. At the latter two sites, however, tholoi appeared during LM IIIC. They are similar to the older ones in plan and dimensions. Additionally, the long-held tradition of using caves and rock shelters as tombs was continued along the mountain slopes of the eastern region (Faure 1964, 51–80; Löwe 1996).

No matter the type of tomb, the manner of burial is usually inhumation, but cremations occurred alongside inhumations after the early LM IIIC period (Figs. 6.4, 6.5). The coexistence between these rites continued for the whole LM IIIC period, and it is attested in tholoi, chamber tombs, and perhaps even in rock shelters. Only one tholos—at Kritsa Kato Lakkoi—exclusively contained only cremated remains. Cremation burials were introduced in this area in LM IIIA at Olous (van Effenterre 1948, 7–13, 47–59; Kanta 2001), where both rituals coexisted in the same cemetery, even if not in the same tomb (cremations were placed in pithoi, whereas inhumations were placed in larnakes).

The tomb was built for family groups, as the number of corpses and the presence of individuals of every age and gender indicates. Gender was

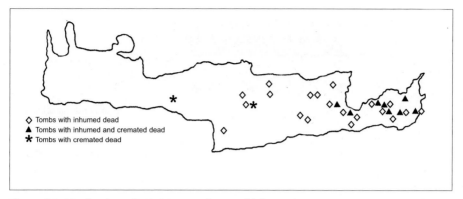

Figure 6.4. Distribution of LM IIIC cremations and inhumations.

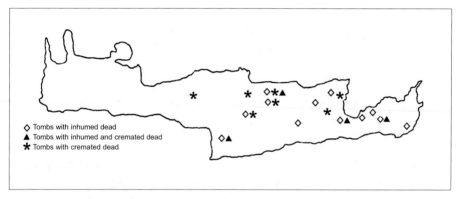

Figure 6.5. Distribution of SM cremations and inhumations.

distinguished in some cases by osteological analysis and by the grave goods in others—jewelry, spindle whorls, and needles for women; weapons or tools and some personal ornaments for men. In the tombs where only one or two bodies were discovered, the skeletons, when sexing was possible, invariably were found to be male.

The grave goods in the majority of the burials consist of a ceramic set that contains few components. The majority of the pottery was represented by common vases: closed vases prevailed (they were present in 60% of the tombs), whereas open vases were attested in 43% of the tombs. Among the closed shapes, the stirrup jars were more numerous (particularly stirrup jars), followed by pouring vessels. The deep bowl was the most common open shape, whereas the kylix was sporadically

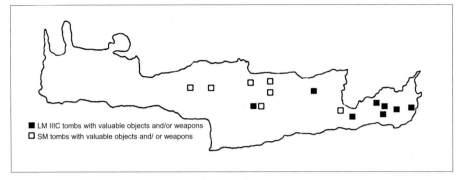

Figure 6.6. LM IIIC/SM tombs with valuable goods.

present. Fibulae and finger rings were the only personal ornaments present in a fair number of tombs, whereas beads and spindle whorls, which had been very numerous among the grave goods of the LM IIIA–B tombs (Perna 2001), became less common in LM IIIC. Bronze pins became more common in the SM period.

Area 1: Lasithi

Many LM IIIC and SM small settlements were located in the heights and in the slopes of the Lasithi Mountains, and tholos tomb cemeteries have been identified there (Figs. 6.1–6.3). Located on the northern side of the mountains is a tomb of a specific type that is unparalleled in the eastern part of Crete. This is the tholos with a square plan built above ground, which is the model of the necropolis of Karphi (Pendlebury, Pendlebury, and Money-Coutts 1937–1938, 100–112), and this square plan is also attested in the nearby town of Siderokephala (Taramelli 1899, 402–406; Eliopoulous 1994, 748) and later at Papoura (Watrous 1980).

Above-ground tholoi with square or round plans have a small stomion and are accessed by a dromos, and their facades were well built. The stomion was blocked from the inside and never reopened; the deceased were introduced by removing the capstone of the vault. In the necropolis of Karphi Ta Mnimata there were some tombs in pairs, sometimes surrounded by low enclosures (tombs 1–2, 7–8) or agglutinated (tombs 16–17). They were similar enough but some were larger than others (e.g., Ta Mnimata tombs 4, 8, and 11); the larger tombs were over 2 m in diameter or length. The construction of small over-ground tholoi, also attested at SM Pantanassa in the central-western region, has precedent in the Mesara Plain, at Apodoulou, in LM IIIB. According to A. Kanta (Kanta 1997a, 247), those tholoi expressly recalled Minoan tradition, and they represented a link with the more recent tholoi of Karphi (contra Belli 1991, 439).

Cremation is totally absent in this area, even if it was present in this period in other parts of the island. Here, the tombs exclusively contained inhumed corpses, usually placed on the ground in a curled or supine position, and only rarely in a larnax. Thirty percent of the tombs at Karphi and the tholos of Siderokephala contained only one inhumed individual; this particularly seems to be the rule in the necropolis of Karphi Astividero. Forty percent contained two or three corpses, and 30% contained four or five.

There were no indicators of status among the burial goods, with the exception of the gold ring in the tholos of Siderokephala (Fig. 6.6); nevertheless, in the settlement at Karphi some valuable objects, such as a Naue II–type sword and a bronze tripod, are attested (Pendlebury, Pendlebury, and Money-Coutts 1937–1938, 72, 92). The deceased was usually accompanied by common vases, among which stirrup jars (38%), deep bowls (10%), cups (12%), and kylikes (10%) prevailed. A kylix could be an alternative to a deep bowl or cup, and it is attested only in tombs 1, 4, 5, 7, and 8 at Karphi Ta Mnimata. Among these, tombs 4 and 8 also contained kraters, a number of bronze objects, and animal figurines. Moreover, tomb 8 contained a lattice-work ware stand. The association of kylix and krater was found in the "Great House" and in shrine 16–17 at Karphi (Day and Snyder 2004). Therefore, in the bigger and better-built tombs of Karphi Ta Mnimata, the grave goods included objects similar to the ones placed in the more important buildings of the settlements.

Tomb 11, one of the largest tombs of the Karphi Ta Mnimata necropolis, also contained an anthropomorphic rhyton similar to the one found in a sacred context of the settlement. These objects perhaps mean that people that were buried in the tombs were involved in the management of the cult places. This could tally with the current opinion that the society of Karphi was characterized by the presence of many groups (that were not subjected to a central authority [D'Agata 2001]), which perhaps competed with each other by constructing special buildings or managing the shrines (for an analysis of architectural features and of social function of Karphi's buildings, see Perna 2004; Wallace 2005).

The general absence of explicit indicators of status in an area where there was competition between clans is surprising. One example to the contrary is the individual buried in the tomb at Siderokephala, who was accompanied by a gold ring and a pottery set composed exclusively of open vases (a kalathos, a cup, and a krateriskos). Since open vases, used for consuming food or drink, were a minority or were absent in the LM IIIC tombs (where closed vases prevailed), this concentration of open shapes is atypical. In Lasithi, generally, they were usually part of the assemblage, probably because funerary banqueting, attested for the whole LM IIIA–B period, was still practiced here.

The visibility of the tombs, the reiteration of funerary banquets, the presence of objects usually placed in religious contexts, and the exclusive adoption of inhumation made the Lasithi area clearly different from the other areas. An echo of the island tradition is also found here in the re-proposal of traditional cults and in the use of traditional architectonical models in the settlements. The absence of indicators of status commits the social definition of the group to the architecture of the tomb (it is in some cases paired with another tomb, probably belonging to the same clan) and also to the presence in the assemblage of votive objects, which could underline the link between clans and the management of religious affairs.

Area 2: Between the Lasithi Massif and the Siteia Mountains

The necropoleis that are related to excavated settlements in this area (Figs. 6.1–6.3) include: the cemetery at Kavousi Vronda (Coulson, Day, and Gesell 1983), located on the borders of the Kavousi settlement and used also after its abandonment (Day 1997, 404–405, n. 32); the LM IIIC tholos at Chalasmenos (Coulson and Tsipopoulou 1994, 86), set 200 m southeast of the settlement; the SM/Protogeometric (PG) cemetery at Vrokastro (Hall 1914, 123–174), located near the settlement; and the tholos at Vasiliki Hagios Teodoros, located near the settlement of Vasiliki Kephala (Seager 1906–1907, 129–132). Other necropoleis have been located at Kritsa Lakkoi and Katharos (Platon 1951; Tsipopoulou and Vagnetti 1997; Tsipopoulou and Little 2001) and at Episkopi Ierapetra (Walter 1942, 198; Amandry 1947–1948, 441; Kanta 1980, 153–154); single tombs have been found at Dreros (van Effenterre 1948, 16–18, 60–61, 63), Elounda Pyrgos (Davaras 1973b, 586–588), and Vasiliki Karamaki (Tsipopoulou and Vagnetti 2003).

The typical small hypogean tholos, with a round or square plan, with or without dromos, was adopted in the newly established cemeteries. In the cemeteries in use from the previous period (e.g., Kritsa Lakkoi), it appeared side by side with the chamber tombs, whereas it was not adopted elsewhere (e.g., at Episkopi). Tholoi in this area were quite similar to one another, except for tomb A at Kritsa Lakkoi, which had a beehive vault and was accessible from a stepped dromos not in line with the chamber. This tomb shows some analogies with Cypriot tombs and older Cretan tombs, such as the LM IIIA ones at Smari Livaditsa (Belli 2006). At Kritsa Lakkoi, the vault projected over the ground and was covered by a mound, which was contained by a square enclosure. Inside the vault a burial with a vase and a fibula was placed.

Inhumation was the most widespread rite in this region. Graves contained one to seven corpses, both adults (men and women) and children. During LM IIIC and SM periods the dead were laid out on the ground. Larnakes were used only in the rich tomb at Vasiliki Hagios Teodoros and in the chamber tombs of Kritsa; in another chamber tomb at Kritsa, an open oblong vase accomplished the same function (Platon 1951). In a pit tomb at Vrokastro Chavga, instead, two pithoi were used as burial containers: one of these contained a child and was placed on its side; the other one contained an adult male and was upside down. The use of burial containers in an upside-down position is attested elsewhere in LM IIIC/SM Crete and has roots in the Minoan tradition, as will be explained further on. Chamber tombs were similar to the older ones, and they were not different from tholos tombs in the method of burial or the grave goods.

Cremation appeared in this area (Fig. 6.4) in an advanced phase of LM IIIC and did not signify a drastic break with the traditional burial ritual. A pyxis was usually used as an ash urn and was placed in tombs containing inhumed corpses. In a plundered chamber tomb at Kritsa Lakkoi, a pyxis, which probably contained a cremated individual, was placed inside a larnax with an inhumed body; this practice is also attested in the tholos at Praisos. In another chamber tomb at Kritsa a pyxis contained cremated bones and fragments of an unburned jawbone and a fragment of the cranium (Tsipopoulou and Little 2001, 87–88). Cremation is also attested in a rock shelter at Pyrgos, in the territory of Olous. There, a pithos—the typical vase used as an ash urn at this site during the LM IIIA–IIIB—contained a cremated corpse with a kylix and a seal. During the SM/PG period at Vrokastro, amphorae were used as urns, as was the case at Knossos and on the mainland (e.g., at Athens and at Perati). Centers that adopted cremation were located around the Mirabello Bay, and for this reason, this zone can be considered a micro-area within the region.

Cremation did not have any hierarchical value, and, in general, status indicators were lacking in this area (Fig. 6.6). The only tomb that contained a rich burial is the tholos of Vasiliki Hagios Teodoros, in which a dagger and a gold pendant were associated with an inhumed man; the tholos at Vasiliki Karamaki (Tsipopoulou and Vagnetti 2003), however, containing a number of metallic and bimetallic objects that are related to Aegean jewelry (found in Attica and Rhodes), reveals the existence of a relationship between the Cretan and the Aegean people and the presence in the isthmus of Ierapetra of people who were able to bury their relatives with valuable goods other than weapons. Except for these cases, the remaining tombs contained the typical grave goods of the period, with a greater presence of open vases (attested in 60% of the tombs) than in other areas. Closed vases, above all stirrup jars, were present in 80% of the tombs. At the end of the period, the flask, a typical Cypriot form, made its appearance.

Among the open shapes, the deep bowl is still the most common vase, but it gradually disappeared, being replaced in the SM period by new forms such as the krateriskos or the belly skyphos. Generally, however, the tendency of putting vases with several functions in the tombs of this region is noticeable, and the prevailing shapes of the vases show they were intended to contain liquids, food, and drink. In some cases, vases that had a high symbolic value in the Minoan-Mycenaean world were preferred (e.g., the kylix [associated in the tomb of Elounda Pyrgos with a heirloom seal]); in other cases, vessels typical of foreign funerary contexts, such as flasks, were inserted into the assemblage.

The variety of the pottery shapes in the grave assemblage seems to confirm the persistence in this area of the practice of funeral banquets: at Dreros, all the vases useful for a banquet (one fruit stand, one deep bowl, one kylix, one spouted cup, one jug, one thelastron, and five stirrup jars) had been placed with five corpses; and at Chalasmenos, four individuals were accompanied by three stirrup jars, five kalathoi, two deep bowls, and three skyphoi. Some burials, though, were different because they consisted of persons accompanied by a few closed vases and some valuable objects. In fact, they seem to indicate a different ideological belief system.

Area 3: Siteia Region and Far Eastern Crete

The richest and most-complex funerary examples of eastern Crete are found in the region around the bay of Siteia, between the eastern slopes of the mountains of Siteia and the eastern edge of the island (Figs. 6.1–6.3). Not far from the coast that marks the eastern corner of the Mirabello Bay is the necropolis of Myrsini Aspropilia (Platon 1959, 372–373), which consists of chamber tombs in use since LM IIIA, and the tholoi of Sellades and Vourlia, in the territory of Mouliana (Xanthoudides 1904); to the east there is the tomb of Piskokephalo Berati (Platon 1952); and to the southeast are the necropolis of Krya (Davaras 1974; 1976; 1977; 1978; Kanta and Davaras 2004), the tholos of Praisos Photoula (Platon 1960, 301–302), the chamber tomb at Praisos Kapsalos (Kanta 1980, 179–181), the chamber tomb at Adromyli Kantemi Kephala (Platon 1954, 367; Kanta 1980, 185), the cave at Hagios Spyridon Kalathiana (Tsipopoulou 1983), and the burials at Zakros Palaimylos (Davaras 1973a, 158–160).

The tholoi of this area were similar to the ones described above for areas 1 and 2, but the tholos of Praisos Photoula is oversized. However, in the necropolis of Krya Orthi Petra, which is contemporary to that of Mouliana, there were other types of tombs alongside the typical tholoi. Prevalent among these tombs types are the "pseudo-tholoi," which essentially were built with stones covering and surrounding the pithos, and, as Kanta and Davaras suggest, combine the typical Cretan pithos burial with the tholos tomb (Kanta and Davaras 2004, 150). In the same necropolis a tholos with a keel vault recalls the tholos of Isopata and the

Royal Tomb at Knossos (Kanta and Davaras 2004, 151); it had been paralleled with some tombs of the Levant (Belli 2006, 276).

The chamber tombs were in line with the older ones and continued side by side tholoi. The coexistence between inhumation and cremation (Fig. 6.4) is also characteristic of this region—it is attested at Mouliana Sellades, Praisos Photoula, Zakros Palaimylos, Krya Orthi Petra, and maybe even at Piskokephalo Berati. The way in which it occurs, however, was different. In Tholos A at Mouliana, which contained an inhumed man placed on a bed of pebbles, there was a krater containing cremated bones, whereas in the tholos at Praisos Photoula, cremation ashes were placed in a pyxis at the feet of a corpse buried in a larnax. The tomb of Zakros Palaimylos, instead, contained a pyxis with a cremated individual and a pithos with an inhumed dead, and the Piskokephalo one contained a burial in a larnax and perhaps cremation ashes under an upside-down basin. Finally, at Krya Orthi Petra, three graves (two tholoi and one pseudo-tholoi) contained inhumed corpses placed on the ground and urns with cremation ashes. With the exception of the tombs at Krya Orthi Petra, the use of a larnax to contain a single corpse was very popular in this area. Pithoi could be used with the same function.

The dead in this zone are accompanied by a deposition of essential grave goods: a few pots (generally stirrup jars, but also jugs, cups, and, in a few cases, deep bowls) and personal objects (rings, fibulae, and pins). Since this was the basic set, weapons and precious objects found in some cemeteries should be taken as indicators of status or as symbols of an ideology of power that had ancient roots on the island. This applies particularly to the tombs of Mouliana. Beside the basic set (three stirrup jars, two fibulae, and other bone and bronze objects), three swords (two of F2 type and a fragmentary third of Naue II type), two spearheads, five or six bronze pots, and two gold rings had been placed with the inhumed dead buried in tholos A. In the same grave, a golden ring highlighted the status of the cremated dead, whose remains were contained in a large krater with a few vessels (a pyxis, a deep bowl, and a flask). The assemblage of tomb B was no less impressive. The individual placed inside a larnax was accompanied by two stirrup jars, shield elements, one gold ring, and a Naue II–type bronze sword, whereas another individual, placed on a "bed" of pebbles, was accompanied by two stirrup jars, another Naue II–type bronze sword, two bronze spearheads, two ivory plaques, and a gold mask, which was placed on his face—a characteristic Mycenaean practice, already adopted on Crete at Knossos during LM II–IIIA:1 (Perna 2001).

Although the tombs of Mouliana are exceptional in comparison to those found in the eastern part of the island, in this region they are less atypical when compared to the tholos of Praisos Photoula and to chamber tombs A and B of Myrsini Aspropilia. In the tholos, in fact, the inhumed man buried in the larnax was accompanied in the vessel by a gold ring, a spearhead, an ivory handle with gold nails, and two stirrup jars; a bronze belt, a gold plaque with the figure of an argonaut, two stirrup jars, and a jug were placed outside the larnax. At Myrsini, a Naue II–type sword, two stirrup jars, one kalathos, and one tankard were in tomb A, while two swords (one of type D and one of type F2) and two stirrup jars were placed in the tomb B. These burials, sometimes defined as "warrior graves" (Kanta 2003), were interpreted (Tsipopoulou 2005) as the sign of the presence of mainlanders in eastern Crete, who were more powerful and richer than Cretan people. Thanks to the presence of typical Cypriot objects, some scholars (Catling 1995; Kanta 2003) have linked these burials to the LM IIIC/SM high-status burials of Knossos, the mainland, and Cyprus.

It can not be forgotten, however, that the corpses in the chamber tombs of Myrsini, which were accompanied by very similar objects to those found in the tombs of Mouliana, were buried in graves already in use in the previous period. Furthermore, the clear reference to typically Mycenaean practices, as indicated by the presence of funeral masks or weaponry, had a long tradition on the island: local people, in fact, after the fall of the last Palace of Knossos in LM IIIA–B, considered these practices an expression of an ideology of power, typical of the Mycenaean world, which had been a code of representation for the rulers of Knossos and was successively diffused throughout the island (Perna 2001).

The presence of the same objects throughout the mainland and in Cyprus, in my opinion, demonstrates that in the late phase of LM IIIC there was better communication between different regions of the Aegean, which was certainly based on trade, but also on the existence of a strong relationship between elite groups that shared common cultural codes. Additionally, the presence of a fragment of the Naue II–type sword in the upland settlement of Karphi clearly shows that foreign resources were more accessible in LM IIIC than in the past.

It is very interesting that in this area, where, during LM IIIA–B, the monumental tholos of Achladia had been built and in which the dead were buried with weapons (e.g., at Palaikastro and Myrsini), the desire for social display was still assigned to the funeral. It is noteworthy that in LM IIIC this custom is found only here and that it was tied to the traditional method of burial—inhumation. The cremated individuals, in fact, were never associated with weapons, although a gold ring sometimes identifies their status. In sum, a social interpretation seems to fit the evidence better than an ethnic one.

Overview of East Crete

The picture emerging from the analysis of burial customs in the eastern part of the island is extremely complex and does not conform to any schematic view. The use of the tholos during the second half of LM IIIC did not cause the disappearance of the chamber tomb (which was still adopted in the cemeteries in use by the LM IIIB) and does not exclude a sort of eclecticism in adopting new architectural types, particularly in the region of Siteia. At Krya, for example, there were six types of tomb, and at Vrokastro different types of graves coexisted. Both cemeteries, however, were also used in the successive periods and it is not easy to discern the phases of use of the various grave types.

The choice of the tholos certainly is a novelty, and it is typical of areas that were inhabited during the LM IIIC. It is likely that the occupation *ex-novo* of the land and the foundation of new small mountain settlements occurred in a climate of reciprocal competition and conflict. The tholoi, visible either because they were built above ground or due to the monumental burial mound when they were hypogean, could have represented a "landmark" (Belli 1997, 252–253). Older tholoi were often used as a sign of elite status or as an ideological symbol of a group, and they were reused for ideological reasons (Cucuzza 2002; Preston 2004, 335). Before LM IIIC, tholoi of various types had been sporadically adopted in the eastern area at Kalamaphka (Dunbabin 1947, 191), Plati (Dawkins 1913–1914, 13–15), Praisos (Bosanquet 1901–1902, 245–248), Sphakia (Platon 1955, 294), Ziros (Davaras

1964, 442), and, in some cases, such as at Achladia (Belli 1995), they had assumed monumental features.

Taking all of this into consideration, the tholos was probably perceived as a traditional tomb and was used—even if in different forms opened to new elaborations—by communities that inhabited new centers and shared a common cultural background in order to legitimize their presence on the land. Moreover, the reference to tradition, as the spread of the cult of the Goddess with Up-Raised Arms also testifies, seems to be important for the newborn mountain communities. The use of caves and rock shelters as burial sites, for example, has a long tradition in this area. In his work on the Cretan caves, Faure asserted that this choice in LM III–SM could have been dictated by defensive and economic needs (Faure 1964, 72–73). The tombs of Elounda Pyrgos and of Piskokephalo Berati, though, seem to be the expression of a choice: the former reiterated a type of burial typical of this area during LM IIIA–B, while the latter, which was also used in later periods, attested the Minoan practice of placing the burial container in an upside-down position.

Some innovating elements were introduced, such as cremation, which never became an alternative method to inhumation. From the oldest graves, like that of Praisos Photoula, until the SM ones of Vrokastro's cemeteries, cremated burials continued appearing in tombs that also contained inhumed dead. This rite, however, seems to be especially typical of the region of Siteia and of the sites overlooking the Mirabello Bay (Olous, Kritsa, Vrokastro); it was completely absent in the mountain cemetery of Lasithi and at the isthmus of Ierapetra. Although cremation does not seem in any way related to high-status burials, it is often related to tombs of rich people, who were accompanied by weapons and precious goods. This phenomenon is most apparent in the region of Siteia, where the richest tombs of the period are located. In the same phase, however, rich burials not related to warriors were attested in the isthmus of Ierapetra at Vasiliki during the LM IIIC, and at Vrokastro later on. Additionally, the tomb at Adromyli Kantami Kephala and one at Siderokephala each contained a precious object—a gold ring.

The existence of coastal sites such as Palaikastro Kastri (Sackett, Popham and Warren 1965) and Elias to Nisi (Hayden 2001) shows that this region maintained an interest for the management of sea products

(Borgna 2003b, 157) and/or trade at the beginning of LM IIIC. During the LM IIIC, though, many imported objects arrived in this region of Crete: Cypriot and mainland pottery (see the vases of Cypriot type at Karphi [Seiradaki 1960] or the Attic pottery in the tholos at Hagios Teodoros Karamaki [Tsipopoulou and Vagnetti 2003, 112–118]); weapons such as Naue II–type swords (Kilian-Dirlmeier 1993, 94–105), lanceolate, short socket, and leaf-shaped spearheads (Snodgrass 1964, 119–120; Catling 1968, 105–106; Höckmann 1980, 67–76; Bouzek 1985, 135–142); bow-violin and bow fibulae (Sapouna-Sakellaraki 1978, 16–19, 34–54; Bouzek 1985, 152–159); and pins (Hood and Coldstream 1968, 212–218, Bouzek 1985, 159–167). This testifies to a flow of communication between this area and the Aegean, probably in consequence to an economic increase that allowed the eastern centers to be competitive and involved in the Aegean trade network.

In the second part of LM IIIC, therefore, a significant difference between the communities of internal upland centers and those living in the lowland can be detected: the former, despite their greater involvement in Aegean trade, kept traditional burial customs alive; the latter sites were more receptive to new funeral rites.

CENTRAL CRETE

In this area (Fig. 6.1), located between the Lasithi Mountains in the east and the Psiloriti Mountains in the west, the mortuary evidence appears very different from that in eastern Crete. In LM IIIC the known necropoleis are those at Liliana near Phaistos (Savignoni 1904, 627–651) and at Erganos (Halberr 1901, 262–281) on the western slope of Lasithi. Contemporaneously in the Knossian area, the tholos of Kephala (Cadogan 1967; Preston 2005), where two burial layers were found, and the Isopata tholos (Evans 1905, 527–530), where a LM IIIC burial was placed in a niche of the dromos, were reused and some burials were placed in the older Nea Alikarnassos tomb (Lembessi 1973); in the hinterland at Kroussonas Rizoplaghia (Dimopoulou 1985, 297), an older building was adapted for funerary purposes.

The necropolis at Liliana seems to continue the local LM IIIA–B burial tradition: it was composed of chamber tombs, and the only rite practiced for all LM IIIC burials was inhumation. The dead, numbering from one to seven, either males or females, were buried in larnakes or placed on the ground. The burial assemblage was made of a pottery set that included closed and open vases (stirrup jars, jugs, cups, bowls, and kalathoi), some personal ornaments (necklaces and rings), and spindle whorls. In comparison with the older cemetery at Kalyvia, which was abandoned in LM IIIA (Savignoni 1904, 505–627), the tombs at Phaistos Liliana present two different elements: the lack of precious objects and weapons, which allowed Savignoni to define them as "tombe della plebe" (pleb tombs), and the use of larnakes as burial containers.

Consistent with what occurs in the eastern part of the island, the square tholos tomb was adopted in the mountain settlement of Erganos, which was founded at this time on the southwest slopes of the Lasithi Mountains. There, the only tomb, which was described by Halbherr (1901, 270–281), contained six corpses, four stirrup jars, and a conical cup, but no personal ornaments. The bones of one corpse were inserted into a pyxis during a secondary burial. The use of this vessel for the second interment of an inhumed corpse shows an interesting analogy with the treatment of cremated remains: evidently, a decomposed corpse and a cremated one could be placed in the same type of urn, which was perhaps in fashion during the late LM IIIC.

A phenomenon that deserves attention is the reuse of old graves during both the LM IIIC and SM periods. It concerns mainly tholos tombs, such as the Isopata and Kephala tombs near Knossos and the tholos at Valis in the Mesara Plain; but reuse is also seen in the chamber tomb at Nea Alikarnassos and in an old house at Kroussonas. The reuse of old tholoi is a practice known in the previous period (Perna 2001) and one that was tied to specific ideological reasons (Cucuzza 2002, 159–160). Unlike LM IIIA–B, though, the dead buried in LM IIIC/SM tholoi were not rich people. However, the choice to reuse this type of tomb while chamber tombs continued to be the most popular type may testify to the will by some people to reconnect to the Minoan past by taking possession of a monumental elitist tomb (Wallace 2003b, 269; 2006, 628; Preston 2005, 90; Perna 2008).

More data is available for the last part of LM IIIC and the SM period. During this period at Knossos, the North Cemetery—an extensive necropolis with chamber tombs, tholoi, pit-caves, and shaft graves (Coldstream and Catling 1996)—and the cemetery at Fortetsa (Brock 1957, 8–15) started to be used. Other burials were placed in older necropoleis, such as the one at Upper Gypsadhes (chamber tombs VIa and VII [Hood, Huxley, and Sandars 1958–1959, 205–210]) and Hagios Ioannis (a reused chamber tomb [Hood and Coldstream 1968]). In the Knossian hinterland at Tylissos Atzolou (Marinatos 1931) and Archanes Kato Lakkos (Sapouna-Sakellaraki 1990, 75–76), cremated individuals were buried in pit tombs. A necropolis of pit graves and tholoi was established at Siderospilia near Prinias (Rizza 1996, forthcoming). In the Mesara Plain, the Early Minoan (EM) tholos of Valis was reopened in order to bury a pyxis containing a cremated individual (Davaras 1973a, 164), and a pyxis with cremated bones was inserted into tomb D at Phaistos Liliana (Savignoni 1904, 643–644; Davaras 1973a, 162–163).

In Central Crete the square or circular tholos had a limited distribution that was restricted to the SM necropoleis of upland sites. The prevailing tomb type remained the chamber tomb, attested at Knossos and Phaistos and also at Hagia Marina Kollyva Metochi (Marinatos 1931–1932, 1–2; Kanta 1980, 22); it decreased in size and showed small architectural differences compared to the oldest tombs (Cavanagh 1996, 653–658). During LM IIIC and especially in the SM period, however, other types of tombs appeared, including shaft graves, pit-caves, and pit tombs (Fig. 6.3).

Shaft graves recalled the simple Mycenaean rectangular graves, which were widespread in Knossos and its territory during LM IIIA–B and were often associated with warriors. During the SM period they appeared in the North Cemetery at Knossos (tombs 149, 153, 160 and 282: Coldstream and Catling 1996, 180–183, 230), in the territory of Phaistos, at Logiadi (Savignoni 1904, 653) and Moni Kalyvianis (Savignoni 1904, 654), and at Archanes Phyties (Sapouna-Sakellaraki 1990, 83–84). The graves were quite small compared to the oldest shaft graves and did not contain rich burials.

Pit-caves formed the oldest nucleus of the North Cemetery at Knossos and had been typical of the LM IIIA–B necropolis of Knossos (especially of the Zapher Papoura's cemetery); they also were widespread in other areas of Crete, such as at Chania during LM IIIA:2–IIIB (Perna 2001). Moreover, they were sporadically present on the mainland and on Cyprus. Compared to the older pit-caves, SM pit-caves were smaller but equal in terms of architecture, and they were intended to accommodate rich burials, like the oldest ones. However, the burial rite with which they were associated markedly differentiates them from the LM IIIA–B pit-caves: the SM pit-caves, in fact, exclusively contained cremations.

Pit tombs were a novelty on Crete; they were typical of the Prinias Siderospilia cemetery and are attested at Tylissos and Archanes Kato Lakkos. At Prinias they consisted of a well-shaped oval pit, usually shallow (0.35–0.40 m), covered with stone slabs, and, in some cases, surrounded by circular stone enclosures that probably encircled a mound of earth. In particular, the oldest tomb of this type was situated in the middle of a large enclosure where there were two other similar tombs surrounded by a small circle of stones. Among the pit tombs at Prinias, pit BA differed from the others in shape and size, being deeper (0.70 m) than the others (ca. 0.30 m) and covered by a stone slab with a hollow in the lower part that resembled a dome.

The coexistence between different types of tombs in Central Crete was not a novelty: at Knossos during LM IIIA–B, three types of tombs were present in the necropolis of Zapher Papoura. It is interesting, however, that in a new funerary site the same types of tombs used in the past were reiterated. The novelty instead was the association of different types of tombs with specific burial methods.

For the whole of the LM IIIC period, inhumation was the only practiced rite (Fig. 6.4); the only exception to this is Prinias, where some pit tombs could be dated to late LM IIIC. The inhumed corpses were buried in chamber tombs or in reopened tholoi inside larnakes or on the ground, either in a supine or contracted position. They were of every age and gender. And, differently from eastern Crete, children could be buried under a house floor, as attested at Knossos, where an upside-down vase covered an infant's corpse in a house of the Stratigraphic Museum (Warren 1982–1983, 73), or at Phaistos, were a child was buried beneath the "Casa ad Ovest del Piazzale I" (Borgna 1997, 210).

Cremated individuals, instead, were usually buried in pit tombs or in pit-caves, and sporadically in chamber tombs; their remains were either placed in vessels or directly in the pit. In the central region cremation appeared quite late (Figs. 6.4, 6.5), and it was adopted as an exclusive ritual by some groups. In fact, despite the prevalence of inhumations in this area, the coexistence of inhumed and cremated corpses within the same tomb is more sporadic than in the eastern area. One exception are the urns placed in the tombs of Phaistos Liliana and Valis, and graves 2, 18, 40 and 112 at the Knossos North Cemetery. At Knossos, pit-caves exclusively contained cremated dead, and the case is the same in the pit tombs at Prinias Siderospilia, Tylissos Atzolou, and Archanes Kato Lakkos.

The analysis of the cremations of the North Cemetery at Knossos (Musgrave 1996, 677–702) revealed that only men (of all ages), were cremated. The exception to this is a group of three tombs (tombs 200–202) that contained a whole family group. Also, at Prinias, Tylissos Atzolou, and Archanes Kato Lakkos, the grave goods buried with the cremated dead primarily consisted of weapons that can be attributed to male individuals. Differently from the eastern area, all the LM IIIC/SM valuable burial goods (Fig. 6.6) in the central area were related to cremated dead. In tombs with inhumed dead, in fact, the offerings consisted of a few closed vases, usually stirrup jars and jugs. Even if it was rare, open vases were present in the chamber tombs (only in four tombs) and in tholoi (tholoi Q and T at Prinias); they were totally absent in the pit-caves and pit tombs.

The North Cemetery of Knossos has provided the richest tombs of the area, all of which date to the SM period. The most interesting one is a group of three pit-caves accessible from the same pit (tombs 200–202). It contained four people, three of whom had been cremated on the same occasion and then buried in the same room (Catling 1996c, 646); on this subject Catling hypothesized that human sacrifices were carried out (Catling 1995, 126–127). This tomb was effectively different from the other tombs of the same type (e.g., tomb 186), which contained only a single individual. The exceptional nature of tombs 200–202 is apparent, without doubt, by the presence of a very rich grave-good assemblage. Individual tomb 200 contained the cremated body of a woman, a stirrup jar, some beads, two gold rosettes, an ivory comb, a bronze pin, and a gold ring. Tomb 202 contained the cremated remains of a man and a woman and, perhaps, a child, and it had a very rich assemblage: a bronze Naue II–type sword, elements of a shield, a spearhead, an iron knife, six arrowheads, an ivory handle, a boar's tusk helmet, a gold ring, a bronze stand, an ivory comb, and a bone inlay. These goods are remarkable in comparison with those of pit-cave 186, which included a stirrup jar, a bronze spearhead, an iron dagger and knife, a shield, a boar's tusk helmet, and two whetstones. Aside from these tombs, only one other in the North Cemetery contained weapons—chamber tomb 2 (an iron dirk and two iron spearheads).

The "warrior graves" located in the hinterland of Knossos and at Prinias were less wealthy, but from an ideological point of view they are similar to the Knossian ones. In a pit tomb at Tylissos the cremated remains of the dead were placed in a bronze lebes that also contained two stirrup jars, two fibulae, a bronze spearhead, and an iron knife; at Archanes Kato Lakkos, in a tomb of the same type, a stone jar contained the ashes of the dead, a stirrup jar, a bronze spearhead, and two iron swords. Finally, at Prinias Siderospilia two stirrup jars, a jug, a gold plaque, a bronze basin, an axe, a few bronze spearheads, an iron sword, and three iron pins were buried with the cremated dead.

The Knossian pit-caves appear as alternatives to the chamber tombs either because they exclusively contained cremated remains or because of the composition of their grave goods. With the exception of tombs 200–202, the other pit-caves, like the shaft grave, contained individual burials. Pit tombs coexisted with tholoi at Prinias. The former differed not only typologically from the latter: they contained only a single cremation and counted weapons among the grave goods. The position of the pits was marked in some cases by a circle of stones, which perhaps were meant to underline the importance of the tomb. Even if these graves were a novelty in this area, pit AI shows that the tradition of placing a basin in an upside-down position over the ashes returned (Rizza and Rizzo 1984, 238–239, fig. 447; Biondi, forthcoming).

In sum, two periods characterized the burial customs of Central Crete. The first is set in the early LM IIIC and is marked by the lack of impressive novelties in the burial customs of the lowland centers. Phaistos, which is located in the Mesara Plain and probably controlled the surrounding area and was in contact with other Aegean people (Borgna 2003a, see 348–350), does not have a corresponding diversification in the burials. However, a tendency to underline the individuality of the dead by placing them in larnakes, which represents a novelty from the previous period, can be noted. Borgna has recently hypothesized that this lack of differentiation in the burial customs of the central-western area during the first half of LM IIIC could have been determined by an ideological strategy employed in order to avoid inopportune displays of economic power and encourage social integration (Borgna 2003a, 171). Owing to the presence of various social components in this center, perhaps this was also true for Phaistos.

On a religious level, in opposition to the eastern area, the central area was characterized for the whole LM IIIC by processes of integration which put together traditional cult features with innovative religious iconographies, such as in the sanctuary at Piazzale dei Sacelli in Hagia Triada (D'Agata 1999b, 236–237; 2001, 351–352) or at Tylissos (Kanta 1980, 11–12; Kanta 2006). In the case of Hagia Triada, the interpretation of it as an open-air sanctuary, controlled by Phaistos, in which many people interacted and offered their cultural contributions, could tally with the reading of the burial customs. In the same period at Knossos, the older cemeteries were still exploited and some ancient and monumental tholoi were reused.

The end of LM IIIC and above all the SM coincided with a period of transformation in the central area. The concentration of prestige burials in the area of Knossos and Prinias seems to reflect the political changes that this region was undergoing, which coincided in the southern part of the area with the progressive decline of Phaistos (Borgna 2003a, 353) and with the emergence of new centers such as Gortyn (Borgna 2003a, 353; Palermo 2003, 276–277) and Prinias. The latter (Perna 2007, forthcoming b, forthcoming c) presented the typical features of the mountain centers of the period, both for the choice of the tholos as the prevailing type of tomb and for the religious cult (it had one or more buildings dedicated to the Goddess with Up-Raised Arms; see Palermo 1999, 2006). But Prinias appears similar to Knossos for the presence of the pit tombs and of cremations. Between the late LM IIIC and the SM periods Prinias was probably a strategic site due to its position between Gortyn and Knossos (Palermo 2003, 276–277); the relationship with the former center could have produced significant changes in the social order. Knossos, on the other hand, is undoubtedly the protagonist of a new cultural climate, as is testified by the creation of more "stable" political structures (Whitley 1991, 352–361) and by its involvement in trade and relations with the mainland and Cyprus—actions that determined the inpour of many of the objects found in its territory.

The presence of alternative rites in the necropoleis of these "emerging" centers could be due to the existence of strong competition among different groups during a period of transformation in the local social-political framework. Some of them probably tried—through the mechanism of subliminal communication acted out during the funeral—to use symbols that referred to different ideologies, (some of which of an elitist type), in order to create and/or affirm their social identity.

Western Central Crete

The LM IIIC/SM burial evidence of the western area (Figs. 6.1, 6.3) of Central Crete is even scanter than in the other parts of the island; the most-western section of the island did not provide any evidence of burials at all. The only known LM IIIC burials are those at Voliones near Rethymnon (Pologhiorghi 1981), where inhumations in larnakes were placed on the ground and accompanied by few objects (a stirrup jar, an incense burner, and few beads in tomb 1, and a jug in tomb 2), and at Atsipades (Petroulakis 1915; Mavrighiannaki 1975), near Pantanassa, which was excavated at the beginning of the last century and recently reconsidered in light of the new findings carried out in the area (Agelarakis, Kanta, and Moody 2001). At this site, vessels containing burial cremations were vertically placed on the ground and supported by stones, as in an urn field. The cremated corpses—adult males and perhaps children—were accompanied by few closed vases (stirrup jars or jugs) and some personal ornaments (fibulae and pins). This cemetery was the only one making exclusive use of cremation in the second half of LM IIIC (Fig. 6.4); there is no comparison elsewhere on the island, but Kanta has noted some similarities with the cemetery at Olous (Agelarakis, Kanta, and Moody 2001, 76–77). In the same area, instead, the only known urn field is the later one at Eleutherna (Stampolidis 1996).

During the SM period, cremations were also placed inside an above-ground tholos tomb (Fig. 6.5) that was built in the Pantanassa area (Tegou 2001). It contained the corpses of two adult males, cremated at different times near the tomb itself, and accompanied by valuable goods (Fig. 6.6), including: weapons (two bronze spearheads and one iron dagger), one bronze krater, one knife, one fibula, and a pottery set composed of one jug, three stirrup jars, two amphorae, two lekythoi, and two kratcriskoi. The architectural features recall the tholoi at Karphi, but the outside of the building was less refined. The character of the burials shows some links with the cremations in the central area, not just for the presence of weapons, the exclusive choice of cremation, and the presence of Cypriot objects. Also, in this case, some grave goods (a bronze amphoroid krater and a jug of Cypriot type) attest to the existence of oversea connections, especially with Cyprus (Tegou 2001; Kanta 2003, 180–181).

These cemeteries are not related to specific settlements. Moreover, for this period only few centers are known in western Crete (for other probable settlements, see Andreadaki-Vlasaki 1991, 405–414). One of these sites, Chania (Hallager and Hallager, eds., 2000), was very powerful during LM IIIB (Kanta 1980, 288–289; Hallager 2000, 171–172) and, although downsized, it was active as a coastal site in LM IIIC (Hallager and Hallager, eds., 2000, 194). In the central-western area there were two important sites: Thronos Kephala (Rocchetti 1994; Prokopiou 1997; D'Agata 1999a), identified with Sybrita, and Chamalevri (Andreadaki-Vlazaki and Papadopoulou 2005). Thronos Kephala arose on a high site in an internal area, set in a territory connecting the northern part of the island to the Amari Valley; Chamalevri arose on a low hill near the coast. After the early LM IIIC, in line with the events taking place on the island, both Chania and Chamalevri were abandoned, but Thronos Kephala continued to grow during LM IIIC and SM until the PG period (D'Agata 1997–2000). Since the evidence in the necropoleis is insufficient, it is not possible to link the burial customs to settlement patterns, but the burials at Voliones and Atsipades show evidence that during LM IIIC, new attitudes related to accentuation of the individuality of the dead also were affirmed. The burials at Pantanassa seem to hint that during the SM period a deep change also occurred in this part of the island. Some centers increased and some groups emerged, which were interested in displaying their economic potential or their social status like other power Cretan groups.

The limited data and the lack of synchronization between the known necropoleis is not sufficient to reconstruct a comprehensive framework of the mortuary customs, but the research conducted on the sites listed above during the last decade has revealed the complexity of this region at the end of LM IIIC. In particular, the graves of Pantanassa insert this area into the political, economic, and ideological system of relationships that the prestigious burials of eastern and Central Crete are related to as well.

Concluding Remarks

Every attempt to generalize the LM IIIC Cretan funerary customs clashes with controversial archaeological evidence. This is not a novelty in Crete, which was for the whole LM IIIA a land where different traditions met and clashed. This happened, for example, during LM II–LM IIIA, when—alongside Mycenaean burial customs, which had been introduced at Knossos and then adopted over the whole of the island—Minoan tholoi were reused by elite who preferred and chose the Minoan tradition over the Mycenaean one.

The significance of the choices made in the burial customs during LM IIIC/SM, however, have to be explained while taking into account the profound crisis that the Aegean world experienced from the end of LM IIIB period that represented a turning point for Crete. The transfer of entire communities from one side of the island to the other and the arrival of Aegean people caused the meeting of various cultural traditions, and this provoked different choices and reactions in the various spheres.

The formation of mixed communities probably encouraged syncretism and perhaps modified some habits, but it is not evident that the substantial changes in Cretan society and funerary customs should necessarily be attributed to the presence of foreigners. Interpretation of the changes that occurred in LM IIIC/SM as the result of a second wave of Mycenaean settlers or of the presence of Cypriot people certainly are plausible and very interesting under many aspects.

This paper aims to contribute to the discussion, therefore, by initiating a different evaluation of the evidence, focusing above all on the mechanisms evidenced in the funerary habits of the communities that were a consequence of the continuity or discontinuity in the occupation of the land. The most innovative choices in the mortuary sphere during the LM IIIC occurred in the territories that were occupied *ex-novo*; nevertheless, new funerary customs often maintained a strong link with tradition. This is the case of the widespread adoption of the tholos. It has recently been suggested that the diffusion of the LM IIIC tholos was the effect of a "Mycenaeanization" of Crete (Tsipopoulou 2005, 327–328). The LM IIIC tholos effectively retained some features of Mycenaean tholoi, which themselves were attested on the island, as at Achladia, for example. On the mainland, instead, the tholos survived only in a few places, mostly peripheral, and it is unclear why the Mycenaeans who arrived on Crete chose just this type of grave. At this stage, the choice of the tholos could be intended as an explicit reference to a traditional model that helped the new settlers to be recognized, and one that legitimated their presence on the territory by establishing a link with the past.

Elsewhere, however, the continued use of settlements determined the maintaining of the same burial customs, with the consequent recurrence of some types of tombs or the reuse of older tombs. This fits the cemeteries of chamber tombs, but also, in my opinion, the burials in rock shelters and caves; these types of tombs had always been used on the island and must not necessarily be considered as extemporaneous or poor graves. As mentioned before, the Minoan practice of turning the burial container upside down is attested (e.g., the rock shelter at Piskokephalo Berati). This practice existed on Crete in the EM period at Voros (Marinatos 1930–1931, 150–151); during the Middle Minoan period at Sphoungaras (Hall 1912, 59), Pacheia Ammos (Seager 1916, 20), Porti (Xanthoudides 1924, 55), Malia (van Effenterre and van Effenterre 1963, 94–95), Mochlos (Seager 1912, 88–89), and Knossos (Evans 1921–1935, 585); and in LM IIIA at Siteia (Platon 1957, 340), Palaikastro (Bosanquet and Dawkins 1923, 155–156), and Malia (van Effenterre and van Effenterre 1963, 97–98). It was revived in LM IIIC at Piskokephalo Berati, in the pit tomb at Vrokastro Chavga, and in a sub-floor burial at Knossos, and it reappeared, again in the late LM IIIC in a pit tomb at Prinias, which contained a cremation. The latter burial shows the existence of an interaction between new and traditional ritual, which is attested in many cases.

The continuation of older customs demonstrates that a crawling conservatism insinuated itself into even the most innovative solutions, such as the cremation of the dead in Crete. The appearance of cremation cannot be interpreted from a unique perspective or generally evaluated as an ethnic indicator. Cremation certainly presupposes a change in the burial procedure; the preparation of the pyre and the execution of the rite created an atmosphere of strong emotional impact, and the fast destruction of the corpse had to suit a particular system of beliefs. Nevertheless, cremation coexisted with inhumation in many cemeteries of the Aegean area (Iakovidis 1970, 423–424; Lemos 2002, 186–187) and Crete. And, even if it appears as the main element of macroscopic discontinuity with the past, cremation was present in this area since the previous period. Moreover, in LM IIIC it was inserted into the traditional burial customs. Cremation emphasized gender difference, given that the cremated dead was a man; and moreover, although it was not associated with rich grave-good assemblages, it was usually found in tombs where rich men were inhumed. At Mouliana, Praisos, and Zakros, moreover, cremations were associated with a gold ring.

Nothing indicates that the cremated dead belonged to another ethnic group. At Kritsa a jaw and part of the cranium of an inhumed woman was inserted in the pyxis containing a cremated young man—an act that recalls an old Minoan custom (Murphy 1998, 35). At Praisos (and perhaps also at Kritsa) the urn with the cremation was put inside the larnax where the inhumed corpse lay, proving once again that tradition and innovation coexisted.

At present, the exact significance of cremation cannot be identified, but some considerations could be attempted. The LM IIIC cremations were confined to the area around the Mirabello Bay and the region of Siteia where, during the LM IIIC, some prestigious burials appeared that reflected an ideology typical of the older warrior graves. In these burials the dead wore gold funerary masks and had next to them offensive weapons such as swords and spears and even boar's tusk helmets and bronze vases—as in the LM IIIA Knossian tombs. Among the funerary goods, the Naue II–type sword, a new type of spear, the flasks, and some bronze vases were linked to other Aegean funerary contexts, especially Cypriot ones. In this case some scholars speculated that these burials belonged to a new generation of Aegean warriors who arrived on the island following the troubles that occurred in the Aegean. As pointed out, the ideology of the Mycenaean warriors had been assimilated by Cretan communities, which had adopted it during the LM IIIA:2–IIIB. Finally, it should not be forgotten that the warrior graves of Myrsini were placed within tombs that were continuously in use since LM IIIA and that "new" objects like the Naue II–type sword were placed in the same graves containing more typical Mycenaean swords (e.g., Sandars types F2 or D), which were widespread throughout the whole Aegean area.

The codes of representation of power acted by the Mycenaean elites have been a model for the entire Aegean. It is not surprising, then, that the LM IIIC Cretan elites used them for expressing their power. The concentration of these tombs in the eastern part of the island and near the coast, and the possession of objects typical of the elite Aegean funerary contexts could mean, instead, that during the second phase of LM IIIC in this part of the island there were groups engaging in trade and perhaps political relationships with other Aegean communities. These groups represented an elite—one that still followed burial tradition, but that gradually adopted new rituals such as cremation.

The case of Atsipades in the central-western region of the island is very different. Here, the exclusive use of cremation and the creation of an urn field shows an ideological attitude that is quite different from that attested in other parts of the island and (perhaps) not exempt from ethnic implications. The cremations attested in the central-western region assumed a different significance during the late LM IIIC and the SM period. In fact, the greater part of them did not coexist in the same grave with inhumed corpses, but they were associated with specific types of tombs and were accompanied by valuable objects and weapons. They were many cases in parts of the necropoleis that were prevalently formed by different types of tombs containing either inhumed corpses only or both inhumed and cremated dead. This form of bi-ritualism implies the existence of dichotomous choices inside the community. Some groups, in fact, openly chose different customs from the common ones. Clearly these groups also had a noticeable economical power, which was stressed at the time of the death of their members through the funeral. The deposition of the dead and all his goods on the pyre probably communicated a strong message to the society and contributed to the group's establishment of economical superiority and power.

As noted above, there are still references to local tradition, as reflected by the choice of pit-caves at Knossos. And that is why Catling has proposed the identification of the wealthy individuals buried in the North Cemetery as Cretan heroes returned home at the end of a war (Catling 1995). While remaining outside the island they would be put in touch with other Aegean warriors, with whom they maintained relations and shared political and ideological choices after they returned back home. Such an explanation could account for the similarities between the rich Aegean burials during the LM IIIC/SM periods.

The exclusive presence of male individuals in the tombs (with the exception of tombs 200–202 in the North Cemetery at Knossos) and their association with weapons, precious objects, and a few closed vases represented the *trait d'union* between the LM IIIC burials of East Crete and the LM IIIC/SM burials of western Central Crete. The main difference between them is the use of cremation. Both the LM IIIC and SM burials seem to be expressions of a specific ideology that was not new on the island (it seems similar to the one of LM II–III shaft grave tombs) and was also connected to other Cretan areas (see below) and Aegean regions (Catling 1995). This ideology emphasized the male individual and his economic power, often defining him as a warrior through the intentional deposition of weapons.

Therefore, the introduction of was perhaps determined by social reasons. The gradual transition from one rite to another means that cremation probably had no roots in different ethnic groups, but that it slowly assumed an ideological value that explicitly connected the representation of power of some men with the possession of an individual tomb and weapons and precious goods.

In conclusion, a reading from a social perspective of the change in funerary habits of the Cretan people since LM IIIC does not claim to be exhaustive, but there is no doubt that in the ideological climate of instability that characterized the island during this period, the demands for recognition and affirmation of the newborn community, the interaction between groups of different origin, and the need to build a system of cultural reference all ensured that old and new symbols and local and external traditions were subject to new elaborations, leading to new codes of social representation.

In this sense, the contribution of people who came from different parts of the island and foreigners who arrived on Crete as a consequence of Aegean micro-mobility was very important, but I think it should be regarded only as one of the elements involved. Paradoxically, in fact, in Central Crete, where the foreign presence seemed to be more conspicuous during the LM IIIC, influencing material production and also religious expression, there is no trace in the cemeteries of ethnic differentiation. Perhaps this is because there remained the presence of a strong central authority that exercised its control over various components of the social body. At the same time, powerful groups emerged from East Crete, a region studded with small towns having unstable political structures. This happened at a time when they were able to establish trade and cultural relationships with other Aegean people, consequently gaining prestige and power, which was made visible when one of them died.

The change in political conditions in western Central Crete in the late LM IIIC and SM periods determined a condition of instability together with a renewed relationship with the rest of the Aegean, and this produced the emergence of groups that then competed with each other. Some of them used the funeral, now centered on the rite of cremation, as a privileged moment of social communication during which their goods, burned on the pyre or inserted in the grave, were turned into symbols of power, underlining not only their social role within the center but also their membership in the Aegean elite.

At the beginning of the Dark Age, in short, Crete was a cultural workshop, which, through the dialectic interaction between different traditions, assumed the eclectic aspect that characterized it for several centuries.

References

Agelarakis, A., A. Kanta, and J. Moody. 2001. "Cremation Burial in LM IIIC–Sub Minoan Crete and the Cemetery at Pezoulos Atsipades," in Stampolidis, ed., 2001, pp. 69–82.

Amandry, P. 1947–1948. "Chronique des fouilles et découvertes archéologiques en Grèce en 1947," *BCH* 71–72, pp. 423–445.

Andreadaki-Vlazaki, M. 1991. "The Khania Area, ca. 1200–700 B.C.," in *La transizione dal Miceneo all'Alto Arcaismo: Dal palazzo alla città. Atti del Convegno Internazionale, Roma, 14–19 marzo 1988*, D. Musti, A. Sacconi, L. Rocchetti, M. Rocchi, E. Scafa, L. Sportiello, and M.E. Giannotta, eds., Rome, pp. 403–423.

Andreadaki-Vlazaki, M., and E. Papadopoulou. 2005. "The Habitation at Khamalevri, Rethymnon, during the 12th Century B.C.," in *Ariadne's Threads: Connections between Crete and the Greek Mainland in Late Minoan III (LM IIIA2 to LM IIIC). Proceedings of the International Workshop Held at Athens, Scuola Archeologica Italiana, 5–6 April 2003*, A.L. D'Agata and J. Moody, eds., Athens, pp. 353–397.

Belli, P. 1991. "Tholoi nell'Egeo dal II al I millennio," in *La transizione dal Miceneo all'Alto Arcaismo: Dal palazzo alla città. Atti del Convegno Internazionale, Roma, 14–19 marzo 1988*, D. Musti, A. Sacconi, L. Rocchetti, M. Rocchi, E. Scafa, L. Sportiello, and M.E. Giannotta, eds., Rome, pp. 425–450.

————. 1995. "L'architettura della tholos," in *Achladia: Scavi e ricerche della Missione greco-italiana in Creta orientale, 1991–1993* (*Incunabula Graeca* 97), M. Tsipopoulou and L. Vagnetti, eds., Rome, pp. 89–104.

————. 1997. "Architecture as Craftsmanship: LM III Tholoi and Their Builders," in Τεχνη: *Craftsmen, Craftswomen and Craftsmanship in the Aegean Bronze Age* (*Aegeum* 16), pp. 251–256.

————. 2006. "Some Architectural Features of the Two Tholos Tombs at Kritsà-Lakkoi (Eastern Crete)," in Πεπραγμένα του Θ' Διενούς Κρητολογικού Συνεδρίου Α' (2), Heraklion, pp. 271–282.

Biondi, G. Forthcoming. "Ricostruire un legame perduto: Elementi di tradizione cretese nella cultura funeraria siceliota di età arcaica," in *Atti del Convegno di Studi "Identità culturale, etnicità, processi di trasformazione a Creta fra Dark Age e Arcaismo"* (*Atene, 9–12 Novembre 2006*), Athens.

Borgna, E. 1997. "Kitchen-Ware from LM IIIC Phaistos: Cooking Traditions and Ritual Activities in LBA Cretan Societies," *SMEA* 32, pp. 189–217.

————. 2003a. *Il complesso di ceramica tardominoico III dell'Acropoli mediana di Festòs* (*Studi di archeologia cretese* 3), Padua.

————. 2003b. "Regional Settlement Patterns, Exchange Systems and Sources of Power in Crete at the End of the Late Bronze Age: Establishing a Connection," *SMEA* 45, pp. 153–183.

————. 2007. "LM IIIC Pottery at Phaistos: An Attempt to Integrate Typological Analysis with Stratigraphic Investigation," in Deger Jalkotzky and Zavadil, eds., 2007, pp. 55–72.

Bosanquet, R. 1901–1902. "Excavation at Praesos. I," *BSA* 8, pp. 231–270.

Bosanquet, R., and R.M. Dawkins. 1923. *The Unpublished Objects from the Palaikastro Excavations 1902–1906* (*BSA Suppl. Paper* 1), London.

Bouzek, J., 1985. *The Aegean, Anatolia and Europe: Cultural Interrelations in the Second Millennium B.C.* (*SIMA* 29), Göteborg.

Brock, J.K. 1957. *Fortetsa: Early Greek Tombs near Knossos*, Cambridge.

Cadogan, G. 1967. "Late Minoan IIIC Pottery from the Kephala Tholos near Knossos," *BSA* 62, pp. 257–265.

Catling, H.W. 1968. "Late Minoan Vases and Bronzes in Oxford," *BSA* 63, pp. 89–131.

————. 1995. "Heroes Returned? Subminoan Burials from Crete," in *The Ages of Homer: A Tribute to Emily Townsend Vermeule*, J.B. Carter and S.P. Morris, eds., Austin, pp. 123–136.

————. 1996a. "The Subminoan Pottery," in Coldstream and Catling, eds., 1996, pp. 295–310.

————. 1996b. "The Objects Other than Pottery in the Subminoan Tombs," in Coldstream and Catling, eds., 1996, pp. 517–637.

————. 1996c. "The Subminoan Phase in the North Cemetery at Knossos," in Coldstream and Catling, eds., 1996, pp. 641–649.

Cavanagh, W. 1996. "The Burial Customs," in Coldstream and Catling, eds., 1996, pp. 651–675.

Coldstream, J.N., and H.W. Catling, eds. 1996. *Knossos North Cemetery: Early Greek Tombs* (*BSA Suppl.* 28), 4 vols., London.

Coulson, W.D.E. 1990. *The Greek Dark Ages: A Review of the Evidence and Suggestions for Future Research*, Athens.

Coulson, W., L.P. Day, and G. Gesell. 1983. "Excavations and Survey at Kavousi, 1978–1981," *Hesperia* 52, pp. 389–420.

Coulson, W., and M. Tsipopoulou 1994. "Preliminary Investigations at Chalasmenos, Crete, 1992–93," *Aegean Archaeology* 1, pp. 65–97.

Cucuzza, N. 2002. "Osservazioni sui costumi funerari dell'area di Festòs ed Hagia Triada nel TM IIIA1–A2 iniziale," *Creta Antica* 3, pp. 133–166.

Cuozzo, M.A. 2003. *Reinventando la tradizione: Immaginario sociale, ideologie e rappresentazione nelle necropoli orientalizzanti di Pontecagnano*, Paestum.

D'Agata, A.L. 1997–2000. "Ritual and Rubbish in Dark Age Crete: the Settlement of Thronos/Kephala (Ancient Sybrita) and the Pre-Classical Roots of a Greek City," *Aegean Archaeology* 4, pp. 45–59.

————. 1999a. "Defining a Pattern of Continuity during the Dark Age in Central-Western Crete: Ceramic Evidence from the Settlement of Thronos Kephala (Ancient Sybrita)," *SMEA* 41, pp. 181–218.

————. 1999b. *Haghia Triada.* II: *Statuine minoiche e post-minoiche dai vecchi scavi di Haghia Triada (Creta)* (*Monografie della Scuola archeologica di Atene e delle missioni orientali in Oriente* 11), Padova.

————. 2001. "Religion, Society and Ethnicity on Crete at the End of the Late Bronze Age: The Contextual Framework of LM IIIC Cult Activities," in *POTNIA: Deites and Religion in the Aegean Bronze Age. Proceedings of the 8th International Aegean Conference, 12–15 April 2000, Göteborg* (*Aegeum* 22), Göteborg, pp. 346–354.

————. 2003. "Late Minoan IIIC–Subminoan Pottery Sequence at Thronos/Kephala and Its Connections with the Greek Mainland," in *LH IIIC Chronology and*

Synchronisms. Proceedings of the International Workshop Held at the Austrian Academy of Sciences at Vienna, October 29th and 30th, 2004, S. Deger-Jalkotzy and M. Zavadil, eds., Vienna, pp. 23–35.

————. 2007. "Evolutionary Paradigms and Late Minoan III: On a Definition of LM IIIC Middle," in Deger Jalkotzky and Zavadil, eds., 2007, pp. 89–118.

Davaras, C. 1964. "Ζῆρος," in "Μικραὶ σκαφικαὶ ἔρευναι περισυλλογὴ ἀρχαιοτήτον," *ArchDelt* 19 (Β', 3 Chronika), pp. 442.

————. 1973a. "Cremations in Minoan and Sub-Minoan Crete," in *Antichità Cretesi: Studi in onore di Doro Levi* (*Cronache di Archeologia* 12), Catania, pp. 158–167.

————. 1973b. "Ἀρχαιοτήτες καὶ μνημεία Ἀνατολικῆς Κρήτης," *ArchDelt* 28 (Β', 2 Chronika) [1977], pp. 585–596.

————. 1974. "Ἀρχαιοτήτες καὶ μνημεία Ἀνατολικῆς Κρήτης," *ArchDelt* 29 (Β', 3 Chronika) [1980], pp. 931–934.

————. 1976. "Ἀρχαιοτήτες καὶ μνημεία Ἀνατολικῆς Κρήτης," *ArchDelt* 31 (Β', 2 Chronika) [1984], pp. 373–382.

————. 1977. "Ἀρχαιοτήτες καὶ μνημεία Ἀνατολικῆς Κρήτης," *ArchDelt* 32 (Β', 2 Chronika) [1984], pp. 334–340.

————. 1978. "Ἀρχαιοτήτες καὶ μνημεία Ἀνατολικῆς Κρήτης," *ArchDelt* 33 (Β', 2 Chronika) [1985], pp. 385–395.

Dawkins, R.M. 1913–1914. "Excavations at Plati in Lasithi, Crete," *BSA* 20, pp. 1–17.

Day, L.P. 1997. "The Late Minoan IIIC Period at Vronda, Kavousi," in *La Crète mycénienne. Actes de la table ronde internationale organisée par l'École française d'Athènes, 28–29 mars 1991* (*BCH Suppl.* 30), J. Driessen and A. Farnoux, eds., Paris, pp. 394–406.

Day, L.P., and L.M. Snyder. 2004. "The 'Big House' at Vronda and the 'Great House' at Karphi," in *Beyond the Palaces. Proceedings of the Crete 2000 Conference* (*Prehistory Monographs* 10), L.P. Day, M.S. Mook, and J.D. Muhly, eds., Philadelphia, pp. 64–79.

Deger Jalkotzy, S., and M. Zavadil, eds. 2007. *LH IIIC Chronology and Synchronisms II: LH IIIC Middle. Proceedings of the International Workshop Held at the Austrian Academy of Sciences at Vienna, October 29th and 30th, 2004*, Vienna.

Desborough, V.R. 1972. *The Greek Dark Ages*, London.

Dickinson, O. 2006. *The Aegean from Bronze Age to Iron Age*, London and New York.

Dimopoulou, N. 1985. "Κρουσώνας," *ArchDelt* 40 (Α', Meletes), p. 297.

Dunbabin, T.J. 1947. "Antiquities of Amari," *BSA* 42, pp. 184–193.

Eliopoulos, T. 1994. "Κερά Πεδιάδος (Θέση Σιδεροκεφάλα Σταυρός)," *ArchDelt* 49 (Β', 2 Chronika), p. 748.

———. 1998. "A Preliminary Report on the Discovery of a Temple Complex of the Dark Age at Kephala Vasilikis," in *Eastern Mediterranean: Cyprus, Dodecanese, Crete, 16th–6th cent. B.C. Proceedings of the International Symposium Held at Rethymnon, Crete, in May 1997*, V. Karagheorghis and N.C. Stampolidis, eds., Athens, pp. 301–313.

Evans, A.J. 1905. "The Prehistoric Tombs of Knossos," *Archaeologia* 59, pp. 391–562.

———. 1921–1935. *The Palace of Minos at Knossos* I–V, London.

Faure, P. 1964. *Fonctions des cavernes crétoises*, Paris.

Gesell, G.C. 1985. *Town, Palace and House Cult in Minoan Crete (SIMA 67)*, Göteborg.

———. 2000. "Popular Religion in Late Minoan III Crete," in *Πεπραγμένα του Η' Διεθνούς Κρητολογικού Συνεδρίου* Α' (1), Heraklion, pp. 497–507.

Haggis, D.C. 1993. "Intensive Survey, Traditional Settlement Patterns, and Dark Age Crete: The Case of Early Iron Age Kavousi," *JMA* 6 (2), pp. 131–174.

———. 2001. "A Dark Age Settlement System in East Crete, and a Reassessment of the Definition of Refugee Settlements," in *Defensive Settlements of the Aegean and the Eastern Mediterranean after c. 1200 B.C. Proceedings of an International Workshop Held at Trinity College, Dublin, 7th–9th May 1999*, V. Karageorghis and C.E. Morris, eds., Nicosia, pp. 41–59.

Halbherr, F. 1901. "Three Cretan Necropoleis: Report on the Researches at Erganos, Panaghia, and Courtes," *AJA* 5, pp. 259–293.

Hall, E.H. 1912. *Excavations in Eastern Crete: Sphoungaras (Anthropological Publications 3.2)*, Philadelphia.

———. 1914. *Excavations in Eastern Crete: Vrokastro (Anthropological Publications 3.3)*, Philadelphia.

Hallager, B.P. 2000. "The Late Minoan IIIC Pottery," in Hallager and Hallager, eds., 2000, pp. 135–174.

Hallager, E., and B.P. Hallager, eds. 1997. *Late Minoan Pottery: Chronology and Terminology. Acts of a Meeting Held at the Danish Institute at Athens (August 12–14 1994)*, Athens.

———, eds. 2000. *The Greek-Swedish Excavations at the Agia Aikaterini Square. Kastelli Khania 1970–1987*. II: *The Late Minoan IIIC Settlement (SkrAth 4°, 47 [II])*, Stockholm.

Hayden, B.J. 2001. "Elias to Nisi: A Fortified Coastal Settlement of Possible Late Minoan IIIC Date in the Vrokastro Area, Eastern Crete," in *Defensive Settlements of the Aegean and the Eastern Mediterranean after c. 1200 B.C. Proceedings of an International Workshop Held at Trinity College, Dublin, 7th–9th May 1999*, V. Karageorghis and C.E. Morris, eds., Nicosia, pp. 61–83.

Höckmann, O. 1980. "Lanze und Speer im spätminoischen und mykenischen Griechenland," *JRGZM* 27, pp. 13–158.

Hodder, I. 1986. *Reading the Past: Current Approaches to Interpretation in Archaeology*, New York.

Hood, M.S.F., and J.N. Coldstream. 1968. "A Late Minoan Tomb at Ayios Ioannis near Knossos," *BSA* 63, pp. 205–218.

Hood, M.S.F., G. Huxley, and N. Sandars. 1958–1959. "A Minoan Cemetery on Upper Gypsades (Knossos Survey 156)," *BSA* 53–54, pp. 194–262.

Iakovidis, S. 1970. *Περατή: Το νεκροταφείον*, Athens.

Jones, S. 1997. *The Archaeology of Ethnicity*, London.

Kanta, A. 1980. *The Late Minoan III Period: A Survey of Sites, Pottery and Their Distribution* (*SIMA* 58), Göteborg.

———. 1997a. "Late Bronze Age Tholos Tombs, Origins and Evolution: The Missing Links," in *La Crète mycénienne. Actes de la table ronde internationale organisée par l'École française d'Athènes, 28–29 mars 1991* (*BCH Suppl.* 30), J. Driessen and A. Farnoux, eds., Paris, pp. 229–247.

———. 1997b. "LM IIIB and LM IIIC Pottery Phases: Some Problems of Definition," in Hallager and Hallager, eds., 1997, pp. 83–101.

———. 2001. "The Cremations of Olous and the Custom of Cremation in Bronze Age Crete," in Stampolidis, ed., 2001, pp. 59–68.

———. 2003. "Aristocrats—Traders—Emigrants—Settlers: Crete in the Closing Phases of the Bronze Age," in *Plóes: Sea Routes. . . Interconnections in the Mediterranean 16th—6th c. B.C. Proceedings of the International Symposium Held at Rethymnon, Crete, September 29th–October 2nd 2002*, N.C. Stampolidis and V. Karagheorghis, eds., Athens, pp. 173–186.

———. 2006. "Tylisos towards the End of the Bronze Age and during the Dark Ages: Elements of History for Central Crete from the Archaeological Evidence." Paper read at the 2006 Convegno di Studi "Identità culturale, etnicità, processi di trasformazione a Creta fra Dark Age e Arcaismo," 9–12 November, Athens.

Kanta, A., and K. Davaras. 2004. "The Cemetery of Krya, District of Seteia: Developments at the End of the Late Bronze Age and the Beginning of the Early

Iron Age in East Crete," in *Το Αιγαίο στην πρώιμη εποχή του Σιδήρου: Πρακτικά του Διεθνούς Συμποσίου (Ρόδος, 1–4 Νοεμβρίου 2002)*, N.C. Stampolidis and A. Ghiannikouri, eds., Athens, pp. 149–157.

Kilian-Dirlmeier, I. 1993. *Die Schwerter in Griechenland (ausserhalb der Peloponnes), Bulgarien und Albanien (Prähistorische Bronzefunde 4°, 12)*, Munich.

Lembessi, A. 1973. "Νέα Ἁλικαρνασσὸς Ἡρακλείου," *ArchDelt* 28 (Β', 2 Chronika) [1977], pp. 564–567.

Lemos, I. 2002. *Protogeometric Aegean*, Oxford.

Löwe, W. 1996. *Spätbronzezeitliche Bestattungen auf Kreta (BAR-IS 642)*, Oxford.

Marinatos, S.N. 1930–1931. "Δύο πρώϊμοι μινωϊκοὶ τάφοι ἐκ Βοροῦ Μεσαρᾶς," *ArchDelt* 13 [1934], pp. 137–170.

―――. 1931. "Μιὰ Ὑστερομινωικὴ καῦσις νεκροῦ ἐκ Τυλίσου," *AM* 56, pp. 112–118.

―――. 1931–1932. "Προτογεωμετρικὰ καὶ γεωμετρικὰ εὑρήματα ἐκ Κεντρικῆς καὶ Ἀνατολικῆς Κρήτης," *ArchDelt* 14 [1934], pp. 1–11.

Mavrighiannaki, K. 1975. "Τό νεκροταφεῖον Ἀτσιπάδων Ἁγίου Βασιλείου Ρεθύμνης," *ArchEph* 1975, pp. 41–56.

Mook, M.S., and W.D.E. Coulson. 1997. "Late Minoan IIIC Pottery from the Kastro at Kavousi," in Hallager and Hallager, eds., 1997, pp. 337–365.

Morris, C. 1987. *Burial and Ancient Society: The Rise of the Greek City-State*, Cambridge.

―――. 1992. *Death, Ritual and Social Structure in Classical Antiquity*, Cambridge.

Murphy, J.M. 1998. "Ideologies, Rites and Rituals: A View of Prepalatial Minoan Tholoi," in *Cemetery and Society in the Aegean Bronze Age*, K. Branigan, ed., Sheffield, pp. 27–40.

Musgrave, J.H. 1996. "The Human Bones," in Coldstream and Catling, eds., 1996, pp. 677–702.

Nowicki, K. 2000. *Defensible Sites in Crete ca. 1200–800 B.C.: LM IIIB/IIIC through Early Geometric (Aegaeum 21)*, Liège.

Palermo, D. 1999. "Il deposito votivo sul margine orientale della Patela di Priniàs," in *Επὶ πόντον πλαζόμενοι: Simposio Italiano di Studi Egei, dedicato a Luigi Bernabó Brea e Giovanni Pugliese*, V. La Rosa, D. Palermo, and L. Vagnetti, eds., Rome, pp. 207–213.

―――. 2003. "Haghia Triada fra il XII ed il VII secolo a.C.," *Creta Antica* 4, pp. 273–285.

————. 2006. "Culti minoici e culti greci sulla Patela di Priniàs: Aspetti di una transizione," in Πεπραγμένα του Θ' Διεθνούς Κρητολογικού Συνεδρίου Α' (3), Heraklion, pp. 355–367.

Pendlebury, H.W., J.D.S. Pendlebury, and M.B. Money-Coutts. 1937–1938. "Excavations in the Plain of Lasithi. III. Karphi: A City of Refuge of the Early Iron Age in Crete," *BSA* 38, pp. 57–145.

Perna, K. 2001. "Rituali funerari e rappresentazione del potere nella Creta del TM IIIA2/B," *Creta Antica* 2, pp. 125–138.

————. 2004. "Karfi: Soltanto un sito di rifugio?" *Creta Antica* 5, pp. 155–179.

————. 2007. "La ceramica TM IIIC dai livelli sottostanti l'edificio tripartito a Sud del tempio B," in "Lo scavo del 2005 sulla Patela di Priniàs: Relazione prelim-inare," D. Palermo, A. Pautasso, S. Rizza, S. Masala, R. Gigli Patanè, K. Perna, and G. Biondi, *Creta Antica* 8, pp. 299–302.

————. 2008. "The Rise of Pre-state Entities in Crete at the End of the Bronze Age: A Socio-Economic Perspective," in *SOMA 2005. Proceedings of the IX Symposium on Mediterranean Archaeology, Chieti (Italy), 24–26 February 2005 (BAR-IS 1739)*, A.M. Giuntella, O. Menozzi, M.L. Di Marzio, and D. Fossataro, eds., Oxford, pp. 391–398.

————. 2009. "Cultural Identity and Social Interaction in Crete at the End of the Bronze Age (LM IIIC)," in *Forces of Transformation: The End of the Bronze Age in the Mediterranean. Proceedings of an International Symposium Held at St. John's College, University of Oxford, 25–26 March, 2006*, C. Bachhuber and R.G. Roberts, eds., Oxford, pp. 37–41.

————. Forthcoming a. "Aspetti rituali e implicazioni sociali del pasto nel culto della dea con le braccia levate." Paper read at the 2005 conference "Cibo per gli uomini, cibo per gli dei: Archeologia del pasto rituale, 4–8 maggio, Piazza Armerina.

————. Forthcoming b. "Nuovi dati sull'occupazione TM IIIC della Patela di Priniàs," in Πεπραγμένα Ι' Διεθνούς Κρητολογικού Συνεδρίου, Chania, October 4–11 2006.

————. Forthcoming c. "Priniàs all'alba della Dark Age: L'evidenza ceramica," in *Atti del Convegno di Studi "Identità culturale, etnicità, processi di trasformazione a Creta fra Dark Age e Arcaismo" (Atene, 9–12 Novembre 2006)*.

Petroulakis, E. 1915. "Κρητικῆς Ἀτσιπάδας τάφοι," *ArchEph* 54, pp. 48–50.

Platon, N. 1951. "Η αρχαιολογικὴ κίνησις εν Κρήτῃ κατὰ τὸ ἔτος 1951," *CretChron* 5, pp. 438–449.

————. 1952. "Ἀνασκαφαὶ περιοχῆς Σητείας," *Prakt* 1952, pp. 630–648.

————. 1954. "Ἀνασκαφαὶ περιοχῆς Σητείας," *Prakt* 1954 , pp. 361–368.

————. 1955. "Ἀνασκαφαὶ περιοχῆς Σητείας," *Prakt* 1955 [1960], pp. 288–297.

————. 1957. "Ἡ ἀρχαιολογικὴ κίνησις εν Κρήτῃ κατὰ τὸ ἔτος 1957," *CretChron* 11, pp. 326–340.

————. 1959. "Ἡ ἀρχαιολογικὴ κίνησις εν Κρήτῃ κατὰ τὸ ἔτος 1959," *CretChron* 13, pp. 359–393.

————. 1960. "Ἀνασκαφαὶ περιοχῆς Πραισοῦ," *Prakt* 1960, pp. 294–307.

Pologhiorghi, M. 1981. "Δύο ταφές ΥΜ III περιόδου στο χωριό Βολιώνες, επαρχίας Αμαρίου," *ArchDelt* 36 (A', Meletes) [1988], pp. 82–105.

Prent, M. 2005. *Cretan Sanctuaries and Cults*, Leiden.

Preston, L. 2004. "A Mortuary Perspective on Political Changes in Late Minoan II–IIIB Crete," *AJA* 108, pp. 321–348.

Preston, L. 2005. "The Kephala Tholos at Knossos: A Study in the Reuse of the Past," *BSA* 100, pp. 61–123.

Prokopiou, N. 1997. "LM III Pottery from the Greek-Italian Excavations at Sybritos Amariou," in Hallager and Hallager, eds., 1997, pp. 371–394.

Rethemiotakis, G. 1997. "Late Minoan III Pottery from Kastelli Pediada," in Hallager and Hallager, eds., 1997, pp. 305–365.

Rizza, G. 1996. "Priniàs in età micenea," in *Atti e Memorie del secondo Congresso internazionale di micenologia, Roma-Napoli, 14–20 ottobre 1991 (Incunabula Graeca 98)*, E. De Miro, L. Godart, and A. Sacconi, eds., Rome, pp. 1101–1110.

————. Forthcoming. "Identità, etnicità, processi di trasformazione a Priniàs," in *Atti del Convegno di Studi "Identità culturale, etnicità, processi di trasformazione a Creta fra Dark Age e Arcaismo," Atene, 9–12 Novembre 2006*.

Rizza, G., and M.A. Rizzo. 1984. "Priniàs," in *Creta antica: Cento anni di archeologia italiana, 1884–1984*, Rome, pp. 227–256.

Rocchetti, L. 1994. "Sybrita: Lo scavo," in *Sybrita: La valle di Amari fra bronzo e ferro*, L. Rocchetti, ed., Rome, pp. 237–248.

Sackett L.H., M.R. Popham, and P.M. Warren. 1965. "Excavations at Palaikastro VI," *BSA* 60, pp. 248–315.

Sapouna-Sakellaraki, E. 1978. *Die Fibeln der griechischen Inseln (Prähistorische Bronzefunde 14°, 4)*, Munich.

————. 1990. "Archanès à l'époque mycénienne," *BCH* 114, pp. 67–102.

Savignoni, L. 1904. "Scavi e scoperte nella necropoli di Phaestòs," *MonAnt* 14, cols. 500–666.

Seager, R.B. 1906–1907. *Report of Excavations at Vasiliki, Crete in 1906* (*University of Pennsylvania Transactions of the Department of Archaeology, Free Museum of Science and Art* 2), Philadelphia.

———. 1912. *Explorations in the Island of Mochlos*, New York.

———. 1916. *The Cemetery of Pachyammos, Crete*, Philadelphia.

Seiradaki, M. 1960. "Pottery from Karphi," *BSA* 55, pp. 1–37.

Snodgrass, A. 1964. *Early Greek Armour and Weapons*, Edinburgh.

———. 1971. *The Dark Age of Greece*, Edinburgh.

Stampolidis, N.C. 1996. *Αντίποινα: Συμβολή στη μελέτη των ηθών και των εθίμων της γεωμετρικής περιόδου* (*Eleutherna* 3.3), Rethymnon.

Stampolidis, N.C., ed. 2001. *Καύσεις στην Εποχή του Χαλκού και την Πρώιμη Εποχή του Σιδήρου. Πρακτικά του Συμποσίου (Ρόδος, 29 Απριλίου–2 Μαΐου 1999)*, Athens.

Taramelli, A. 1899. "Ricerche archeologiche cretesi," *MonAnt* 9, pp. 297–446.

Tegou, E. 2001. "Θολωτός τάφος της πρώιμης Εποχής του Σιδήρου στην Παντάνασσα Αμαρίου Ν. Ρεθύμνης," in Stampolidis, ed., 2001, pp. 121–153.

Tsipopoulou, M. 1983. "Ταφική σπελιά στον Άγιο Σπυρίδονα Σητείας," *ArchDelt* 38 (A', Meletes) [1990], pp. 78–104.

———. 2005. "'Mycenoans' at the Isthmus of Ierapetra: Some (Preliminary) Thoughts on the Foundation of the (Eteo)Cretan Cultural Identity," in *Ariadne's Threads: Connections between Crete and the Greek Mainland in Late Minoan III (LM IIIA2 to LM IIIC). Proceedings of the International Workshop Held at Athens, Scuola Archeologica Italiana, 5–6 April 2003*, A.L. D'Agata and J. Moody, eds., Athens, pp. 303–333.

Tsipopoulou, M., and L. Little. 2001. "Καύσεις του τέλους της εποχής του Χαλκού στην Κριτσά Μιραμπέλου, Ανατολική Κρήτη," in Stampolidis, ed., 2001, pp. 83–98.

Tsipopoulou, M., and L. Vagnetti. 1997. "Ricerche greco-italiane in Creta orientale (Kritsà Mirabello): Campagna 1997," *SMEA* 39, pp. 281–282.

———. 2003. "New Evidence for the Dark Ages in Eastern Crete: An Unplundered Tholos Tomb at Vasiliki," *SMEA* 45, pp. 85–124.

van Effenterre, H. 1948. *Nécropoles du Mirabello* (*ÉtCrét* 8), Paris.

van Effenterre H., and M. van Effenterre. 1963. *Fouilles exécutées à Mallia* (*ÉtCrét* 13), Paris.

Wallace, S.A. 2003a. "The Changing Role of Herding in the Early Iron Age of Crete: Some Implications of Settlement Shift for Economy," *AJA* 107, pp. 601–628.

———. 2003b. "The Perpetuated Past: Re-Use or Continuity in Material Culture and the Structuring of Identity in Early Iron Age Crete," *BSA* 98, pp. 251–277.

———. 2005. "Last Chance to See? Karfi (Crete) in the Twenty-first Century: Presentation of New Architectural Data and Their Analysis in the Current Context of Research," *BSA* 100, pp. 215–274.

———. 2006. "The Gilded Cage? Settlement and Socioeconomic Change after 1200 B.C.: A Comparison of Crete and Other Aegean Regions," in *Ancient Greece: From the Mycenaean Palaces to the Age of Homer* (*Edinburgh Leventis Studies* 3), S. Deger-Jalkotzy and I.S. Lemos, eds., Edinburgh, pp. 619–664.

Walter, O. 1942. "Griechenland von Früjhar 1940 bis herbst 1941," *AA* 1942, cols. 99–258.

Warren, P.M. 1982–1983. "Knossos: Stratigraphical Museum Excavations, 1978–82. Part II," *AR* 29, pp. 63–87.

———. 2007. "Characteristics of Late Minoan IIIC from the Stratigraphical Museum Site at Knossos," in Deger Jalkotzky and Zavadil, eds., 2007, pp. 329–343.

Watrous, L.V. 1977. "Aegean Settlements and Transhumance," *TUAS* 2, pp. 2–6.

———. 1980. "J.D.S. Pendlebury's Excavations in the Plain of Lasithi: The Iron Age," *BSA* 75, pp. 169–283.

Whitley, J. 1991. "Social Diversity in Dark Age Greece," *BSA* 86, pp. 341–365.

Xanthoudides, S. 1904. "From Crete," *ArchEph* 1904 [1905], pp. 1–56.

———. 1924. *The Vaulted Tombs of Mesara*, London.

7 | Regionalism in Early Iron Age Cretan Burials

MELISSA EABY

The Early Iron Age (EIA) on Crete represents an important phase of cultural change, comprising the years after the final collapse of the pala-tial system in Late Minoan (LM) IIIB up to the development of the city-state before or during the Archaic period.* Over the course of this period, significant changes occurred in settlement patterns, settlement forms, ritual contexts, and most strikingly, in burial practices (e.g., Nowicki 2000; Borgna 2003; Wallace 2003b; Prent 2005). Early Iron Age burial practices varied extensively throughout Crete, not only from region to region, but also often at a single site. For example, both inhumation and cremation, as well as single and multiple burial, were practiced on the island during this period (Fig. 7.1) In addition, numerous distinct tomb types were used, including the tholos tomb, chamber tomb, pseudotho-los tomb, pit grave, pit-cave, shaft grave, cist grave, burial enclosure, burial in natural caves and rock shelters, pithos burial, mounds/pyres, intramural burial, open burials, and cremation under a cairn of stones (Figs. 7.2, 7.3) (cf. Snodgrass 1971, 142–143). Furthermore, a signifi-cant number of EIA burials have been identified on the island thus far

*This paper is derived from my doctoral dissertation (Eaby 2007). Funding for my research was pro-vided by the Fulbright Foundation, the Archaeological Institute of America, and the University of North Carolina at Chapel Hill.

(e.g., Pendlebury 1939; Pini 1968; Snodgrass 1971; Desborough 1972; Kanta 1980; Tsipopoulou 1984, 1987, 2005; Sjögren 2001); roughly 1,200 EIA tombs have been found in the vicinity of approximately 122 modern villages or towns (Fig. 7.1). An examination of the burial methods, architecture, assemblages, and spatial contexts of these tombs and cemeteries provides new evidence regarding the extent of cultural diversity present on the island during this period.

Although numerous tomb types existed on EIA Crete, several were very limited in use, appearing at only one or two sites; for example, true shaft graves and pit-caves occurred only at Subminoan (SM) Knossos (Coldstream and Catling, eds., 1996), intramural burial of children or infants only at Late Minoan (LM) IIIC–SM Knossos (Warren 1983, 73, 80) and Vrokastro (Hall 1914, 106, 112), and open burials and mounds/pyres only at Eleutherna in the Early Orientalizing (EO) period and later (Stampolidis 1993, 1994). Cremation under a small cairn of stones, pseudotholoi, and true cist graves also appeared relatively infrequently (Eaby 2007, 32–325, 332). Thus, these tomb types are of limited value when seeking regional patterns within the funerary material. This paper therefore focuses on the evidence presented by the most common tomb types—primarily tholos tombs, but also chamber tombs, caves and rock shelters, pithos burials, pit graves, and burial enclosures.

The tholos tomb is perhaps the most significant tomb type for understanding regionalism in EIA burials and requires further definition (see also Pendlebury 1939, 306–308; Belli 1991, 439–450; Kanta 1997; Kanta and Karetsou 1998, 170). Two distinct types of tholos tomb were used in EIA Crete (Eaby 2007, 197–264; 2009)—small (type one) and large (by EIA standards, type two). The two tholos types differ from each other in that type one tombs have square, rectangular, circular, and ellipsoidal chambers of small diameter (<2.5 m) built of irregular, un-worked fieldstones, while type two tombs are exclusively circular in plan with diameters >2.5 m, especially 3 m or more. In addition, the large tombs tend to be of much better craftsmanship than the smaller examples with more regular, rectangular courses of stone. A total of over 200 EIA tholos tombs are known from as many as 49 sites on the island (Fig. 7.4); most of these tombs (ca. 85%) are of the first type, while the second type is much rarer, occurring at only nine possible sites with 12–15 total known examples (Fig. 7.5). Furthermore, the majority of small examples were constructed

Figure 7.1. Map of EIA burial sites on Crete (* indicates sites at which the presence of EIA tombs is uncertain; site numbers correspond to the catalog numbers in Eaby 2007). (1) Hagios Georgios Papoura, (2) Kaminaki*, (3) Karphi, (4) Lagou*, (5) Mesa Lasithi*, (6) Plati*, (7) Adrianos, (9) Anavlochos, (10) Dreros, (11) Kastri, (12) Kritsa, (13) Milatos, (14) Olous*, (15) Vrachasi, (16) Vrokastro, (17) Zenia, (18) Hagios Ioannis, (19) Braimiana, (20) Chalasmenos, (21) Episkopi, (22) Kalamaphka, (23) Kavousi, (24) Meseleroi, (25) Parsa, (26) Schoinokapsala, (27) Vasiliki, (28) Achladia (offerings only), (29) Adromyloi, (30) Hagios Georgious (Tourtouloi), (31) Hagia Photia (offerings only), (32) Hagios Spyridon, (33) Hagios Stephanos, (34) Chamaizi, (35) Chandras, (36) Itanos, (37) Karydi, (38) Koutsouras*, (39) Krya, (40) Lastros, (41) Makrygialos, (42) Mesa Mouliana, (43) Mochlos (offerings only), (44) Myrsini, (45) Orino, (46) Palaikastro, (47) Pefkoi, (48) Piskokephalo, (49) Praisos, (50) Sklavoi, (51) Skopi, (52) Sphakia, (53) Tourloti, (54) Zakros, (55) Zou, (56) Hagia Deka, (57) Ampelouzos, (58) Gortyn, (59) Kourtes, (60) Petrokephali, (61) Valis*, (62) Hagia Marina, (63) Hagia Pelagia, (64) Kavrochori, (65) Krousonas, (66) Prinias, (67) Stavrakia, (68) Tylissos, (69) Arkalochori, (70) Ligortynos, (71) Rotasi, (72) Hagies Paraskies, (73) Aitania, (74) Alitzani, (75) Anopolis, (76) Arkades, (77) Elia, (78) Episkopi, (79) Erganos, (80) Gonies*, (81) Kato Vatheia, (82) Kounavoi, (83) Koxari, (84) Krasi, (85) Lyttos*, (86) Malia, (87) Nipiditos*, (88) Panagia, (89) Smari, (90) Stamnioi, (91) Vatheianos Kambos*, (92) Zinda, (93) Hagia Triada (offerings only), (94) Kamares, (95) Kamilari (burials and offerings), (96) Phaistos, (97) Sivas*, (98) Hagios Syllas*, (99) Hagios Vlasis*, (100) Archanes, (101) Herakleion, (102) Katsamba, (103) Knossos, (104) Mt. Juktas, (105) Nea Halikarnassos, (106) Phoinikia, (107) Prophetes Elias, (108) Tsangaraki, (109) Arvi*, (110) Viannos, (111) Atsipades, (112) Koxare*, (113) Orne, (114) Mesonisia*, (115) Pantanassa, (116) Thronos*, (117) Eleutherna, (118) Mesi*, (119) Rethymnon, (120) Aptera, (121) Astrikas, (122) Gavalomouri, (123) Kavousi, (124) Kissamos, (125) Vouves, (126) Chania, (127) Modi, (128) Mousouras, (129) Vryses.

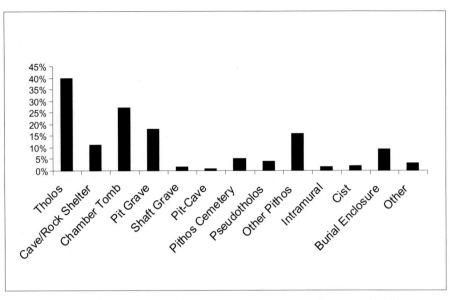

Figure 7.2. Relative frequency of EIA tomb types by percentage of sites at which they appear.

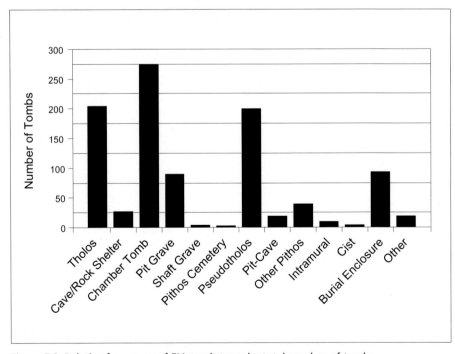

Figure 7.3. Relative frequency of EIA tomb types by total number of tombs.

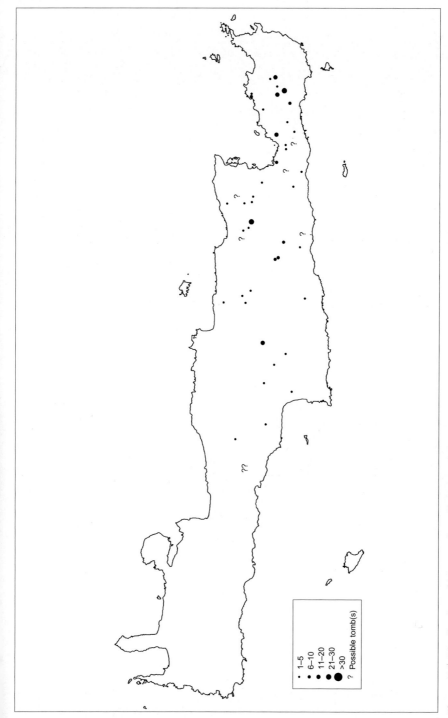

Figure 7.4. Distribution of large and small tholos tombs.

1–5
6–10
11–20
21–30
>30
? Possible tomb(s)

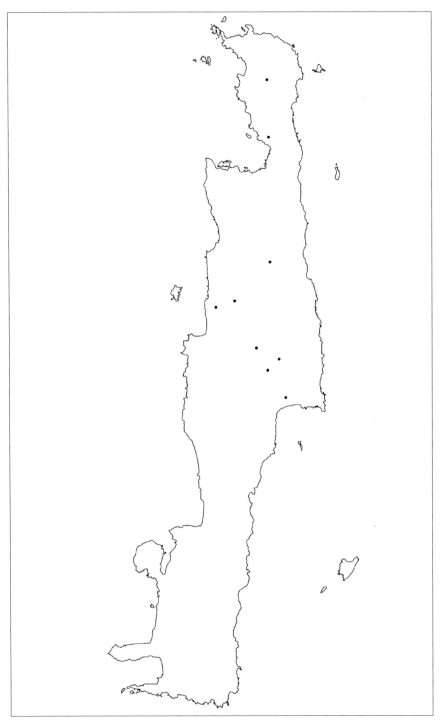

Figure 7.5. Distribution of large tholos tombs.

in LM IIIC–SM and only used for a brief period of time, though a limited number of tombs were constructed or continued to be used in the Protogeometric (PG) and Geometric (G) periods; the earliest examples of the large type, however, date to PG in Central Crete and Late Geometric (LG) in eastern Crete (Fig. 7.6).

The EIA is defined here as ca. 1200–700 B.C., encompassing the LM IIIC–EO periods (cf. Nowicki 2000, 16–17, 223–247; Whitley 2001, 60–74; Tsipopoulou 2005; Dickinson 2006, 10–23). In this analysis, the dates for tombs and cemeteries are derived primarily from published material (i.e., original excavation reports and more recent analyses when available). Whenever possible, precise dates or ceramic phases are used, though the vast majority of burial sites can be only broadly dated due to the nature of the evidence (e.g., a high degree of tomb robbing, poor publishing and inconsistent recording, or the presence of only a single tomb from a site). In addition, while the majority of tombs have been at least partially excavated, burials from many sites are merely inferred on the basis of survey information or chance finds brought to a museum. Despite the limitations of the data, a study of the existing evidence reveals clear overall trends in mortuary behavior on the island during the EIA.

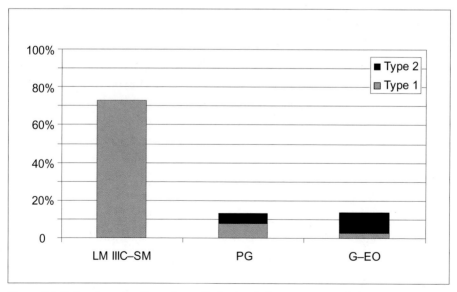

Figure 7.6. Date of construction of new tholos tombs by percentage of sites.

Crete was characterized by profound regionalism in the EIA. In previous discussions, the island has been divided into two large regional groups (West/Central and East) on the basis of ceramic styles (Coldstream 1968, 258; 1977, 275; Snodgrass 1971, 164; Desborough 1972, 234; Tsipopoulou 2005, 547; see also Nowicki 1994, 238); in these studies, the division between Central and eastern Crete is generally considered to occur at the mountain passage near modern Neapolis, with the Lasithi Plateau thus being more closely associated with Central Crete. The basic division between the central and eastern parts of the island has been maintained in recent investigations of EIA settlement patterns (Borgna 2003) and cult dedications (Prent 2003, 2005), though in these studies the Lasithi area is typically considered to be more closely associated with the east. In addition, scholars such as Pendlebury (1939), Nowicki (2000), and Sjögren (2001, 2003) have used geography as a means of examining settlement patterns or identifying culture-regions on the island. One goal of this paper is to supplement these recent studies by investigating patterns of regionalism in EIA Crete as revealed by the funerary material.

In addition to the basic division between Central and eastern Crete observed in recent ceramic, settlement, and cult studies, I have been able to identify six distinct mortuary regions (Lasithi, far eastern, Mirabello/West Siteia Mountains, Central, west-central, and far western Crete) and three border (or transition) zones on the island (Figs. 7.7, 7.8). Factors such as sociopolitical organization, cultural identity, previous tradition in a region, settlement type, and the development of the city-state/urban nucleated center appear to have played important roles in creating mortuary regionalism on the island during the EIA. In this paper, I examine each of the six EIA mortuary regions separately. I first define each region, briefly summarizing its characteristics. I then offer preliminary observations regarding the significance of these regional distinctions, focusing on the evidence provided by the most common tomb types, in particular the tholos tomb. Due to space limitations, the emphasis here is primarily on tomb type, and only to a limited extent on burial type and grave goods; a more detailed examination of grave goods may be found in my dissertation (Eaby 2007) and is the subject of future research.

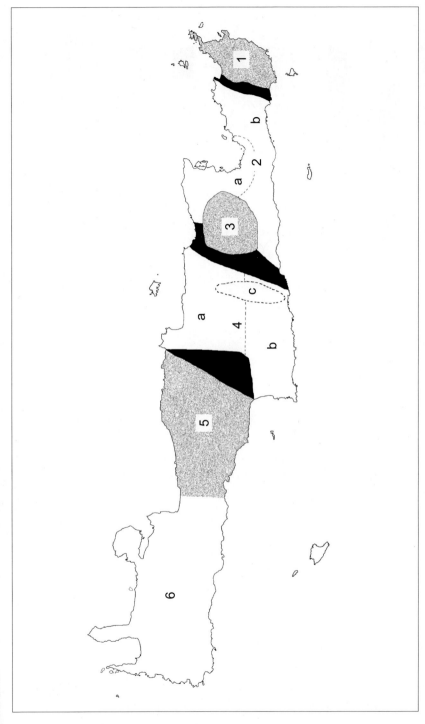

Figure 7.7. Potential EIA burial regions. (1) Far eastern, (2) Mirabello/West Siteia Mountains, (3) Lasithi, (4) Central, (5) West-Central, (6) Far western.

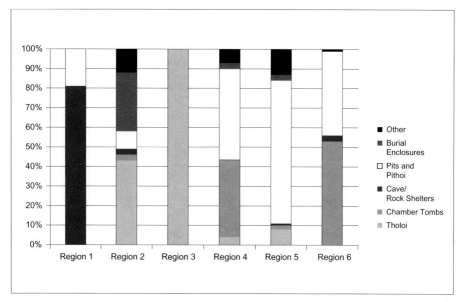

Figure 7.8. Relative frequency of EIA tomb types by region.

Lasithi

Over 35 EIA tombs have been confirmed thus far from six sites (Hagios Georgios Papoura, Karphi, Krasi, Kastri, Zenia, and Adrianos) in the Lasithi Plateau (Fig. 7.7, region 3; Eaby 2007, 23–28, 31, 36, 47–48, 126–128). In terms of mortuary practices, this region is very homogeneous. For example, all known burials were found in small tholos tombs, and all tombs appear to have held a small number of inhumations, usually between one and five individuals. In addition, all Lasithi tholoi appear to have shared a characteristic feature—the masonry enclosure (defined by Pendlebury [1939, 308] as a mass of rough masonry approximately square in shape covering the exterior of the tomb on three sides); only a limited number of tholos tombs outside this region are known to have had masonry enclosures. Furthermore, with the exception of Hagios Georgios Papoura, all of these tombs date to LM IIIC (and sometimes into SM) and were associated with short-term defensible settlements (Nowicki 2000). No known polis developed in this area, though Papoura became a relatively large town in the later part of the period (Sjögren 2001, 123–124).

While minor architectural variations do exist among these small tholoi, such as chamber shape and size, stomion dimensions, presence or lack of a dromos, orientation, location, architectural features (i.e., built facades, monolithic lintels, door jambs, thresholds) and/or better construction (more regular coursing), as well as number and type of grave goods, the overall similarity of the Lasithi tombs and their contents, both within and among the sites, is the most prominent feature. This overall homogeneity, which is distinct from the pattern observed at several other regions on the island, could have resulted from the presence of limited to no social stratification at these sites at the beginning of the EIA. For much of LM IIIC–SM Crete, in fact, a relatively loose sociopolitical organization, more egalitarian than hierarchical, is assumed to have existed, with the household or extended family forming the basic unit, though with some differentiation of wealth possibly present (Haggis 1993, 151; Nowicki 2000, 226–227, 250; Prent 2005, 615–623). The architecture of the associated defensible settlements can also be interpreted as reflecting very little or no social stratification, as the houses show only slight differences in size or construction techniques (Nowicki 2000, 237–239).

The overall picture may be slightly more complicated, however. Although no clear correlation exists between specific architectural features and tomb size, date, or location, there may have been a minor association between tomb size and wealth; for example, the slightly larger-sized small tholoi (e.g., M.4 and 8 at Karphi; Pendlebury, Pendlebury, and Money-Coutts 1937–1938, 102–105) appear to have been slightly wealthier in grave goods than other tombs. These larger tombs thus potentially could have been distinguished from others in a cemetery, perhaps reflective of differing levels of social status, though more likely of greater wealth or larger family size (Nowicki 2000, 237–239); in fact, those slightly larger tholoi tended to have a greater number of burials than other tombs. In addition, Wallace (2005, 252–255) sees the slightly larger houses at Karphi as belonging to the largest or most powerful families of the settlement. While the minor distinctions in house and tomb size do not appear to mark clear social diversity in LM IIIC–SM, they may have led to its development later on. There is, however, no clear evidence in settlement or tomb architecture for "big man" organization in this region during the EIA, though the existence of some form of ranking or the presence of elites remains possible even if not clearly revealed in the settlements or burials (Haggis 1993, 151; Nowicki 2000, 238–239; Day and Snyder 2004; Prent 2005, 120–126; cf. Whitley 1991; Borgna 2003, 164–168).

The large number of small tholos tombs (several dozen or more are estimated at Karphi alone) and the lack of a single example of another tomb type imply that this was the standard tomb form for the Lasithi area in the EIA. In this area, the small tholos tomb was clearly not a form of burial used exclusively by elites, although, if elites existed, they would have been buried in these tombs as well. The consistent use of the tholos tomb in this region could reflect a conscious local or community effort to retain an old or create a new cultural identity, rather than a method of distinguishing certain groups of people or elite families within the community (cf. Wallace 2006, 643). On the one hand, the EIA small tholos tomb can be seen as reflecting a traditional "Minoan" form of burial, the descendant of the Early Minoan (EM) large circular structures (Belli 1991; Kanta 1997; Kanta and Karetsou 1998, 170); the EIA inhabitants could thus have deliberately chosen this tomb type as a means of showing a continuing link to the past or of distinguishing themselves from others outside the region, especially the neighboring inhabitants of Central Crete. On the other hand, the use of a single tomb type may have been related to the fact that all of the associated settlements in this area were founded at roughly the same time. In fact, the very limited differentiation of the buildings and tombs could be related to the formation of a new community identity; social cohesion would have been important in these newly formed communities, and "proscriptions on extreme differentiation" may have existed with respect to architecture (Wallace 2005, 252–253).

In contrast to other areas on the island, the Lasithi region is most prominent in its lack of variation in mortuary practices. No clear evidence of social stratification or complex political organization exists in the burials from this area, but it is true that burials are not necessarily direct reflections of such features. Although the slightly larger tholos tombs may reflect small distinctions in family size, wealth, or status, their exact significance remains unclear. Regardless, it does not appear that burials were used in this region as avenues for display or as obvious status symbols; rather, the consistent use of a single tomb type and method of interment may reflect an adherence to old traditions or an attempt to create a new community/regional identity in the midst of the changes resulting from the collapse of the Late Minoan palatial system.

Far Eastern Crete

A minimum of 15 EIA tombs are known from at least five sites in far eastern Crete: Itanos, Karydi, Palaikastro, Zakros, and Zou (Fig. 7.7, region 1; Eaby 2007, 72, 81, 93–95). At the majority of sites in this region, burials have been found thus far only in caves and rock shelters (e.g., Faure 1964, 66–69). The caves and rock shelters are rarely altered (i.e., given architectural features), the method of interment is inhumation (usually multiple), and the grave goods are typically poor. In addition, the use of this tomb type does not appear to be confined to any particular phases within the EIA. The final burial site in this region is coastal Itanos, where a few LG cremation burials in pits, apparently placed in a clearly designated cemetery area, have been identified (Greco et al. 1997, 817–818). Itanos is exceptional for this region in that it was founded at a late date and ultimately (by the early 5th century at the latest, though probably much earlier) became a polis (Sjögren 2003, 102–103). The associated settlements of many caves and rock shelters are unknown, however, and the burials themselves tend to be in relatively isolated locations; while the Zakros burials were associated with a defensible settlement, the burials from the other sites may have been associated either with similar inaccessible sites with small farms and hamlets (Nowicki 2000, 46–48, 54–55; Sjögren 2001, 129).

As in the Lasithi Plateau, far eastern Crete also reveals a high level of homogeneity in its mortuary practices, but the sample of known burials is admittedly much smaller. Burial in caves and rock shelters was a traditional "Minoan" practice in far eastern Crete (Faure 1964, 51–80; Branigan 1970, 152–154), and this tomb type may have been an easy choice, given the frequency with which caves and rock shelters naturally occur in this area. Like the Lasithi Plateau, with its small tholos tombs, the far eastern region may have held on to traditional practices for the longest period of time, perhaps being an area for refugees from other locations after new people or outside influences came, especially from the mainland (Nowicki 2000, 235–241). The use of caves and rock shelters for burial in the EIA clearly distinguishes this area from Central Crete, where caves were used primarily in this period for religious or cult practices and not for burial (Prent 2005, 615–623). The burial practices of far eastern Crete in the EIA may also reflect the fact that the region was characterized by a different settlement pattern than that observed farther west, with small farms and hamlets apparently being more predominant than defensible settlements. The use of caves in relatively isolated locations could also potentially reflect a greater role of pastoralism in this area (e.g., Wallace 2003a).

Throughout much of the EIA in far eastern Crete, it would appear that limited social diversity and a relatively simple sociopolitical organization existed among those individuals using caves and rock shelters for burial. This is supported by the consistency of tomb type, burial method, and poor grave goods, as well as the fact that this tomb type requires no labor and is easily accessible and reusable. As the evidence is limited, it cannot be definitively stated whether or not this tomb type was used by the entire population of the area in the EIA. At Zakros this tomb type appears to represent the characteristic form of burial, with at least 10 known examples (Tsipopoulou 2005, 221–223). Zakros Koukou Kephali Tomb A (Hogarth 1900–1901, 148), however, may be distinguished from others at the site in the number of burials and relative wealth of grave goods, including the only known iron objects from a cave or rock shelter burial, as well as its location at the mouth of the gorge rather than inside where most of the other burials are found. This noteworthy tomb thus may hint at minor differences in wealth, family size, or status level, as also potentially seen in certain Lasithi tombs (Hogarth 1900–1901, 148).

Aside from the Koukou Kephali tomb, no evidence exists in the known far eastern burials for increasing social complexity or changing sociopolitical organization over the course of the period; there is no apparent precursor to the sudden appearance at Itanos in LG of pit graves with cremations. With the exception of Itanos, the burials in far eastern Crete are characterized by their lack of variation throughout the EIA. Unfortunately, the limited nature of the evidence makes any conclusions about social complexity, political organization, or the exact nature of a possible regional identity extremely tentative for this area. It is possible, however, that the consistent use of a traditional tomb type and method of burial may reveal a desire to maintain an old regional identity or create a new one, as also suggested for the Lasithi tombs.

Border Zone between Far Eastern Crete and Mirabello/West Siteia Mountains

Unlike most sites in the far eastern area, those located on the border between far eastern Crete and the West Siteia Mountains (in the vicinity of the modern north–south road from Siteia to Ierapetra) show a much greater variety in tomb type, method of interment, and wealth of grave goods. The modern road is placed along one of the traditional communication routes for this area—its location being dictated primarily by topography—and the associated sites are thus notable for their close proximity to this transportation or communication route. As many as 50 tombs from up to seven sites have been identified in this area (Eaby 2007, 66–69, 72, 76, 83–92). Among these sites, small tholos tombs were the primary form of burial at Sphakia (Platon 1955a, 292–296) and Praisos (in the beginning of the period), though Praisos also had burials in rock shelters and caves, burial enclosures, chamber tombs, a pit or shaft grave, and a large tholos tomb. In contrast to other sites in the area, the basic form of the city-state appears to have been established at Praisos by the end of the period (Whitley, Prent, and Thorne 1999, 253). Clear distinctions may also have existed in the use of different tomb types; for example, the cave burials found in the vicinity of this site appear to be dispersed from other tomb types and distinguished by a "more restricted range of grave goods" (Whitley, Prent, and Thorne 1999, 245–253, 260–261). The tradition of cave burial also existed at Piskokephalo (Platon 1952, 639–642; 1953, 292–293), though this site stands out from those found in the far east in that both inhumation and cremation were practiced and the grave goods were relatively wealthy (by cave standards, at least). Finally, the burials at Hagios Georgios (Tourtouloi) were placed primarily in rock-cut chamber tombs and a small number of tholoi of EO date (Tsipopoulou 1987, 259; 2005, 126–193). The use of the chamber tomb was unusual for eastern Crete in the EIA, though it was the primary form of burial at this site in LM III, and the late date of the small tholos tombs is also atypical for Crete in general.

The diversity in mortuary practices observed at sites in the border zone could represent a confluence of traditions, perhaps the movement of various peoples or extra-regional cultural influences. For example, while no definite imports have been recovered from the far eastern cave and rock shelter burials, many imports are present among the grave goods from the sites located near the main transportation route, as would be expected. Also, even in LM III, the population living in the vicinity of the transportation routes was likely mixed and heterogeneous, with Minoan, Mycenaean, and possibly Cypriot elements influenced by factors such as trade, travel, immigration, and native population (see Borgna 2003, 156 for additional references). The burial sites found in this border zone were thus likely influenced by the tradition of burial in small tholos tombs found immediately to the west in the Siteia mountains, the "Minoan" tradition of burial in caves and rock shelters found farther east, as well as the mixed Minoan and Mycenaean tradition of the area, as illustrated, for example, in the continuation of the LM III tradition of chamber tombs at Hagios Georgios.

Mirabello and West Siteia Mountains

Thus far, over 230 EIA tombs have been identified at more than 31 sites in the West Siteia Mountains and Mirabello area (Fig. 7.7, region 2a, b; Eaby 2007, 32–66, 68, 70–83, 91–92, 171–172). This region is characterized by a greater variety of tomb types than the Lasithi Plateau or far eastern Crete. For example, chamber tombs or pit graves were the only tomb types found at Tourloti, Myrsini, Episkopi, and Milatos during the EIA, though the majority of these burials appear to date to the final phases of use in a LM IIIA–IIIC cemetery (Kanta 1980, 125–128, 146–160, 163–173); these tombs would thus represent the end of the old, pre-EIA tradition, rather than EIA-constructed tombs for a new defensible settlement. There was also a very limited presence of pits (LG Meseleroi) and pseudotholoi (Krya and possibly Meseleroi) in this region. In addition, a single burial cave or rock shelter was found at Lastros, Hagios Stephanos,

Orino, Pefkoi, Vrokastro, and Parsa (Faure 1964, 66–69). Small tholos tombs, however, characterized the majority of sites in this area (e.g., Hagios Ioannis, Chalasmenos, Schoinokapsala, Chamaizi, Skopi, Mesa Mouliana, Adromyloi, Vasiliki, Viannos, Kalamaphka, Braimiana, Kritsa, Orino, Pefkoi, Krya, and possibly Arvi); some of these tholoi were distinguished from examples found in the Lasithi Plateau by the use of cremation, though inhumation remained the dominant form of interment. In addition, nearly all sites in this region were associated with defensible settlements, many of which remained inhabited throughout the EIA (Nowicki 2000).

A significant exception in this region is the site of Kavousi, which has one large and several small tholos tombs, burial enclosures, cremations under cairns of stone, and a pithos burial (Boyd 1901; Gesell, Day, and Coulson 1995). Several other sites also display burial practices somewhat distinct from those found in the rest of the region. At Dreros (van Effenterre 1948), Anavlochos (Demargne 1931, 368–379), and Vrokastro (Hall 1914, 124–168), the earliest tombs appear to have been small tholos tombs; as early as Protogeometric B (PGB), however, a change occurs at these locations to primarily burial enclosures, though none of the above sites has a tholos of the large type. In addition, the shift in burial type was accompanied by a change in interment practice from primarily inhumation to cremation. The burial enclosure may, in fact, represent an eastern regional type for northern Mirabello in the second half of the EIA (see area 2a on Fig. 7.7); this same tomb type later appears at Kavousi (Gesell, Coulson, and Day 1991, 148–167; Gesell, Day, and Coulson 1995, 70–90) in the Middle/Late Geometric period and possibly at Praisos (Tsipopoulou 1987, 265) in the EO period.

Although a greater variety of tomb types is present in Mirabello and the West Siteia Mountains than in other eastern regions, the majority of sites show an overall similarity at the beginning of the EIA in their adherence to old traditions, manifested especially in the predominant use of the small tholos tomb and the limited use of caves and rock shelters. Most small tholos tombs in this region appear to show little diversity in tomb construction and grave goods in LM IIIC–SM, a feature also seen in the Lasithi Plateau. A few tombs at only a handful of sites, however, stand out in wealth of grave goods during this early phase. The Mesa Mouliana tholoi (Xanthoudides 1904, 21–52) and a single tomb from Praisos

Photoula (Platon 1960, 302–305), for example, are especially noteworthy in the richness of their contents. While the owners of these tombs may have been warriors or local chieftains, the early LM IIIC date of the burials could actually reflect the final phase of the previous (LM IIIA–IIIB) "Mycenaean" hierarchy, rather than complex social stratification at the beginning of the EIA (Nowicki 2004, 277–279; cf. Kanta 2003). For the majority of sites in the Mirabello/West Siteia Mountain region, however, the overall similarities in the funerary material reveal no clear evidence of ranking or elites during LM IIIC–SM.

Many of the defensible sites in the Mirabello/West Siteia Mountain region were abandoned by or during the PG period (Nowicki 2000, 241–247; Wallace 2003b, 256–262). Clear changes begin to occur in mortuary practices at many of the continuing sites, however, as early as PG; for example, one or more tholos tombs, apparently PG or later, from Adromyloi (Platon 1954a, 365–368), Chamaizi (Davaras 1972, 44–45), and Vrokastro (Hall 1914, 124–153) appear to have been slightly larger in size and significantly more wealthy than the other tholoi at the site. Unfortunately, the individual tombs from two of these sites have not been adequately published and their chronology and contents remain poorly understood. Regardless, the cemeteries at these same sites and several others in the region remained in use for a much longer period of time than those found in the Lasithi Plateau. It is thus possible that the apparent increase in grave good diversity at these sites, longer continuity of tomb use, and the later date of the most noteworthy tombs may reveal the early phases of the increasing social complexity and changing sociopolitical structure that eventually led to the development of the polis or urban nucleated center at other sites. A comparable situation may be visible at Argos, where LG burial customs are considered to be related to the emergence of the polis; at this site, the earliest signs of change occur by Early Geometric (EG), when some larger sized cist graves appear with richer contents than those observed in PG (Hägg 1983).

The switch from inhumation in small tholoi to cremation in burial enclosures—which begins at several northern Mirabello sites as early as PGB—may also be significant for this area. The introduction of new burial practices does not in and of itself necessarily indicate a changing sociopolitical structure or the presence of new people. At most sites, in fact, the use of burial enclosures actually shows little distinction from the basic practices observed in the former small tholos tombs, aside from the obvious new tomb form and widespread use of cremation. In other words, the presence of multiple burials in most tombs, as well as the frequent association with earlier tholos tombs, implies that no significant change in ideology has yet taken place; the basic unit of social organization still seems to have been the household or extended family (Haggis 1993, 151–152; 1996, 410–415; Wallace 2006, 643). These tombs thus show no signs of developing the larger "group" or community identity often attributed to the polis, although the apparent overall, widespread adoption of a new burial method and form may be indicative of the fact that changes in this direction are beginning to occur at certain sites (e.g., Morris 1987; Whitley 2001, 185–188). On the other hand, the placement of burials within abandoned houses at Kavousi Vronda could be interpreted as illustrating a need for individual family groups to preserve their own specific identities due to the increasing importance of the extended lineage—a result of the formation of larger-scale authorities (Wallace 2003b, 268). At Dreros, however, the presence of a single, defined cemetery area and a lower number of burials per tomb could signify the beginning of an ideological change, with the focus shifting to a larger group or community, possibly even the clan, as the site develops toward the polis by the 7th century (Sjögren 2003, 98–107).

Another indicator of increasing social complexity at certain sites in this region can be observed in the use of a single large tholos tomb at Kavousi and Praisos (in the border zone) in LG; at the time that these large tholoi were in use, the small tholos was no longer the primary form of burial at either site, and settlements at both sites appear to have become poleis or at least urban nucleated centers in the LG or Archaic period (Whitley, Prent, and Thorne 1999, 252–253; Haggis et al. 2004, 390–393). Also, Kavousi, as well as Praisos, is characterized by a diversity of tomb types and varying degrees of wealth in grave goods. These factors, considered along with the presence of distinct burial areas, some of which may have represented elite cemeteries (e.g., Aloni/Plai tou Kastrou, and Skouriasmenos), may be indicative of a changing sociopolitical structure, including the development of different social status levels (Haggis 1993, 151–152). This variability would seem to provide a good predictor of the changes to come—the eventual urban nucleation at Azoria in the Archaic period (Haggis et al. 2004, 2007).

This practice is even more clearly illustrated by certain sites in Central Crete in the EIA. In addition, a similar diversification of tomb types at LM II Knossos, as well as on the mainland in Late Helladic (LH) I and II, is interpreted by Preston (1999) as reflecting or even contributing to the social changes occurring at the time, with mortuary practices beginning to be employed as a forum for status display.

Finally, a few LG vases were found associated with a single LM III tomb at Mochlos (Soles 2001) and Achladia (Vagnetti and Tsipopoulou 1995, 126), and possibly above one of the EM graves at Hagia Photia (Davaras 1971, 396). The placement of these vases as offerings potentially illustrates, at the end of the period, a renewed interest in the "Minoan" or "ancient" past and a desire for association—either real or perceived—with it (Wallace 2003b, 268–271). Although the exact significance of these offerings remains uncertain, it is noteworthy that the examples from eastern Crete all date to the LG period, the time when the polis/urban nucleated center was developing in this area, and that offerings seem to have been made only once and at a single tomb per site (Antonaccio 1994, 1995). Also, no known EIA settlement was located in the vicinity of any of these three sites. The formation of a new, larger, and shared identity within the city-state may have created a need to fashion new, smaller "group" identities, or assert old family ones, accomplished by forming a connection to the local "ancestral" past (Wallace 2003b, 271). These offerings—possible examples of ancestor or tomb cult—could also reflect competition for authority among the emerging elites in eastern Crete at the very end of the EIA. In other words, elites may have attempted to legitimize their authority by claiming links with the past (an actual kinship or knowledge of the deceased was not necessary) (Morris 1992, 8–15; Antonaccio 1994, 410). Asserting a link with the past at a location distant from a settlement could have been especially significant for emerging elites at sites such as Itanos which were founded at the end of the period.

The Mirabello/West Siteia Mountain region is thus distinguished from other areas in eastern Crete by its diversity of tomb type, use of inhumation and cremation, and greater variety in grave goods. Many sites and tombs remained in use for much longer periods of time in this area, though no site in eastern Crete appears to have become a polis before LG (Whitley, Prent, and Thorne 1999, 252–253; Haggis et al.

2004, 390–393). The late development of the polis/urban nucleated center at eastern sites may be partially attributable to the nature of the village organization present at sites such as Kavousi and Vrokastro (Haggis 1993; 1996; Hayden 2004; Wallace 2006, 648). The cluster type of site pattern and the strength of the family institution appear to have created a much more stable environment at these sites than in Central Crete, the result of which may have been a relatively smooth, or at least slower, transition towards urbanization and the development of poleis-like towns, with sociopolitical changes and new traditions being more gradually assimilated (cf. Whitley 1991). There may also have been fewer outsiders in this area than in Central Crete, or else their arrival or influence was later, making any competition or power struggles less intense (Nowicki 2000, 241–247). A similar situation is seen in Middle–Late Helladic Messenia, where the funerary evidence appears to reveal a much smoother transition to the emergence of the palatial system than in the Argolid (Voutsaki 1998). Regardless of the rate of transition toward urbanization in eastern Crete, a clear increase in social diversity and evidence of an increasingly complex sociopolitical organization is visible at some Mirabello/west Siteia sites by the end of the EIA; this is observed in longer continuity of tomb use, greater diversity in tomb type and wealth of grave goods, as well as the appearance of the large tholos tomb.

Central Crete

Early Iron Age burials have been found in Central Crete at approximately 47 sites, with a minimum of 585 tombs, the majority of which are located in the north (Fig. 7.7, region 4a–c; Eaby 2007, 95–170). The most common tomb types are the rock-cut chamber tomb and the pit or pithos burial. As many as 300 chamber tombs have been identified from across the island; 68% of these (roughly 170) come from the area of Knossos/Herakleion alone (only 19 are known from Phaistos and nine from Kounavoi). The chamber tombs of Central Crete are in many ways similar to the tholoi found farther east in that they show considerable variation in shape, tend to be of small diameter (ca. 1–<3 m, esp. 1.5–2.0 m), and typically contained only a small number of burials (fewer than 10; usually one to five, thus likely representing family tombs), which usually were cremations rather than inhumations (for Knossos, see Coldstream and Catling, eds., 1996, 643). They were also carved and used throughout the period (from LM IIIC to EO, particularly in PG) and frequently located in defined cemeteries, although they were also often in scattered locations. Pits and pithos burials, on the other hand, tended to be later in date, particularly G (LG), though examples do exist as early as LM IIIC. Pits/pithos burials also typically contained only one (or two) cremated individuals per tomb and were frequently relatively poor in grave goods—often with only one or two vases (notable exceptions do occur, e.g., Petrokephali: Levi 1957–1958, 358–361; Rocchetti 1967–1968). Additionally, while these burials tended to be scattered early in the period, they were frequently found in designated cemeteries by the LG period.

The current evidence suggests that the majority of known EIA burial sites in Central Crete utilized only a single form of burial. For example, only chamber tombs have been found thus far at Elia, Phoinikia, Aitania, Tylissos, and possibly Kavrochori, Hagia Marina, and Kato Vatheia; while only pits or pithos burials were found at Stavrakia, Stamnoi, Arkalochori, Alitzani, Anopolis, Koxari, and possibly Episkopi, Smari, Krousonas, and Kamilari Alisandraki (Kanta 1980; Sjögren 2001). It is possible, however, that some of the sites had burials of both types; these tombs are often poorly described in the sources, and it is sometimes difficult to distinguish between them. The extent of EIA burial at these sites is difficult to determine because none has been completely excavated, and most of the finds and tomb information have not been published. A few sites in Central Crete, however, show a variety of tomb types in the EIA, a pattern distinct from that observed at the majority of sites in the region. Knossos, Prinias, and Kounavoi in the north each have examples of four to five different tomb types, while Phaistos and Gortyn in the south have two to three. Although these distinct tomb types do not necessarily date to the same phases within the period, their presence is nevertheless significant.

The associated settlements for the majority of Central Cretan burial sites have not yet been located, though the large number of sites and scattered distribution of the tombs may reflect a settlement pattern of small, widespread villages and farmsteads—at least for the 8th century (Sjögren

2001, 111–114). Fewer defensible settlements existed in this area than in eastern Crete, and few to none of the central sites founded in LM IIIC appear to have been abandoned at the end of that phase; in fact, many sites expanded their borders rapidly during PG, perhaps partially related to an influx of outsiders (Nowicki 2000, 241–247). As early as PG, the foundations for the later system of the city-state were developing at the strongest sites of this type; nucleated centers developed much faster in Central Crete than in the east, possibly because the cluster type settlement pattern identified at several eastern sites did not exist in this area (Nowicki 2000, 246–247). Nucleation may have begun at Phaistos, for example, as early as LM IIIC (Watrous, Hadzi-Vallianou, and Blitzer 2004, 309), and Knossos is sometimes considered to have been an urban nucleus throughout the period (Coldstream 1991). Regardless, by the 8th century, the northern region appears to have been dominated by two urban centers (Knossos and Prinias) and the south by three (Gortyn for the central Mesara, Phaistos for the west, and Arkades, in the border zone between Central and eastern Crete, for the east) (Sjögren 2003, 80–84).

As a result of the nucleation process and rapid population growth occurring at certain central sites during this period, more complex social structures were developing, one aspect of which was the rise of emerging elites. This rapid development of new social and political structures thus likely involved attempts by individuals or families to gain new dominance or maintain old authority (Wallace 2003b, 268–271). Changing sociopolitical organization may be reflected in some instances by an increasing distinction in burial types, grave goods (especially at Knossos and Phaistos), and funerary rituals (cf. Preston 1999, 2004), as well as changes in ceramic shapes and motifs (e.g., LM IIIC Phaistos; see Borgna 2003, 158–164). Those sites with the greatest variety in tomb types (Knossos, Prinias, Kounavoi, Gortyn, and Phaistos), for example, tend to be those which develop into poleis at some time during the EIA or at least make significant developments toward the city-state during that period. While this diversity in tomb type may be an indicator of social organization becoming increasingly complex at these sites, in this area it could also show the presence of a mixed population (Coldstream and Catling, eds., 1996, 715–720).

The central sites with the greatest variety in tomb type all also had at least one large tholos tomb, typically constructed as early as PG and containing many cremations; the three northern sites had at least one small tholos. The tholos tomb is not the primary form of burial at any of these sites in the EIA, but it does appear to represent the second phase of burial at Prinias rather than a few isolated examples (Prinias is in general unique in its burial practices, and the use of several tholoi may have resulted from its location near the border with the Rethymnon area; Rizza and Rizzo 1984, 152). An elite distinction—or desire to be perceived as such—thus seems to have been associated with tholoi of the large variety in all areas of Crete in which they appear, in part due to their size, wealth, and rarity. In contrast to eastern Crete, however, in the central part of the island there may also have been a special meaning or significance attached to the tholos tomb in general, especially when used late in the period. The fact that tholos tombs were so rare in this area in the EIA may indicate that they were used by emerging and potentially competing elites as a source of, or justification for, power or sociopolitical status; the tholos would thus have functioned for these elites as a symbol of the past and/or former authority. The use of the tholos tomb would therefore appear to provide a clear reflection of the increasing social diversity and complexity that were occurring at certain central sites relatively early in the period (see also Borgna 2003; Prent 2003; Wallace 2003b, 268–271, 275–277).

A similar meaning/significance can potentially also be attributed to a limited number of large chamber tombs, carved in either LM IIIC or PG, from this area: Knossos Kephala 1957 (4.2 m in diameter; Coldstream 1963, 42–43), Phaistos tou Phygiote to Aloni T.1 (6 m diameter; Savignoni 1904, 503), and Phaistos Kalyviani (9.5 x 10 m; Chatzi-Vallianou 1979, 384). These three tombs are significantly larger than all other examples from the area and are located in the vicinity of former palace sites/future urban centers. Being relatively wealthy, these few large tombs (both the chambers and tholoi) would seem to indicate even more clearly the emergence of elite groups or families, rather than individuals, when compared to the more common small pits or pithos burials that typically contained only one or two individuals and few grave goods. In addition, a similar attempt at forming an association with the Bronze Age past and perhaps legitimizing claims to power by the rising aristocracy may further be revealed in the presence of ruin cults, which were more prevalent in Central Crete than eastern

(Prent 2003, 90, 97), as well as the re-use of certain Bronze Age tombs as at Knossos (e.g., Coldstream 1998; Preston 2005) and offerings placed in the Middle–Late Minoan tholos at Kamilari Gligori Koriphi (Wallace 2003b, 268–271; Lefèvre-Novaro 2004) and near Tholos A at Hagia Triada (D'Agata 1998, 22).

In addition, the sites of Rotasi, Hagies Paraskies, and Ligortynos may form a small sub-region within the larger area of Central Crete (area 4c on Fig. 7.7). Each of these sites contains a single tomb that shares many features with the large tholoi of the nearby Mesara and North-Central Crete but on a smaller scale. Rotasi (Platon 1958, 468) and Hagies Paraskies (Platon 1945–1947) each had a single well-built small tholos with circular chamber of PG–EO/O date, and both tombs contained a large number of cremation burials. Although two other small tholoi are known from Rotasi, the majority of burials from the site appear to have been in a pithos cemetery (Platon 1954b, 516; 1955b, 567; Galanaki 1993, 466–467). A single chamber tomb has also been excavated at Ligortynos (Platon and Davaras 1961–1962, 284–285), but it had many features of the large tholoi, namely monolithic jambs and lintel, a circular chamber, late date (PGB–LG), and probably a large number of cremation burials. The selected tombs from these sites thus show more similarities in style, construction, date, and manner of burial with the large tholos tombs of the Mesara and its northern border than with any other area. It is possible that the presence at each of these sites of a single noteworthy tomb may reflect an imitation, albeit on a smaller scale, of the "elite" practices observed at the larger, more dominant sites in North and South-Central Crete.

In conclusion, while the majority of Central Cretan sites were characterized by burial in only small chamber tombs or pits/pithoi, poor publication and lack of excavation make further analysis of these sites on a regional basis difficult. The use of the chamber tomb, and possibly also the pit grave, would appear, however, to represent a continuation of the previous LM III burial practices of this area, though now with cremation as the dominant form of interment (Pini 1968, 36–46). On the other hand, a small number of sites from Central Crete stand out in their variety of tomb types and the rare use of the tholos tomb. A limited number of settlements appear to have become dominant, or at least larger than most other sites in the area, relatively early in the period, and the rapid nucleation observed at these sites likely caused competition between emerging elites. The limited use of the large tholos tomb, as well as the presence of offerings at certain Bronze Age tombs and former palatial ruins, appears to have served the same function throughout Central Crete—namely deliberate association with the past. These tombs were potentially used as a means of acquiring or justifying authority or status in the midst of the developing social and political structures of the EIA. Furthermore, the tholos tomb was particularly associated with those sites that eventually became poleis/urban centers. Changes occurred much more swiftly in Central Crete than in the east, thus making the use of such symbols potentially even more significant or influential in this area.

Border Zones between Central and Eastern Crete and Central and West-Central Crete

The majority of sites in the border zone between central Crete and Lasithi, such as Erganos, tend to follow the same pattern as that observed within the Lasithi Plateau, in that they were short-term defensible settlements with small tholoi containing a few inhumation burials. Arkades (Levi 1927–1929) differs from this pattern slightly, however; this site began as a small defensible settlement like other sites in Lasithi, but it developed into a polis, or at least an urban center, by the end of the EIA (Sjögren 2003, 100–101). In addition, while the earliest tombs at this site consist solely of small tholoi, the later tombs are comprised mainly of pithos burials and a few large tholoi, as seen at several sites in South-Central Crete. Clear distinctions are thus visible at Arkades in the small number of large, wealthy tholoi with multiple burials, imported grave goods, and elaborate architectural constructions, and the typical covered pithoi with single burials and few grave goods. Furthermore, these large tholoi, as at certain central sites, may illustrate an attempt by current aristocratic families or members of the ruling class to assert their authority or status, or else a desire by old notable families, not necessarily currently in power, to present an image of retained influence and authority. Such distinctions, however, are really just beginning to appear at the end of the EIA at Arkades, as at the few polis/urban sites in the eastern part of the island, and they become more pronounced in the period immediately following.

The burials in the mountainous border zone between Central and West-Central Crete show many similarities to those observed in southern Lasithi and other areas of eastern Crete, as well as in the Amari region immediately to the west. For example, Kamares and Kourtes were both characterized by the use of small tholos tombs, which were likely associated with defensible settlements. Each site, however, has features which distinguish it slightly from others with small tholoi. Kourtes is unusual in that its tombs appear to date primarily to PG; in addition, one large tholos tomb may have existed at the site (Halbherr 1901; Mariani 1901; Taramelli 1901a). The Kamares tholoi, on the other hand, appear to date primarily from LM IIIA–IIIC, and one PG pithos burial from a tomb of unknown type has also been recovered (Taramelli 1901b; Alexiou 1964, 284). The tombs from Kamares and Kourtes thus illustrate well the mix of traditions often found in border zone sites, in that the small tholos form is like that commonly found to the west in the Amari area, while the possible large tholos and pithos burial are more reminiscent of tomb types found immediately to the southeast in the Mesara.

Far Western Crete

Relatively few EIA burials have been identified thus far from the westernmost region of Crete. A minimum of 31 tombs have been uncovered from 10 possible burial sites in this region, and all known tombs have been found in the north (Fig. 7.7, region 6; Eaby 2007, 187–196). No EIA tholos tombs have yet been found in this area of the island, nor have any tombs built in LM IIIC yet been published. The majority of sites, however, apparently contained tombs of only a single type, either chamber tombs or pits/pithos burials, similar to the pattern seen in the North-Central region. Astrikas, Gavalomouri, Kavousi, Vouves, and possibly Kissamos are currently known to have had only chamber tombs (e.g., Andreadaki-Vlasaki 1985; 1991; 2000, 32–35); these tombs range in date from Late Protogeometric–Early Orientalizing, and inhumation appears to have been the primary form of burial, though cremation did also occur. Pithos burial in pits is the sole form of interment found thus far at Aptera (LG–EO), Chania (PG, LG), and possibly Mousouras (SM/PG), and inhumation also appears to have been the primary funerary rite at these sites (e.g., Andreadaki-Vlasaki 1985; 1991; 2000, 32–35). Both forms of burial were found at Vryses (chamber tombs and a child burial in a pithos), while Modi (SM–G) showed the greatest variety in tomb type, with chambers, pits, a burial under overhanging rock, and pithos burials.

Unfortunately, the far western sites are not well published, making an analysis or identification of patterns in burial practice difficult for this region. The limited available information does, however, suggest that these tombs contained few imports, and that the chamber tombs were in some cases relatively wealthy in grave goods. Settlements in the westernmost region of Crete were primarily dispersed in the lowland and in general not of the defensible type (Nowicki 2000; Moody 1987, 2004), as was also typical of many north-central sites. In fact, nucleation seems to have begun much later in this area than in Central Crete, perhaps not becoming a significant factor for most of the region until the 6th century (Sjögren 2001, 118–119); Chania and Aptera, however, may have become urban centers as early as the 8th century (see also Andreadaki-Vlasaki 1985, 12–14, 30, 33; 1991, 420).

The lack of tholoi in the Chania region during the EIA would seem to represent a continuation of the predominant LM tradition in the area of burial in large and small rock-cut chamber tombs. Many similarities exist between the burials of the westernmost region and those found in North-Central Crete; this is perhaps due to the level of previous "Mycenaean" presence or influence in both areas, as partially illustrated by the elements of continuity in the burial tradition. One of the primary factors distinguishing the westernmost burials from those of Central Crete is the apparent persistence of inhumation throughout the period; the presence of certain unusual grave goods, such as skuttles and loomweights, may also represent significant variations in the funerary tradition between these two areas. While such distinctions do exist, the overall mortuary traditions of North-Central and far western Crete exhibit many similarities; far more differences in funerary tradition are visible between the westernmost and the west-central regions. Unfortunately, the nature of the evidence makes a more detailed analysis of sociopolitical organization or social stratification unfeasible for the region at this time.

West-Central Crete

Approximately 50–100 EIA tombs are currently known from as many as nine sites in West-Central Crete, and the majority of these burial sites were associated with defensible settlements (Eaby 2007, 173–186). The small tholos may have been the primary tomb type at several sites: Orne (Kanta and Stampolidis 2001, 98–103); Pantanassa (Tegou 2001), where a pithos burial was also found; and possibly Koxare (Hood and Warren 1966, 177, 179). All known tholoi from this area are LM IIIC–SM in date; unfortunately, the existing evidence and number of recorded tombs is very limited, and the presence of other tomb types at these sites remains unknown. The use of small tholoi in this area may, however, represent a direct continuation of the LM III Amari tradition (Kanta 1997). An EIA date for the burials in the rock shelter at Mesonisia (Faure 1963, 503–504) is by no means certain, and any potential EIA presence at Mesi (a single LM IIIC amphora; Tzedakis 1976, 372) would merely reflect the final phase of burial in a LM III cemetery. In addition, cremation urn cemeteries were found at Atsipades (e.g., Petroulakis 1915; Agelarakis, Kanta, and Moody 2001), which is unusual in its early (LM IIIC) use of cremation, and Rethymnon (possibly Geometric; Woodward 1929, 235). Finally, Eleutherna is the most striking site of this region in its unusual burial types, which include a large chamber tomb, burial mounds, open burials, pithoi, and enclosures (Stampolidis 1993, 1994); this site also belonged to a defensible settlement in the EIA, though it later became a polis (Sjögren 2003, 100–102). The Eleutherna cemetery is unusual in its apparent distinctions of burial type and grave goods based upon age and sex. It is unclear, however, exactly what percentage of the burials from this cemetery are from the EIA; many, in fact, appear be slightly later in date.

Based on the limited available information, West-Central Crete in the EIA thus appears to have been a mixed area, as illustrated by the simultaneous use of several different tomb types and burial traditions. For example, a few early sites in the southeastern part of the region appear to have been influenced by the previous LM III tradition of small tholos tombs, as also seen slightly farther east at Kourtes and Kamares. On the other hand, the LM IIIC cremation urn cemetery at Atsipades is unique for the entire island, as are certain later burial practices from Eleutherna. It is difficult, however, to determine any regional patterns in the funerary data or to make suggestions regarding sociopolitical organization and social stratification on a regional level due to the small number of known and published burial sites.

Conclusions

In the EIA, the island of Crete was characterized by a high level of regionalism, not only in ceramic styles, settlement patterns, and cult practices, but also in mortuary practices. Six distinct funerary regions (Lasithi, far eastern, Mirabello/West Siteia Mountains, Central, far western, and West-Central) and three border zones have been identified on the island. Factors such as geography, previous tradition in a region, cultural identity, settlement type, and sociopolitical organization appear to have played significant roles in the development of mortuary regionalism on Crete in the EIA. In many cases, for example, variations in funerary tradition seem to follow geographical boundaries; sites in the vicinity of transportation or communication routes often show the greatest degree of diversity from site to site, while traditional burial practices, or at least consistency in tomb and interment type, are sometimes retained for the longest in the most mountainous or isolated areas. Furthermore, the primary tomb type used in a region, especially in far eastern, Central and far western Crete, frequently reflects a continuation of the previous LM III funerary tradition in the area. In other cases, such as Lasithi and possibly Mirabello/West Siteia Mountains, the use of the tholos tomb may indicate a return to an even older tradition, possibly representing a deliberate choice to maintain or create a new regional/community identity as part of the recovery process after the collapse of the LM palatial structure.

In addition, the homogeneity of EIA mortuary practices in Lasithi and far eastern Crete would appear to reflect limited social diversity and relatively simple sociopolitical organization, at least during the beginning of the period. On the other hand, the funerary practices of Mirabello/West Siteia Mountains and Central Crete are distinguished, over the course of the period, by an increasing diversity in wealth of grave goods, variety of tomb types at a single site, greater continuity of tomb and settlement use, and/or presence of the large tholos tomb.

These distinctions would appear to reveal a changing sociopolitical organization and increasing social stratification at certain sites in these regions; also, elites may have used the large tholos tomb as a means of justifying or acquiring power or social status in the midst of such changes. Mortuary variability may thus reflect the changes that accompanied the development of the polis or urban nucleated center at certain sites, especially in Central Crete. Sociopolitical developments, as well as the concomitant changes in settlement patterns and burial practices, did not occur consistently throughout the island; some areas adopted new features at a slower rate than others, and outside or new influences were manifested in a variety of ways depending upon location and previous tradition in a region. The purpose of this paper is to provide an initial analysis of mortuary regionalism on the island, thus supplementing recent ceramic, settlement, and cult studies. The ideas presented are preliminary in nature; further research is needed, particularly in the area of grave goods, in order to better understand mortuary regionalism on Crete during the EIA.

References

Agelarakis, A., A. Kanta, and J. Moody. 2001. "Cremation Burial in LM IIIC–Sub Minoan Crete and the Cemetery at Pezoulos Atsipadhes, Crete," in *Καύσεις στην Εποχή του Χαλκού και την Πρώιμη Εποχή του Σιδήρου, Ρόδος, 29 Απριλίου–2 Μαΐου 1999*, N.C. Stampolidis, ed., Athens, pp. 69–82.

Alexiou, S. 1964. "Χρονικά," *CretChron* 18, pp. 279–290.

Andreadaki-Vlasaki, M. 1985. "Γεωμετρικὰ νεκροταφεῖα στὸ Νομὸ Χανίων," in *Πεπραγμένα του Ε' Διεθνούς Κρητολογικού Συνεδρίου* A' (1), Herakleion, pp. 10–35.

———. 1991. "The Khania Area, ca. 1200–700 b.c.," in Musti et al., eds., 1991, pp. 403–423.

———. 2000. *The County of Khania through Its Monuments from the Prehistoric Period to Roman Times*, 2nd ed., Athens.

Antonaccio, C.M. 1994. "Contesting the Past: Hero Cult, Tomb Cult, and Epic in Early Greece," *AJA* 98, pp. 389–410.

———. 1995. *An Archaeology of Ancestors: Tomb Cult and Hero Cult in Early Greece*, Lanham, Md.

Belli, P. 1991. "Tholoi nell'Egeo dal II al I millennio," in Musti et al., eds., 1991, pp. 425–450.

Borgna, E. 2003. "Regional Settlement Patterns, Exchange Systems and Sources of Power in Crete at the End of the Late Bronze Age: Establishing a Connection," *SMEA* 45, pp.153–183.

Boyd, H.A. 1901. "Excavations at Kavousi, Crete, in 1900," *AJA* 5, pp. 125–157.

Branigan, K. 1970. *The Foundations of Palatial Crete: A Survey of Crete in the Early Bronze Age*, New York.

Chatzi-Vallianou, D. 1979. "Εφορεία προϊστορικών και κλασικών αρχαιοτήτων Ηρακλείου," *ArchDelt* 34 (Β΄, Chronika) [1987], pp. 382–385.

Coldstream, J.N. 1963. "Five Tombs at Knossos," *BSA* 58, pp. 30–43.

———. 1968. *Greek Geometric Pottery*, London.

———. 1977. *Geometric Greece*, London.

———. 1991. "Knossos: An Urban Nucleus in the Dark Age?" in Musti et al., eds., 1991, pp. 287–300.

———. 1998. "Minos Redivivus: Some Nostalgic Knossians of the Ninth Century B.C. (A Summary)," in *Post-Minoan Crete. Proceedings of the First Colloquium on Post-Minoan Crete Held by the British School at Athens and the Institute of Archaeology, University College London, 10–11 November 1995*, W.G. Cavanagh and M. Curtis, eds., Nottingham, pp. 58–61.

Coldstream, J.N., and H.W. Catling, eds. 1996. *Knossos North Cemetery: Early Greek Tombs* (*BSA Suppl.* 28), 4 vols., London.

D'Agata, A.L. 1998. "Changing Patterns in a Minoan and Post-Minoan Sanctuary: The Case of Agia Triada," in *Post-Minoan Crete. Proceedings of the First Colloquium on Post-Minoan Crete Held by the British School at Athens and the Institute of Archaeology, University College London, 10–11 November 1995*, W.G. Cavanagh and M. Curtis, eds., Nottingham, pp. 19–26.

Davaras, C. 1971. "Πρωτομινωικόν νεκροταφείον Αγιάς Φωτιάς Σητείας," *AAA* 4, pp. 392–397.

———. 1972. "Η Αρχαιολογική κίνησις στην ανατολική Κρήτη κατά το 1971," *Amaltheia* 3, pp. 33–52.

Day, L.P. and L.M. Snyder. 2004. "The 'Big House' at Vronda and the 'Great House' at Karphi: Evidence for Social Structure in LM IIIC Crete," in *Crete Beyond the Palaces: Proceedings of the Crete 2000 Conference* (*Prehistory Monographs* 10), L.P. Day, M.S. Mook, and J.D. Muhly, eds., Philadelphia, pp. 63–80.

Demargne, P. 1931. "Recherches sur le site de l'Anavlochos," *BCH* 55, pp. 365–407.

Desborough, V.R.d'A. 1972. *The Greek Dark Ages*, London.

Dickinson, O. 2006. *The Aegean from Bronze Age to Iron Age: Continuity and Change between the Twelfth and Eighth Centuries B.C.*, London.

Eaby, M. 2007. *Mortuary Variability in Early Iron Age Cretan Burials*, Ph.D. diss., University of North Carolina at Chapel Hill.

———. 2009. "Early Iron Age Cretan Tholoi," in *SOMA 2007. Proceedings of the XI Annual Symposium on Mediterranean Archaeology, 24–29 April 2007, Istanbul Technical University (BAR-IS* 1900), Ç. Özkan-Aygün, ed., Oxford, pp. 98–105.

Faure, P. 1963. "Cultes de sommets et cultes de cavernes en Crète," *BCH* 87, pp. 493–508.

———. 1964. *Fonctions des cavernes crétoises (TravMém* 14), Paris.

Galanaki, K. 1993. "Επαρχία Μονοφατσίου," *ArchDelt* 48 (B΄, Chronika) [1998], pp. 466–467.

Gesell, G.C., W.D.E. Coulson, and L.P. Day. 1991. "Excavations at Kavousi, Crete, 1988," *Hesperia* 60, pp. 145–177.

Gesell, G.C., L.P. Day, and W.D.E. Coulson. 1995. "Excavations at Kavousi, Crete, 1989 and 1990," *Hesperia* 64, pp. 67–120.

Greco, E., T. Kalpaxis, A. Schnapp, and D. Viviers. 1997. "Travaux menés en collaboration avec l'École française en 1996: Itanos (Crète orientale)," *BCH* 121, pp. 809–824.

Hägg, R. 1983. "Burial Customs and Social Differentiation in Eighth Century Argos," in *The Greek Renaissance of the Eighth Century B.C.: Tradition and Innovation (SkrAth* 4°, 30), R. Hägg, ed., Stockholm, pp. 27–31.

Haggis, D.C. 1993. "Intensive Survey, Traditional Settlement Patterns, and Dark Age Crete: The Case of Early Iron Age Kavousi," *JMA* 6, pp. 131–174.

———. 1996. "Archaeological Survey at Kavousi, East Crete: Preliminary Report," *Hesperia* 65, pp. 373–432.

Haggis, D.C., M.S. Mook, R.D. Fitzsimons, C.M. Scarry, and L.M. Snyder. 2007. "Excavations at Azoria, 2003–2004, Part 1: The Archaic Civic Complex," *Hesperia* 76, pp. 243–321.

Haggis, D.C., M.S. Mook, C.M. Scarry, L.M. Snyder, and W.C. West III. 2004. "Excavations at Azoria, 2002," *Hesperia* 73, pp. 339–400.

Halbherr, F. 1901. "Cretan Expedition XI: Three Cretan Necropoleis. Report on the Researches at Erganos, Panaghia, and Courtes," *AJA* 5, pp. 259–293.

Hall, E.H. 1914. "Excavations in Eastern Crete Vrokastro," *Anthropological Publications* 3 (3), Philadelphia, pp. 79–185.

Hayden, B.J. 2004. *Reports on the Vrokastro Area, Eastern Crete.* II: *The Settlement History of the Vrokastro Area and Related Studies* (*University Museum Monograph* 119), Philadelphia.

Hogarth, D.G. 1900–1901. "Excavations at Zakro, Crete," *BSA* 7, pp. 121–149.

Hood, S., and P. Warren. 1966. "Ancient Sites in the Province of Ayios Vasilios, Crete," *BSA* 61, pp. 163–191.

Kanta, A. 1980. *The Late Minoan III Period in Crete: A Survey of Sites, Pottery, and Their Distribution* (*SIMA* 58), Göteborg.

———. 1997. "Late Bronze Age Tholos Tombs, Origins and Evolution: The Missing Links," in *La Crète mycénienne. Actes de la table ronde internationale organisée par l'École française d'Athènes, 28–29 mars 1991* (*BCH Suppl.* 30), J. Driessen and A. Farnoux, eds., Paris, pp. 229–247.

———. 2003. "Aristocrats—Traders—Emigrants—Settlers: Crete in the Closing Phases of the Bronze Age," in *Πλόες: Sea Routes. . . Interconnections in the Mediterranean 16th–6th c. B.C. Proceedings of the International Symposium Held at Rethymnon, Crete, September 29th–October 2nd 2002*, N.C. Stampolidis and V. Karagheorghis, eds., Athens, pp. 173–186.

Kanta, A., and A. Karetsou. 1998. "From Arkadhes to Rytion: Interactions of an Isolated Area of Crete with the Aegean and the East Mediterranean," in *Eastern Mediterranean: Cyprus, Dodecanese, Crete, 16th–6th cent. B.C. Proceedings of the International Symposium Held at Rethymnon, Crete, in May 1997*, V. Karagheorghis and N.C. Stampolidis, eds., Athens, pp.159–173.

Kanta, A., and N.C. Stampolidis. 2001. "Orné (ΑΙΠΥ) in the Context of the Defensive Settlements of the End of the Bronze Age," in *Defensive Settlements of the Aegean and the Eastern Mediterranean after c.1200 B.C. Proceedings of an International Workshop Held at Trinity College, Dublin, 7th–9th May 1999*, V. Karageorghis and C.E. Morris, eds., Nicosia, pp. 95–113.

Lefèvre-Novaro, D. 2004. "Les offrandes d'époque géométrique/orientalisante dans les tombes crétoises de l'âge du Bronze: Problèmes et hypothèses," *Creta Antica* 5, pp. 181–198.

Levi, D. 1927–1929. "Arkades: Una città cretese all'alba della civiltà ellenica," *ASAtene* 10–12, pp. 78–387.

———. 1957–1958. "Gli scavi a Festòs nel 1956 e 1957," *ASAtene* 35–36, pp. 193–361.

Mariani, L. 1901. "Cretan Expedition XIII: The Vases of Erganos and Courtes," *AJA* 5, pp. 302–314.

Moody, J. 1987. *The Environmental and Cultural Prehistory of the Khania Region of West Crete: Neolithic through Late Minoan III*, Ph.D. diss., University of Minnesota.

——. 2004. "Western Crete in the Bronze Age: A Survey of the Evidence," in *Crete Beyond the Palaces: Proceedings of the Crete 2000 Conference (Prehistory Monographs* 10), L.P. Day, M. Mook, and J.D. Muhly, eds., Philadelphia, pp. 247–264.

Morris, I. 1987. *Burial and Ancient Society: The Rise of the Greek City-State*, Cambridge.

——. 1992. *Death-Ritual and Social Structure in Classical Antiquity*, Cambridge.

Musti, D., A. Sacconi, L. Rocchetti, M. Rocchi, E. Scafa, L. Sportiello, and M.E. Giannotta, eds. 1991. *La transizione dal miceneo all'alto arcaismo: Dal palazzo alla città. Atti del convegno internazionale, Roma, 14–19 marzo 1988*, Rome.

Nowicki, K. 1994. "A Dark Age Refuge Center near Pefki, East Crete," *BSA* 89, pp. 235–268.

——. 2000. *Defensible Sites in Crete c. 1200–800 B.C. (LM IIIB/IIIC through Early Geometric) (Aegaeum* 21), Liège.

——. 2004. "South of Kavousi, East of Mochlos: The West Siteia Mountains at the End of the Bronze Age," in *Crete Beyond the Palaces: Proceedings of the Crete 2000 Conference (Prehistory Monographs* 10), L.P. Day, M. Mook, and J.D. Muhly, eds., Philadelphia, pp. 265–280.

Pendlebury, H.W., J.D.S. Pendlebury, and M.B. Money-Coutts. 1937–1938. "Excavations in the Plain of Lasithi. III. Karphi: A City of Refuge in the Early Iron Age in Crete," *BSA* 38, pp. 57–145.

Pendlebury, J.D.S. 1939. *The Archaeology of Crete: An Introduction*, New York.

Petroulakis, E.N. 1915. "Κρητικής Άτσιπαδες τάφοι," *ArchEph* 1915, pp. 48–50.

Pini, I. 1968. *Beiträge zur Minoischen Gräberkunde*, Wiesbaden.

Platon, N. 1945–1947. "Γεωμετρικός τάφος Αγίων Παρασκιών Ηρακλείου," *Arch Eph* 1945–1947, pp. 47–97.

——. 1952. "Ανασκαφαί περιοχής Σητείας," *Prakt* 1952, pp. 630–648.

——. 1953. "Ανασκαφαί εις την περιοχήν Σητείας," *Prakt* 1953, pp. 288–297.

——. 1954a. "Ανασκαφαί περιοχής Σητείας," *Prakt* 1954, pp. 361–368.

——. 1954b. "Χρονικά," *CretChron* 8, pp. 499–517.

——. 1955a. "Ανασκαφαί περιοχής Σητείας," *Prakt* 1955, pp. 288–297.

————. 1955b. "Χρονικά," *CretChron* 9, pp. 547–569.

————. 1958. "Ἔκθεσις Πεπραγμένων του Δ.Σ. της Ε.Κ.Ι.Μ κατά το ἔτος 1958," *CretChron* 12, pp. 453–483.

————. 1960. "Ἀνασκαφαί περιοχής Πραισοῦ," *Prakt* 1960, pp. 294–307.

Platon, N., and C. Davaras. 1961–1962. "Ἀρχαιότητες και μνημεία Κρήτης," *ArchDelt* 17 (Β΄, Chronika) [1963], pp. 281–291.

Prent, M. 2003. "Glories of the Past in the Past: Ritual Activities at Palatial Ruins in the Early Iron Age Crete," in *Archaeologies of Memory*, R.M. Van Dyke and S.E. Alcock, eds., Malden, pp. 81–103.

————. 2005. *Cretan Sanctuaries and Cults: Continuity and Change from Late Minoan IIIC to the Archaic Period*, Leiden.

Preston, L. 1999. "Mortuary Practices and the Negotiation of Social Identities at LM II Knossos," *BSA* 94, pp. 131–143.

————. 2004. "A Mortuary Perspective on Political Changes in Late Minoan II–IIIB Crete," *AJA* 108, pp. 321–348.

————. 2005. "The Kephala Tholos at Knossos: A Study in the Reuse of the Past," *BSA* 100, pp. 61–123.

Rizza, G., and M.A. Rizzo. 1984. "Prinias," in *Ancient Crete: A Hundred Years of Italian Archaeology (1884–1984)*, Rome, pp. 143–167.

Rocchetti, L. 1967–1968. "Il deposito protogeometrico di Petrokephali presso Festòs," *ASAtene* 45–46), pp. 41–70.

Savignoni, L. 1904. "Scavi e scoperte nella necropoli di Phaestos," *MonAnt* 14, pp. 501–666.

Sjögren, L. 2001. *Sites, Settlements and Early Poleis on Crete (800–500 B.C.)*, Ph.D. diss., University of Stockholm.

————. 2003. *Cretan Locations: Discerning Site Variations in Iron Age and Archaic Crete (800–500 B.C. (BAR-IS* 1185), Oxford.

Snodgrass, A. 1971. *The Dark Age of Greece*, New York.

Soles, J. 2001. "Reverence for Dead Ancestors in Prehistoric Crete," in *POTNIA: Deities and Religion in the Aegean Bronze Age. Proceedings of the 8th International Aegean Conference, 12–15 April 2000, Göteborg (Aegeum* 22), Göteborg, pp. 229–236.

Stampolidis, N.C. 1993. *Ελεύθερνα: Γεωμετρικά–αρχαϊκά χρόνια (Eleutherna* 3.1), Rethymnon.

————. 1994. *Ελεύθερνα: Γεωμετρικά–αρχαϊκά νεκροταφείο της Ορθής Πέτρας (Eleutherna* 3.2), Rethymnon.

Taramelli, A. 1901a. "Cretan Expedition XII. Notes on the Necropolis of Courtes," *AJA* 5, pp. 294–301.

———. 1901b. "Cretan Expedition XX: A Visit to the Grotto of Camares on Mount Ida," *AJA* 5, pp. 437–451.

Tegou, E. 2001. "Θολωτός τάφος της πρώιμης εποχής του Σιδήρου στην Παντάνασσα Αμαρίου Ν. Ρεθύμνης," in *Καύσεις στην Εποχή του Χαλκού και την Πρώιμη Εποχή του Σιδήρου, Ρόδος, 29 Απριλίου–2 Μαΐου 1999*, N.C. Stampolidis, ed., Athens, pp. 121–154.

Tsipopoulou, M. 1984. "Τάφοι της πρώιμης εποχής του σιδήρου στην ανατολική Κρήτη," *ArchDelt* 39 (Α΄, Meletes) [1990], pp. 232–245.

———. 1987. "Τάφοι της πρώιμης εποχής του σιδήρου στην ανατολική Κρήτη," in *Ειλαπίνη: Τόμος τιμητικός για τον καθηγητή Νικόλαο Πλάτωνα*, L. Kastrinaki, G. Orphanou, and N. Giannadakis, eds., Herakleion, pp. 253–269.

———. 1995. "LMIII Sitia: Patterns of Settlement and Land Use," in *Achladia: Scavi e ricerche della Missione greco-italiana in Creta orientale, 1991–1993 (Incunabula Graeca* 97), M. Tsipopoulou and L. Vagnetti, eds., Rome, pp. 177–192.

———. 2005. *Η ανατολική Κρήτη στην πρώιμη εποχή του σιδήρου*, Herakleion.

Tzedakis, Y. 1976. "Αρχαιότητες και μνημεία δυτικής Κρήτης," *ArchDelt* 31 (Β΄, Chronika) [1984], pp. 364–372.

Vagnetti, L., and M. Tsipopoulou. 1995. "I materiali rinvenuti nella tomba," in *Achladia: Scavi e ricerche della Missione greco-italiana in Creta orientale, 1991–1993 (Incunabula Graeca* 97), M. Tsipopoulou and L. Vagnetti, eds., Rome, pp. 115–128.

van Effenterre, H. 1948. *Nécropoles du Mirabello (ÉtCrét* 8), Paris.

Velho, G. 2008. "Retour sur les 'Bone enclosures' de Vrokastro: Éléments de datatión et pratiques funéraires," *Creta Antica* 9, pp. 209–244.

Voutsaki, S. 1998. "Mortuary Evidence, Symbolic Meanings and Social Change: A Comparison between Messenia and the Argolid in the Mycenaean Period," in *Cemetery and Society in the Aegean Bronze Age*, K. Branigan, ed., Sheffield, pp. 41–58.

Wallace, S. 2003a. "The Changing Role of Herding in the Early Iron Age of Crete: Some Implications of Settlement Shift for Economy," *AJA* 107, pp. 601–627.

———. 2003b. "The Perpetuated Past: Re-use or Continuity in Material Culture and the Structuring of Identity in Early Iron Age Crete," *BSA* 98, pp. 251–277.

———. 2005. "Last Chance to See? Karfi (Crete) in the Twenty-First Century: Presentation of New Architectural Data and Their Analysis in the Current Context of Research," *BSA* 100, pp. 215–274.

————. 2006. " The Gilded Cage? Settlement and Socioeconomic Change after 1200 B.C.: A Comparison of Crete and Other Aegean Regions," in *Ancient Greece: From the Mycenaean Palaces to the Age of Homer* (*Edinburgh Leventis Studies* 3), S. Deger-Jalkotzy and I.S. Lemos, eds., Edinburgh, pp. 619–664.

Warren, P.M. 1983. "Knossos: Stratigraphical Museum Excavations, 1978–82. Part II," *AR* 29, pp. 63–87.

Watrous, L.V., D. Hadzi-Vallianou, and H. Blitzer. 2004. *The Plain of Phaistos: Cycles of Social Complexity in the Mesara Region of Crete* (*Monumenta Archaeologica* 23), Los Angeles.

Whitley, J. 1991. "Social Diversity in Dark Age Greece," *BSA* 86, pp. 341–365.

————. 2001. *The Archaeology of Ancient Greece*, Cambridge.

Whitley, J., M. Prent, and S. Thorne. 1999. "Praisos IV: A Preliminary Report on the 1993 and 1994 Survey Seasons," *BSA* 94, pp. 215–264.

Woodward, A.M. 1929. "Archaeology in Greece 1928–1929," *JHS* 49, pp. 220–239.

Xanthoudides, S. 1904. "Ἐκ Κρήτης," *ArchEph* 1904, pp. 1–55.

Index

Achladia, tholos of, 128, 138, 139, 149, 184

Adrianos, 174

Adromyli Kantemi Kephala, 135, 139

Adromyloi, 181, 182

Aegean-connected objects, 67, 73

Aegean trade, in LM IIIC period, 124–125, 140, 145, 153–154

agency
  of landscape, 26
  and mortuary studies, 8

agnosticism, 27

Aitania, 186

Akrotiri, 112

Alexiou, S., 35, 36, 39

Alitzani, 186

Amari region, 191, 193

Amnisos, 124

amphorae, 134, 147

ancestors, 6, 39, 40, 42, 96, 98, 184

Anopolis, 186

antechambers, Lebena tombs, 35

anthropological archaeology, 8, 9

anthropological functionalism, 5

Apache, 26

Apesokari, 59, 65, 67, 69

Apodoulou, 131

Aptera, 191, 192

Archaeological Institute of America (AIA), 10

Archaic period, 183

Archanes Kato Lakkos, 142, 143, 144, 145

Archanes-Phourni, 51, 52, 60–61, 66, 67, 69, 71

Archanes Phyties, 142

Archibald, R., 26

Argos, 182

Arkades, 187, 190

Arkalochori, 186

Arnold, B., 7

arrowheads, 144

artifact distribution. *See also* grave goods
  at Lebena tombs, 35, 37–38, 38, 39, 41, 42
  at Mochlos tombs, 30–31, 42

Arvi, 181

Ashanti tribe, 5

Asterousia Mountains, 35, 63
Astrikas, 191
atheism, 27
Atsipades, 147, 148, 152, 193
Azoria, 183

Barrett, J.C., 7
Basso, K., 26
bedrock, Mochlos, 33
bench-sanctuaries, 125
Betancourt, P., 12, 110
Binford, L., 5, 6, 8
bone objects, 136, 144
bones, animal, 126
bones, human
  Erganos, 141
  Kritsa, 134
  Lebena, 35, 36, 37, 38–41
  Mochlos, 30
  Mouliana, 136
  Myrtos-Pyrgos, 12, 107–108, 113, 116
  osteological analysis, 121, 129
  Phaistos Liliana, 142
  Pseira, 89, 97
Borgna, E., 145
Bourdieu, P., 26
bowls, 111
  bird's-nest, 61
  deep, 129, 131, 134, 135, 136
  pottery, 116, 141
  stone, 113
Braimiana, 181
Branigan, K., 38
bronze objects, 31
  belts, 137
  daggers, 113
  knives, 113
  kraters, 147, 148
  pins, 130, 144
  plaques, 137
  pots, 136
  spearheads, 136, 144, 145, 147
  stands, 144

bronze objects, cont.
  swords, 136, 144
  tripods, 131
  vases, 151
built environment, and cultural narratives, 26, 27
burial containers, 133, 136, 139, 143, 145, 150. *See also* larnakes; pithoi
burial enclosures, in EIA, 166, 181, 182–183, 193

Cadogan, Gerald, 12
calcrete, 88, 93, 98
Catling, H.W., 144, 152
cave tombs, 77, 128, 139, 142, 144, 152, 166, 177–181
cemeteries, 8, 11, 12, 54, 55, 126. *See also* and specific cemeteries; tholos cemeteries
  Lebena, 35–36, 40
  Mochlos, 28, 30–34, 42
Central Crete, 171, 190, 191. *See also* South-Central Crete; West-Central Crete
  as EIA mortuary region, 172, 176, 178, 184, 185–190, 192, 194
  in LM IIIC, 140–147, 153, 187
Chalasmenos, 124, 125, 132, 135, 181
Chamaizi, 181, 182
Chamalevri, 124, 148
chamber tombs, 150, 166, 179–180, 191, 192, 192
  in Central Crete, 140–142, 143, 144, 145, 185–186, 188, 189
  in East Crete, 128, 133–134, 135, 136, 137, 138
Chania, 124, 142, 148, 191, 192
Chapman, R., 6–7
children, and mortuary practices, 107, 116, 133, 143, 144, 147, 166, 192
cist graves, 86–87, 96, 97, 166, 182
city-states, 13. *See also* settlement patterns

Clarke, D., 4, 8
classical archaeology, 8–9
clay objects, 31
copper objects, 31, 69
cremations, 166, 177, 179, 191
  in Central Crete, 141, 142, 143–144, 145, 146, 186, 188, 189
  in East Crete, 128, 131, 133–134, 136, 138, 139, 153
  in Mirabello/West Siteia Mountains, 181, 182, 183, 184
  and traditional burial customs, 150, 151, 152
  in West-Central Crete, 147, 148, 153, 193
cultural anthropology, 5, 7
cultural historical approaches, 10
cultural syncretism, 121, 149
cups
  pottery, 89, 90, 94, 108, 112, 116, 131, 136, 141
    carinated, 94
    conical, 71, 112, 141
    spouted, 135
  stone, serpentine, 113
Cyclades, 61
Cypriot objects, 134, 137, 140, 148, 151
Cypriot people, 121, 149
Cyprus, 137, 142, 146

D'Agata, A.L., 122, 126
daggers, 67, 69, 70–71, 95, 134
  bronze, 113
  iron, 144, 147
  silver, 60, 62
Davaras, C., 135
death, 3, 4–13, 54, 96, 98, 120, 148
diachronic studies, 1–2, 11
diadems, gold, 31, 37
doorways, 31
Dreros, 133, 135, 181, 183
Durkheim, É., 4, 5–6

Eaby, M., 12–13
Early Bronze Age (EBA), 49, 51, 52, 56, 90
Early Geometric (EG), 182
Early Iron Age (EIA), 165–166, 171, 172, 175, 194, 195. See also specific regions of Crete
Early Minoan (EM), 97, 150, 184
  tholos cemeteries, 49, 56, 142, 176
Early Minoan (EM) I, 59
  Koumasa, 59, 60
  Lebena cemeteries, 35, 40
  Platanos, 67
  Pseira, 90
Early Minoan (EM) II, 59
  Hagia Triada, 69, 70
  Koumasa, 59, 60, 62, 63
  Lebena cemeteries, 35, 36, 37
  Mochlos cemetery, 28
  Myrtos-Pyrgos, 104, 106–107, 109, 110
  Platanos, 65, 66, 67, 72
Early Minoan (EM) IIA
  Koumasa, 60, 61–62, 66, 72, 73
  Koumasa's Tomb Gamma, 59, 61
  Platanos, 67, 72
Early Minoan (EM) IIB
  Myrtos-Pyrgos, 104
  Pseira, 89, 90
Early Minoan (EM) III
  Archanes-Phourni, 71
  Hagia Triada, 59
  Koumasa, 59, 61, 62, 63
  Mochlos cemetery, 28
  Myrtos-Pyrgos, 108, 110
  Platanos, 65, 66, 67, 69
Early Orientalizing (EO), 12, 166, 179, 181, 186
East Crete, 127–140, 190–191
economics, 11, 148
  in LM IIIC period, 124, 139, 140, 145–146, 152
Egyptian scarabs, 37, 69, 70

Eleutherna, 147, 166, 193
Elia, 186
elite structures, 3, 4, 9,
    and Central Crete, 147, 187, 188–189,
        190
    and East Crete, 137, 154
    in Lasithi Plateau, 76
    and Lebena, 38, 40
    in Mirabello/West Siteia Mountains,
        183, 184
    and Mochlos, 32, 42
    Myceanean, 151–152
    and Myrtos-Pyrgos, 114, 115, 116
    and tholos tombs, 138, 141, 149, 195
Elounda Pyrgos, 133, 134, 139
Episkopi, 128, 180, 186
Episkopi Ierapetra, 133
Erganos, 140, 141, 190
ethnic groups, 121, 150, 151, 152, 153
ethnographic analogy, 5

far eastern Crete, 172, 177–180, 194
far western Crete, as EIA mortuary
    region, 172, 191–192, 194
Faure, P., 139
feasting, 9, 132, 135
figurines, 60–61, 62, 67, 131
Final Neolithic (FN)
    Pseira, 85–86, 88, 90, 93–94, 99
    Zakros, 97
fires, Lebena, 39
flasks, 134, 136, 151
Fortetsa cemetery, 141–142
Foucault, M., 25
funerals, 5–6, 8, 120
    funerary banquets, 132, 135
    Lebena, 37–38, 41, 42

Gavalomouri, 191
gender, 8, 143
    and cremation, 144, 147, 151, 153
    and elite structures, 12, 113–114, 115

gender, cont.
    and grave goods, 128–129, 144, 147,
        152–153, 193
Geometric (G), tholos tombs, 171
Girouard, M., 103
Goddess with Up-Raised Arms, 125–
    126, 139, 146
gold objects, 61, 63, 67, 69–70, 95
    diadems, 31, 37
    masks, 137, 151
    nails, 137
    pendants, 134
    rings, 131, 132, 136, 137, 138, 144, 151
    rosettes, 144
    sheathing, 31
Goldstein, L., 6
Gortyn, 124, 146, 186, 187
grave goods. *See also* artifact distribution
    in border zones, 179, 180, 190
    in Central Crete, 144, 145, 186, 187,
        194
    in East Crete, 128, 129, 130, 131, 136
    in far eastern Crete, 177, 178
    in far western Crete, 192
    and gender, 128–129, 144, 147, 152–
        153, 193
    at Koumasa, 58, 60, 62, 73
    in Lasithi Plateau, 175, 181
    at Lebena, 35, 38, 39, 41, 42
    in Mirabello/West Siteia Mountains,
        181–182, 183, 184, 185, 194
    at Myrtos-Pyrgos, 111–112
    at Platanos, 60, 65–67, 69–70
    at Pseira, 90
    in West-Central Crete, 147, 148, 193
Greek archaeology, role of data in, 9
Gulf of Mirabello, 85, 98–99

habitus, 26
Hagia Kyriaki, 7, 36–37, 59, 63, 67
Hagia Marina, 186
Hagia Marina Kollyva Metochi, 142
Hagia Photia, 184

Hagia Triada, 51, 52, 59, 61, 62, 65, 69, 71, 99, 126, 146, 189
Hagies Paraskies
Hagio Forango Valley, survey of, 36–37
Hagios Antonios, 97
Hagios Georgios, 179, 180
Hagios Georgios Papoura, 174
Hagios Ioannis, 142, 181
Hagios Nikolaos, 97
Hagios Onouphrios, 52
Hagios Spyridon Kalathiana, 135
Hagios Stephanos, 180
Halbherr, F., 141
Halbwachs, M., 26
Hatzaki, Eleni, 112
hearths, Myrtos-Pyrgos, 110–111
helmets, boar's tusk, 144, 151
Hertz, R., 4
Hierapytna, 104
high-value objects
    in East Crete, 128, 131, 139
    at Koumasa, 55, 60, 61, 62, 74
    at Platanos, 55, 69, 74–75
Hodder, I., 5, 7
house tombs
    at Mochlos, 28, 31–32
    at Myrtos-Pyrgos, 106
    at Pseira, 87, 95, 96
Huntington, R., 4, 5–6

identity construction, 11, 26, 38, 39, 41, 42, 116, 147, 176, 177, 179, 183, 184, 194
ideologies, 11, 25, 120, 138, 141, 148
    and Central Crete, 145, 145–146, 147
    and East Crete, 135, 137
    and landscapes, 25, 27–28
    and Lebena, 35, 38, 40, 41, 42, 43
    and Mochlos, 28, 34, 41, 43
    Mycenaean ideologies of power, 137, 151–152
    and Myrtos-Pyrgos, 113, 114, 115
    warrior graves, 151, 152–153

Ierapetra, isthmus of, 104, 134, 139
incense burners, 147
inhumations, 147, 174, 177, 179
    in Central Crete, 140, 141, 143–144, 150, 151, 152, 186
    in East Crete, 128, 131, 132, 133, 134, 136, 137, 138, 139
    in far western Crete, 191, 192
    in Mirabello/West Siteia Mountains, 181, 182, 184
Iron Age (IA), mortuary practices, 12–13, 120
iron objects, 144, 145, 147
Isopata, 135, 140, 141
Itanos, 177, 178, 184
ivory objects, 31, 69, 136, 144

jar burials, at Pseira, 87, 96, 99
jars
    bridge-spouted, 111, 112, 115, 116
    stirrup, 129, 131, 134, 135, 136, 137, 141, 144, 145, 147
    stone, 145
jewelry, 129, 134
    beads, 95, 130, 144, 147
    fibulae, 130, 133, 136, 140, 145, 147
    necklaces, 141
    pendants, 95
    pins, 136, 140, 144, 147
    rings, 131, 132, 136, 137, 138, 141, 144, 151
jugs, 90, 108, 112, 135, 136, 137, 141, 144, 147

Kalamaphka, 138, 181
kalathoi, 135, 137, 141
Kalyvia, 141
Kamares, 191, 193
Kamilari, 59, 67, 71
Kamilari Alisandraki, 186
Kamilari Gligori Koriphi, 189
Kanta, A., 131, 135, 147

kantharoi, 92
Karphi, 124, 125, 126, 130–131, 138, 147, 175, 176
Karphi Astividero, 131
Karphi Ta Mnimata, 130–131
Karydi, 177
Kastri, 174
Kastro, 124
Kata Lakkoi, 128
Kato Symi, 126
Kato Vatheia, 186
Kavousi, 124, 181, 183, 185, 191
Kavousi Vronda, 124, 125, 132, 183
Kavrochori, 186
Kephala, tholos of, 140, 141
kernos, 60, 108
Kinnes, I., 6–7
Kissamos, 191
knives, 113, 144, 145, 147
Knossos, 104, 134, 137, 146, 150, 184
    chamber tombs, 142, 185
    grave goods, 151, 187
    in LM IIIC, 124
    Mycenaean burial customs, 149
    North Cemetery, 141–142, 144–145, 152
    Palace of, 128, 137
    political structures, 98, 146
    Royal Tomb, 136
    settlement patterns, 187
    shaft graves, 142
    in SM, 125, 142, 166
    Temple Repositories, 99
    tholos tombs, 146
    tomb types, 186
Knossos Kephala, 188
Koumasa, 11, 51, 55–63, 69, 74
Kounavoi, 186, 187
Kourtes, 191, 193
Koxare, 193
Koxari, 186
Krasi, 67, 174
krateriskoi, 134, 147
Kritsa, 139, 151, 181
Kritsa Kato Lakkoi, 128

Kritsa Kratharos, 128, 133
Kritsa Lakkoi, 133–134
Krousonas, 186
Kroussonas Rizoplaghia, 140
Krya, 135, 138, 180, 181
Krya Orthi Petra, 135, 136
kylikes, 129–130, 131, 134, 135

lamps, pedastalled, 111
landscapes, 8, 11, 23, 25–28
    of Lebena, 27–28, 35, 37, 38, 40, 41, 42, 43
    of Mochlos, 27–28, 33–34, 42, 43
larnakes, 99, 108, 128, 131, 133–134, 136, 137, 141, 143, 145, 147
Lasithi/Mirabello, 104
Lasithi Mountains, 130, 132–135
Lasithi Plateau, 172, 174–177, 181, 190, 194
Lastros, 180
Late Geometric (LG), 171, 177, 178, 182, 183, 184, 186
Late Helladic (LH) I, 184
Late Helladic (LH) II, 184
Late Minoan (LM), 66
Late Minoan (LM) I
    Myrtos-Pyrgos, 106, 113, 115, 116
    Pseira, 96–97
Late Minoan (LM) IA, Myrtos-Pyrgos, 111, 112, 115
Late Minoan (LM) IB, Myrtos-Pyrgos, 112, 115
Late Minoan (LM) II, 149, 184
Late Minoan (LM) IIIA, 125, 128, 133
    chamber tombs, 135, 140
    cremations in, 128, 134
    grave goods, 130, 132, 137, 138
    Mycenaean burial customs, 149, 151
    political structures of, 127–128
    shaft graves, 142
    tholos tombs, 141
Late Minoan (LM) IIIB, 124, 125, 127–128, 149, 165
    chamber tombs, 138, 140

Late Minoan (LM) IIIB, cont.
    Chania, 148
    cremations in, 134
    grave goods, 130, 132, 138
    Mycenaean burial customs, 151
    shaft graves, 142
    tholos tombs, 131, 141
Late Minoan (LM) IIIC, 122, 124, 126,
    137
    economics in, 124, 139, 140, 145–
        146, 152
    grave goods, 130
    mortuary practices, 12–13, 119, 120–
        122, 149–150, 152, 186
    overseas trade in, 124–125, 137, 140,
        145, 146, 148, 152, 153–154
    political structures of, 119, 124–125,
        154, 175
    religious expression in, 119, 121, 125–
        126
    settlement patterns, 121, 124–125,
        128, 130, 138, 139, 148, 149–150
    social structures, 12, 124
lattice-work ware, 131
lead objects, 31
Lebena, 11, 23, 27–28, 34–43
    Aginaropapoura, 36
    Gerokampos, 35, 36, 59, 65, 71
    Gerokampos II, 35, 39, 40, 66
    Gerokampos IIa, 35, 39, 66
    Papoura, 35, 36, 62
    Papoura I, 35, 36, 37, 39, 40
    Papoura Ia, 35, 40
    Zervou, 35, 36, 39
Legarra Herrero, B., 11
lekythoi, 147
Ligortynos, 189
Liliana, 140–141
limestone, blue-gray, 32
Logiadi, 142
loomweights, 192

Malia, 71, 104, 111, 114, 115, 150
Mann, M., 25

memory, 8, 23, 25, 26
Mesa Mouliana, 181–182
Meseleroi, 180
Mesi, 193
Mesonisia, 193
Messenia, 185
metacarbonate, 87, 88, 96
metal objects, 134
Metcalf, P., 4, 5–6
Middle Bronze Age (MBA)
    Pseira, 97, 98, 99
    tholos cemeteries, 49, 51, 52
Middle Minoan (MM)
    Koumasa, 58
    Pseira, 97
    tholos cemeteries, 49, 56, 59
    upside-down burials, 150
    Zakros, 97
Middle Minoan (MM) I
    Apesokari, 65, 67
    Archanes-Phourni, 71
    Hagia Triada, 59, 62, 67, 69, 70
    Koumasa, 59, 60, 61, 62, 63
    Platanos, 65, 66–67, 69, 70, 71, 72–
        73
    in South-Central Crete, 74
Middle Minoan (MM) IA
    Koumasa, 63
    Lebena cemeteries, 35
    Mochlos cemetery, 28, 30
Middle Minoan (MM) IB
    Lebena cemeteries, 35
    Myrtos-Pyrgos, 111, 116
    Platanos, 66
Middle Minoan (MM) II
    Malia, 115
    Platanos, 66
    Pseira, 85, 86, 89, 91, 92, 93, 94, 97,
        98
Middle Minoan (MM) IIB, Pseira, 93–
    94, 98, 99
Middle Minoan (MM) III
    Mochlos cemetery, 30
    Pseira, 95, 98
Milatos, 180

Mirabello/West Siteia Mountains, 179–180, 172, 180–185, 194
Mochlos, 11, 27–35, 36, 41, 42, 43, 150, 184
Modi, 192
Monastiraki Katalimata, 99
Moni Kalyvianis, 142
Moni Odigitria, tholos cemeteries, 51, 59, 71
Morgan, L.H., 4
Morris, I., 6
mortuary practices, 1–9, 11, 13, 120, 121
  and children, 107, 116, 133, 143, 144, 147, 166, 192
  in EIA, 165–166, 171
  in EO, 12, 166, 179, 181, 186
  in IA, 12–13, 120
  in LM IIIC, 12–13, 119, 120–122, 149–150, 152, 186
  and regional studies, 1–2, 10, 11, 120, 121, 166, 172, 194
  in SM, 119, 121, 149, 152
mortuary studies, 2–13
mortuary systems, 23, 27–41
Mouliana, 135–137, 151
Mouliana Sellades, Tholos A, 136
Mousouras, 192
Murphy, J., 11
Mycenaean people, 121 137, 149, 151–152, 180
Myrsini, 151, 180
Myrsini Aspropilia, 135, 137, 138
Myrtos-Phournou Koriphi, 104, 106
Myrtos-Pyrgos, 106–116

Nea Alikarnassos tomb, 140, 141
Neopalatial period, Myrtos-Pyrgos, 115, 116
New Archaeology, 9
Nowicki, K., 172
Nyakyusa of Tanzania, 6

Olous, 128, 139, 147
open-air sanctuaries, 126
orientalia, Platanos, 69, 70
Orino, 181
Orne, 193
orthostates, 31, 32
ossuaries, 39, 65
overseas trade, in LM IIIC period, 124–125, 137, 140, 145, 146, 148, 152, 153–154

Pacheia Ammos, 99, 150
Palaikastro, 150, 177
Palaikastro Kastri, 124, 138, 139
Pantanassa, 131, 147, 148, 193
Papoura, 130, 174
Parsa, 181
peak sanctuaries, 99
Pefkoi, 181
Pendlebury, J.D.S., 172
Perna, Katia, 12
Phaistos, 124, 126, 142, 143, 145, 146, 186, 187, 188
Phaistos Liliana, 141, 142, 144
Phaistos tou Phygiot, 188
Phoinikia, 186
phyllite formation, 87
Piskokephalo, 179
Piskokephalo Berati, 135, 136, 139, 150
pit burials, 28, 150, 152, 166
  in Central Crete, 142–145, 146, 185, 186, 188, 189
  in East Crete, 133
  in far eastern Crete, 177, 178
  in far western Crete, 191, 192
  in Mirabello/West Siteia Mountains, 180
pithoi, 181, 190
  in Central Crete, 185, 186, 188, 189
  in East Crete, 128, 133, 134, 135, 136
  in EIA, 166

pithoi, cont.
  in far western Crete, 191, 192
  Myrtos-Pyrgos, 107, 108
  in West-Central Crete, 193
Platanos, 11, 51, 55, 63–72, 74–75
Plattenkalk, 87
political structures, 120–121, 179
  in Central Crete, 146–147, 154, 187,
    190
  in East Crete, 127
  in EIA, 172, 194, 195
  in far eastern Crete, 178
  in LM IIIC period, 119, 124–125, 154,
    175
  in Mirabello/West Siteia Mountains,
    182, 183, 185
  in West-Central Crete, 148
Porti, 150
post-modernism, 4, 7, 8, 9, 10
post-processualism, 9, 11, 120
pottery, 31, 90, 93–94, 126
  bowls, 116, 141
    deep, 129, 131, 134, 135, 136
  cups, 89, 90, 94, 108, 112, 116, 131,
    136, 141
    carinated, 94
    conical, 71, 112, 141
    spouted, 135
  fruit stands, 135
  goblets, 94
  jars, 111, 115
    bridge-spouted, 112, 115, 116
    stirrup, 129, 131, 134, 135, 136,
      137, 141, 144, 145, 147
  jugs, 90, 108, 112, 135, 136, 137, 141,
    144, 147
  kalathoi, 135, 137, 141
  kantharoi, 92
  krateriskoi, 134, 147
  kylikes, 129–130, 131, 134, 135
  lekythoi, 147
  pyxis, 66, 90, 94, 133–134, 136, 141,
    142, 151

pottery, cont.
  rhyta, 108, 110, 112, 116, 131
  skyphoi, 134, 135
  thelastron, 135
  vases, 89, 90, 93, 94, 96, 129, 131
    closed, 129, 132, 134, 135, 141,
      144, 147, 153
    open, 129, 132, 134, 141, 144
  vessels, 60, 66, 85, 90, 92, 94, 98, 136
    pouring, 129
  wares
    coarse, 112–113
    cooking pot, 112–113
    fine, 37
    lattice-work, 131
power, 11, 25, 35, 116, 137, 151–152,
  154, 188
Praisos, 124, 134, 138, 151, 179, 181, 183
Praisos Kapsalos, 135
Praisos Photoula, 128, 135, 136, 137, 139,
  181–182
Prepalatial period, 11, 27–28, 41, 115.
  See also Lebena; Mochlos
Preston, L., 184
Prinias, 124, 125, 144–146, 150, 186–
  188
Prinias Siderospilia, 142, 143, 144
Protogeometric B (PGB), 181, 182
Protogeometric (PG), 148, 182
  in Central Crete, 186, 187
  in East Crete, 132, 134
  tholos tombs, 171, 187–188
Protopalatial period, 11, 34–35, 115, 116
Pseira, 85–86
Pseira cemetery, 86–87, 89, 93–95
  Tomb 2, 94, 97, 98
  Tomb 4, 12, 85, 87–93, 94, 97, 98, 99
  Tomb 6, 92
Pyrgos, 103–104, 112, 113, 115, 134
Pyrgos I, 104, 109
Pyrgos II, 106, 107, 109, 110, 114
Pyrgos IIc, 110, 111
Pyrgos IId, 110, 111

Pyrgos III, 109, 111, 114, 115
Pyrgos IV, 111, 112
pyxis, 66, 90, 94, 133–134, 136, 141, 142, 151

Radcliff-Brown, A.R., 5
Randsborg, K., 6–7
Rappaport, R.A., 27
regional studies
  and mortuary practices, 1–2, 10, 11, 55, 114, 115, 116 120, 121, 166, 172, 194
religion, 27, 132. *See also* rituals
  in Central Crete, 146, 153, 178
  in LM IIIC, 119, 121, 125–126
Renfrew, C., 8, 9
resource control, 11
Rethymnon, 193
rhyta, 108, 110, 112, 116, 131
rituals, 27, 99, 126, 150, 165. *See also* religion
  bi-ritualism, 127, 152
  interpretations of, 5, 13
  in Koumasa, 72, 73
  and Platanos, 71–73, 74
  and Pseira, 94, 99
  relating to death, 4–5, 7, 9, 12, 98, 120
rock shelter tombs, 150, 180, 181, 192
  in East Crete, 128, 134, 139
  in EIA, 166, 177–178
  in far eastern Crete, 177–178, 180
  at Mochlos, 28, 32
  at Pseira, 85, 87–93, 96, 97, 98, 99
roofed house tombs, 28, 31–32
Rotasi, 189
ruin cults, 188–189

Saudi Arabia, 5
Savignoni, L., 141
Saxe, A., 6
Schoinokapsala, 181
Seager, R., 30, 31, 32, 34, 96

seals, 31, 37, 61, 66, 67, 69, 70, 95, 134
sealstones, 37
Sellades, 135
settlement patterns, 178, 192, 193
  in border zones, 190, 191
  in Central Crete, 186–187, 189–190, 194, 195
  in EIA, 165, 172, 174
  in LM IIIC, 121, 124–125, 128, 130, 138, 139, 148, 149–150
  in Mirabello/West Siteia Mountains, 181, 184–185, 194
shaft graves, 142, 153, 166
shells, triton, 113, 115
shield elements, 136, 144
Siderokephala, 130, 131, 132
silver objects, 31, 60, 62, 67, 69
single-site examinations, 10
Siteia, 135–138, 139, 150, 151. *See also* Mirabello/West Siteia Mountains
Sjögren, L., 172
skeletal remains. *See* bones, human
Skopi, 181
skull veneration, Myrtos-Pyrgos, 108
skuttles, 192
skyphoi, 134, 135
slabs, stone, 31–32
Smari, 186
Smari Livaditsa, 133
social hierarchies, 25, 27, 28, 53, 56, 142, 148, 151, 175, 178. *See also* elite structures
  and East Crete, 132, 136, 138, 139
  and Koumasa, 62, 63, 73–74
  and Lebena, 35–38, 39, 40, 41, 42–43
  and Mirabello/West Siteia Mountains, 181–182, 184
  and Mochlos, 28, 30, 31, 32, 33, 34, 42, 43
  and mortuary practices, 3, 4, 6–7, 9, 11, 13, 120, 121
  and Myrtos-Pyrgos, 103, 113–114, 115, 116
  and Platanos, 70–71, 74, 75

social memory, and landscapes, 25, 26
social structures, 5, 23, 54, 98
    Koumasa, 63, 72, 73–74
    in LM IIIC period, 12, 124
    and mortuary studies, 3–4, 5, 6, 7–8,
        9, 11, 13
    Myrtos-Pyrgos, 113, 114
    Platanos, 72, 73, 74
    of South-Central Crete, 23, 53, 56
social unit of burial, 183
    in East Crete, 128–129
    at Koumasa, 62, 73–74
    at Lebena, 35, 36–37, 40
    at Mochlos, 30, 36
    at Myrtos-Pyrgos, 113–114
    at Platanos, 70, 73, 75
    at Pseira, 89, 96
sociology, 4–5, 7
socles, stone, 32
Soles, J., 30, 32
South-Central Crete, 36, 37, 71, 74. See
    also Lebena
    pattern of tombs in, 35, 36, 40, 42
    social structure in, 23, 53, 56
    tholos cemeteries in, 49, 53, 55–56
Spencer, H., 4
Sphakia, 138, 179
Sphoungaras, 99, 150
spindle whorls, 129, 130, 141
Stamnoi, 186
stands, handmade perforated, 91
Stavrakia, 186
stone objects, 31, 113, 145
    vases, 31, 32, 37, 66, 69, 113
    vessels, 61, 63, 66–67, 69–71, 74, 85,
        93–94, 98
Stratigraphic Museum, 143
Subminoan (SM), 124, 126, 141, 142,
    147, 148
    and Central Crete, 142–143, 144, 146
    and East Crete, 134, 139
    mortuary practices of, 119, 121, 149,
        152
    pit-caves, 142–143, 144
    settlement patterns of, 125, 130

Subminoan (SM) I and II, 122
swords, 136, 144, 145
    Naue II–type, 131, 136, 137–138, 140,
        144, 151

tankards, 137
Teke-Knossos, 60
terraces
    Myrtos-Pyrgos, 106, 109, 110
    Pseira, 91, 92, 93, 94, 97, 98, 99
    West Terrace at Mochlos, 28, 30,
        31–32, 33, 34, 42
thelastron, 135
tholos cemeteries, 11, 49, 51–56, 59,
    127, 130. See also Koumasa; Platanos
tholos tombs, 149–150, 166, 174, 179,
    180, 190, 191
    in Central Crete, 141, 142, 143, 145,
        146, 187–188, 189, 190
    dromos, 128, 130, 133, 175
    in East Crete, 128, 132–133, 134,
        135–139
    in EIA, 166, 171
    in Lasithi Plateau, 174–177, 181, 194
    in Mirabello/West Siteia Mountains,
        181, 182, 183, 185, 194
    pseudo-tholoi, 135, 136, 166, 180
    reuse of, 141, 143, 146, 149, 150
    square plan, 130–131, 133, 141, 142,
        166
    stomion, 128, 130, 175
    in West-Central Crete, 147, 193
thresholds, stone slab, 32
Thronos Kephala, 124, 126, 148
tomb architecture, 2–3, 35, 126, 147, 190
    in Central Crete, 142–143
    in East Crete, 128, 132, 138
    in EIA, 166, 175
    and Koumasa, 58, 59, 62, 63
    in Lasithi Plateau, 175, 176
    and Mochlos, 28, 31–33, 42, 43
    and Platanos, 65–67, 71–73, 74
    and Pseira, 85, 86, 95
tomb distribution, 28, 32–36, 42–43

Tourloti, 180
Turner, V., 4
Tylissos, 124, 126, 143, 145, 146, 186
Tylissos Atzolou, 142, 144
Tylor, E., 4

Ucko, P.J., 5
Upper Gysadhes, 142

Valis, tholos tomb, 141, 142, 144
van Gennep, A., 4
vases, 61, 66, 151
    pottery, 89, 90, 93, 94, 96, 129, 131
        closed, 129, 132, 134, 135, 141,
            144, 147, 153
        open, 129, 132, 134, 141, 144
    stone, 31, 32, 37, 66, 69, 113
Vasiliki, 139, 181
Vasiliki Hagios Tedoros, 132, 133, 134
Vasiliki Karamaki, 133, 134
Vasiliki Kephala, 124–126
Vasiliki Ware, 89
veneration rituals, Tomb 4, Pseira, 12
vertical slabs, at Pseira, 86
vessels
    pottery, 60, 66, 85, 90, 92, 94, 98, 129,
        136
    stone, 61, 63, 66–67, 69–71, 74, 85,
        93–94, 98
Viannos, 181
Voliones, 147, 148
Voros, 150
Vorou, North Deposit, 71
Vourlia, 135
Vouves, 191

Vrokastro, 124, 132, 134, 138, 139, 181,
    185
Vrokastro Chavga, 133, 150
Vryses, 192

Wallace, S., 175
walls, 65, 66, 88, 92–93, 109, 115
Warren, P., 66
warrior graves, 137, 139, 142, 145, 151,
    152, 153, 182
weapons, 144
    in East Crete, 128, 129, 131, 136, 138,
        139, 153
    Naue II-type swords, 131, 136, 137–
        138, 140, 144, 151
    spearheads, 136, 137, 140, 144, 145,
        147, 151
    type D and F2 swords, 137
West-Central Crete, 191
    as EIA mortuary region, 172, 193–194
    in LM IIIC, 147–148, 193
whetstones, 145

Xanthoudides, S., 56, 58–61, 63, 65–67,
    69–70

Zakros, 97, 151, 177, 178
Zakros Koukou Kephali Tomb A, 178
Zakros Palaimylos, 135, 136
Zapher Papoura, 142, 143
Zenia, 174
Ziros, 138
Zou, 177